Cyber War and Terrorism

Cyber War & Terrorism

Capt. Mithilesh Kumar Singh

Prashant Publishing House
DELHI - 110094 (INDIA)

PRASHANT PUBLISHING HOUSE
C-34, 28 Foota Road, Gali No. 3
West Karawal Nagar, Delhi-110094
Phone : 9810396373, 22963970

Cyber War & Terrorism

First Published : 2009

ISBN : 978-81-908282-7-7

PRINTED IN INDIA

Published by Mr. R. K. Jha M/s. Prashant Publishing House, Delhi and Printed at H.S. Offset Press, Delhi.

Preface

Gaining importance of information systems in today's warfare shows that information security is being a key to success of a conflict or even a war. Cyber warfare is becoming more and more powerful on today's battlefield and affects development of armies in many countries as well as development of weapon technologies. It's use should not be underestimated as it is highly flexible and hard to detect. Its costs allow any country to train or hire a team capable of doing more than a complete army. Effective use of such teams can gain dominance on battlefield or force the enemy to retreat by shutting down its command infrastructure or communication network. Value of cyberwarfare is growing and with digitization of conventional warfare technologies as well as using more complex devices creates risks and weaknesses that allow cyberwarfare units to do more damage than they could in past.

Information age is taking over conventional industries and with growing needs for automation and digitization nations realize lack of skilled people able to control them. Governments realize that this problem is slowing economy but they don't realize that it also creates risks and holes in national security strategy. Shuting down nuclear powerplants may destroy the whole economy in a mattter of minutes; opening water dams may kill thousands of people or releasing poisonous chemicals destroy country's nature. Cyberwarfare units have a important mission to ensure country's survivability, prosperity and stability. They need to ensure national security and in worst case help with disaster recovery.In past countries relied on strength of convetional military units but now future of a country may depend on how well trained cyberwarfare units are and how much practice they have.

— *Author*

Contents

1
Introduction

Every country has it's right to defend itself by all appropriate means. Defence industries arose to satisfy demand for armies and doesn't seem to stop growing. This industry is driven by daily progress in advanced defence or offence technologies that make all the previous advancements obsolete. There are very few countries whose wealth allows to keep up with this speed. Even the best economic countries can't afford to develop technologies too advanced due to high expenses required for such programms.

Any conventional army needs to be well equipped and well organized. Equipment is not the only expense because organization of the army is much more important. Organization is distribution of correct information in exact scale and timing. Every army needs information and telecomunication network, every army is based on logistics and every army needs to know the enemy. Information age doesn't show only in business but also on the battlefield. The information distribution needs to be done much faster; enemy movement must be communicated more precisely; troops need to be deployed more exactly and decisions have to be based on more accurate information. This shows that armies rely more and more on information, but they don't realize that information is an asset with great value that needs to be protected.

All the efforts to protect the information was targeted on physical security (eg. Limiting access to the information), but today with inernetworking and teleworking there are other risks that need to be taken into account. Weaknesses in logical security enable attackers do all what is possible with conventional weapons (destruction of infrastructure) as well as weapons of mass destruction (nuclear reactor meltdown)

Cyberwarfare

Cyberwarfare is a relatively new type of weaponry with varous effects on the target. It doesn't have any limitations of use and can achieve most of the goals set. Weapons

Cyber weapons are usually basic programs that have the objective to defend or attack a target. Most of them are freely available on the internet but some more sophisticated or newer ones are kept privately or are commercial.

Detection

Systems in this category have the goal to detect possible attackers and identify what are they trying to do and possible where they are. Detection can be based on expert knowledge (if I hear bullets flying then somebody is attacking us) or based on standard behavior (if a patrol doesn't come back from recon mission on time there might be an attack imminent).

Tools in this category are:

- Intrusion detection systems
- Security monitoring
- Log analysis
- Prevention

Stopping the attacker is the primary concern even if the attack has not been identified (locking the entrance door is always a good idea). Most of the attacks are very simple and straightforward just like testing each door if it is open and a good prevention is to simply lock it, unless somebody expects an army trying to enter (but then other preventive measures apply).

Main tools in this category are:

- Firewalls
- Authentication systems
- Authorization systems
  - Target Identification

- Network scanners
- System scanners
- Vulnerability scanners

Attack

Here come all the tools that use the vulnerability of the system or application and achieve the objective an attacker wants. There are too many tools here to mention them as for every vulnerability there is more than one tool available. It is also important to mention internet worms, that are automated tools misusing certain vulnerabilities and self-replicating themselves from one system to the other. Another group are Trojan horses that can be deployed on the system to gain access to it later or to create a covert channel to obtain important information.

Deception tools

Deceiving the enemy is also important in case a distraction is needed to perform an attack or to slow the detection time of it. Here belong these subcategories:

- Log modifiers
- Distributed attack systems
- Root-kits
- Stealth tools

Strategy and Tactics

The acclaimed British strategic thinker B.H. Liddell-Hart approached strategy from two different perspectives. He differentiated between a grand strategy and military strategy. Liddell-Hart s grand strategy focused on a nation s ability to coordinate and direct all resources of a nation toward the attainment of a political objective. Military strategy was more narrow, related to the execution of a battle plan or the projection of military force.

In Cybersecurity there is no difference between military and civilian infrastructure as many targets are non-military but indirectly are involved in military infrastructure. Disrupting economy or damaging image of a public infrastructure can wield much larger effect as weapons of mass destruction and therefore it is necessary not to limit the tactics or a strategy with any boundaries in order to get a global understanding of what attackers can gain or loose.

Strategies are based on certain behavior that defines the acting party. In cyber-security there are 3 major types (if not counting chaotic behavior)

Reactive Behavior

Here strategy is based on action that can be seen or reported in any way. It reacts upon it with the apropriate response by increasing the awarenes on that weakness. As an example US security started to concentrate on airport security after September 11th incident. Or increasing awareness on information security after extensive cyber-attacks from china and other not "pro-american" countries.

This behavior strengthens those points in defence where attacks already happened, which means that there will be always several succesful penetrations at the beginning. Although it seems as in longterm infrastructure may reach a point where the systems would be secured sufficiently, but the fact is that with introduction of new software or new updates (and this happens very often) there are new security holes introduced which may be misused in time.

Infrastructures with limited security resources are very often using this behavior to manage security. This means that security team in charge is either not very experienced or there is not enough people devoted to maintain IT systems. Depending on the response on a system breach there might be conclusions drawn upon their cybersecurity strategy (especially incident handling and security monitoring).

By analyzing the security vulnerabilities of their systems it is possible to see the history of attacks upon their infrastructure. There is also another alternative to this behavior, which is learning from mistakes of others, but not always can solutions of others be used to increase security of a bit different infrastructure.

Planned Behavior

Importance of planning is already well known to project managers, but due to the nature of IT infrastructure it is not always applicable. IT infrastructure can't be kept strictly static and not change to fit the work needs of its owner. To keep up with the progress in IT field as well as match the requirements for functionality in a very short time it is not possible to keep everything planned and well documented.

It is similar in national security planning where detailed plans won't work as expected as they cover huge economic; military and other systems that are changing very often and are not well documented. In a best case with appropriate security planning well thought of and implemented appropriately can achieve decent level of security defense. In former communist countries planning was done in almost every part of the state, but although many scenarios were thought of one aspect wasn't so much covered and that was human resources. Due to unexpected deviations in human behavior the whole system collapsed.

Cyber-security can be very well planned but the plan can't cover all scenarios and by not employing capable and experienced security people who can adopt the response there would always be a risk of a break-in. If companies lack skilled people to operate defensive security measures or keep the systems secured (this is very ofthen the case) apropriate response would follow after a long period of investigation and escalation. By knowing the procedures used by external companies an attacker can predict specific behaviors that would follow and adjust the cyberattack to prevent any response.

A risk may be to underestimate the possibility of having outsourced managed security system that might be difficult to overcome. This trend gains importance in middle-sized or progressively thinking companies and if implemented nation-wide can be a very effective measure.

Proactive Behavior

Previous behaviors were trying to cover known risks and vulnerabilities, but what if there is something new that wasn't reported or documented? In such case this attacks would remain undetected and would be identified as anomalies. For detecting and preventing also unknown new attacks it is necessary to be highly flexible and "be the first to know" your weakness.

A security strategy that concentrates on identifying its own potential weaknesses and covering its own holes is based on proactive behavior. There are many functions that fall under proactive behavior category:

- source code review
- formal functionality proving
- traffic analysis
- self penetration testing
- self-adaptable security measures

There are already some security solutions and products on the market but are not very capable due to lack of skilled people to operate it. Formal functionality testing and source code review is not done in necessary scope to insure the safety of such system. Several countries already started investigating this field and started adapting some parts of their systems.

China already invested a lot into building large and well trained cyber-security force or USA has built national cyber-security research centers to concentrate security experts and skilled engineers to improve bits and pieces of national cyber-security.

Proactive behavior needs highly skilled people and verytight security system in place and therefore it is important to keep highly skilled people in the country to either ensure its own security or to develop security systems that do it.

NATIONAL SECURITY STRATEGY

This is more an utopistic approach as it is not possible to integrate and synchronise all the parts of one nation into one cyber-defense initiative, but it should be the goal of any cyber-security initiative.

The main goal here is to secure the nation from the network provider side up to the end-user. There is one general security standard and security policy which is being implemented and audited by authorized experts. Central electronic warfare center is responsible of handling incidents that are reported by any entity in the country. Educational system is capable of providing sufficient number of security experts and research capabilities to ensure implementation of national security strategy in every important infrastructure.

Attacking such system is extremely hard and may be only done from inside near by the target in order to minimize the possibility of detection or prevention. Such attacks require cooperation with conventional special forces that help the cyber-attack team to get to the target as close as possible and gain access to its data or functionality.

People

Security is based on 3 aspects: people; systems and procedures. As systems and procedures are developed by people, human resources are the key to cyber-security defense initiative.

Experts

The core of a cyber-security defense force are the people with security knowledge. These are not administrators who are able to install a firewall, but these are people who design and develop firewalls and other security measures. Without these people a country or a company needs to rely upon external help that may or may not be successful. Position of a security expert is similar to a nuclear scientist, who can invent and develop deadly weapon for any state that is willing to pay for his research.

Intelligence

Information about the enemy is according to Sun Tzu the key to success in the battle or warfare. Gathering information about enemy tools and cyber-security systems is as valuable as knowing what kind of weapons and soldiers enemy has. Even on a company level it is important to know what kind of new security tools are on the market and what kind of security problems were discovered recently. Also information about security experts may be valuable in case of recruiting needs.

Hackers

Defense force is one side of cyber-security but it is also necessary to have offense capabilities. For the training scenarios as well as for identification of existing and new security holes in systems hackers are important. Very often ex-hackers tend to do security consulting but the major difference between a hacker and security expert is that a hacker needs to identify one hole while the security expert has to cover them all.

System Programmers

With all the knowledge of security requirements and new security holes, there needs to be somebody who integrates and modifies the software/hardware or a solution. Knowledge of a system and skills in programming are necessary for progress of the IT industry as well as cyber-security.

Defense

Information systems have many potential weaknesses, but whatever they are if they don't operate there is a problem. It is the scale of this problem that determines the importance of such system and necessary security measures to protect it.

Minimizing the risk of such problem or the scale of it requires security measures that cover all the potential initiators of the problem. Here security experts tend to differentiate 3 main categories, although some security measures are in more than one and there is no clear definition which security measure belongs where.

Physical Security

For thousands of years people, goods, towns or states were protected by physical security measures starting with stone walls up to nuclear bunkers. But no matter how smart or good the defense was there were always ways to get through. Therefore combination of each category is necessary to prevent the accident. A good example of physical security is detecting and preventing EMP weapons getting in contact with logical security measures and switching them off. A EMP blast can disable C3 (command

and communication center) communication system and herewith stop the attack or prevent defensive force from operating efficiently. A good physical countermeasure may be anti air defense or air patrols in the area. A company level physical security countermeasure may be storing information system in a shielded datacenter with UPS.

Logical Security

This is the main cyber-security battlefield where digital information is being exchanged or stored. Every security measure that is performed by a non-human device in the digital world is a member of this group.

There are many sub-fields here:

- Encryption
- Network security
- System security
- Application security
- Security monitoring/auditing

Organizational Security

Even if information is sealed behind the blast doors there might be a risk that somebody would open the door and let the attacker take it. That is why security procedures are in place to ensure that in case other security measures fail people would know what to do and by following procedures ensure the safety of the information. Very often in stressful situations with lack of expertise people tend to do more mistakes than ever. Procedures are there to help people do the right thing even if they don't know what to do these guidelines would show them how to prevent the worst.

Offence

Strike Scenario

The cyber-attack requires detailed structure and a plan in order to achieve the expected objective. Such plan should have this structure:

1. General Target analysis
2. Choosing specific objectives
3. Selection of team members with sufficien qualification
4. Detailed target analysis
5. Attack planning
6. Training the attack
7. Execution of the attack
8. Observing the target to ensure the obectives were met

At first point analysts collect as much information about the target as possible by standard means (eg. Newspapers, web-sites; newsgroups;..). This information should help identify: Target's mission (what is the goal of system's existance) Content and structure of the target's systems (network structure; geographical location; external systems connected; customers ;..) Technologies used (systems used; software and hardware implemented; defensive measures) -

History of system implementation (system integration times; upgrade dates; vendors) Human resources (how many people are employed; how well trained are they; what kind of information they collect; what are their interests;..) All the information above should help to pick up the best (or the weakest) target and possible source of attack as well as time plan of action.

Second point should identify all the weakest spots or interesting spots that should be looked into more deeply. These targets do not have to be specific systems they also can be information sources or people. In third point the team should be assembled containing specialists for every type of system used at the target. As it is not always possible to collect all the information necessary to choose the team all the starting members in the team should be able to call in any specialists they need for target analysis or strike.

Point four should gather all the necessary information about the target to create a specific plan of action to achieve the objectives specified in point two. This point identifies specific target structure and validates the information collected at point one. This is done by scanning the target systems and identifying operation systems, network elements as well as services and daemons running on them.

At point five the above information is processed and specific weaknesses identified for possible break-in. It is not always possible to identify them up to the detail necessary, but with correlation of other information collected it may be possible to make the attack plan more specific. The plan can contain further testing and scanning as there may be other systems that are not identifiable from outside. Training the attack at point six is a preparation for the attack that optimizes and tests the cyber-weapons as well as the plan for the attack on a group of ssimilar systems. This also helps to develop a certain level of automation that speeds up the attack and minimizes the probability of human intervention.

Attack plan is usually very simple:

1. use a system vulnerability detected
2. gain the autorization level required
3. achieve the objectives
4. remove all the clues (if the objective was other than destroy the target)

Verification of achieving the objectives is dependant on their contents, but can be proved by analyzing the information collected or checking the target's services that should have been disrupted or analyzing the local information sources (eg. Newspapers).

TRAINING

Building cyber army from volunteers can't be a solution for national security even if they are the elite of computer security experts. It is the same as if best sportsmen or hunters were to build an army. They may run fast or excell in precision shooting, but they will not succeed in logistics and tactics.

In order to train a cyber army there needs to be a structure created that will use them efficiently. There have to be procedures created to help handle the situations effectively. All this needs to be built first before any training can begin. It is already clear that standard army field manuals can't be used to help build the cyber troops as here quality matters not quantity. Also tactics has to be built from scratch in order to achieve objectives necessary. Separation of offensive and defensive training is more clearer and distinctive than in real combat training.

Defensive Training

Infrastructure protection requires training in security technologies.

- Field
- Technologies
- Roles
- Network Security
- Firewalls
- NIDS
- Network design
- Firewalls specialist
- NIDS specialist
- Network designer
- System Security
- System installation and configuration
- HIDS (system monitoring, integrity checking)
- Authentication
- Auditing and logging
- System programming
- System administrator
- HIDS specialist
- Authentication specialist
- System auditor
- System coder
- Application Security
- Application installation and configuration
- Application design and development
- Data encryption
- Application administrator
- Application developer

- Encryption specialist
- Organization Security
- Security policies
- Disaster recovery planning
- Incident handling
- Forensics
- Auditing
- Policy writer
- Disaster recovery planner
- Incident manager
- Forensics officer
- Auditor
- Other
- Security monitoring
- Surveilance crew

All the roles described above are already existant in many companies and government agencies. There are many trainings for technologies specified above, but in order to use them in cyberwarfare they need to be integrated together. For example there is a potential target detected and commanding officer decides it is important to protect the target.

Here is a general plan that needs to be executed:

1. Auditors are sent onsite to investigate current status of security
2. Every area specified above is assessed and commanding officer decides what area needs improvement and what experts would join the taskforce.
3. Experts start improvements in organizational security (priority nr.1)
4. After improving security policy other areas start improving systems and networks accordingly.
5. Incident reporting (if possible also security monitoring) is linked to a defence center with security surveilance crew.
6. General advisory is given to the target's security crew.

7. After deescalation of security alert monitoring and incident reporting is given back to target's security team.

This all needs to happen in a very short time as cyber attacks may start immediatelly after warning. Also cooperation with target's security team is vital due to the fact that they know their systems better. Defence teams need to be trained in various technologies on the market and practice their skills on most of the common systems on the market. Trainings on specific technologies need to be done by external companies who have resources and skills for it, but trainings in tactics should be done locally with cooperation of offensive warfare teams.

There are 3 types of training:

1. Proactive securing of a target
2. Immediate reaction on a attack and securitg of the target
3. Security forensics after attack and securing of target's infrastructure to prevent more attacks

Type 1 training start with deployment of a system with application and a function defined for it. It continues with performing security checklists in order to bring the system and network components to a securely configured level. Next there are active security measures deployed in order to prevent majority of standard attacks. After that there are passive security measures deployed to monitor the system as well as provide sufficient auditing data to identify what happened.

Type 2 trainings are very similar to security drills on a military base. After an alert is issued team members have to gain control over the system and remove all the attackers from the system. This can be done with cooperation with offensive warfare teams.

After allert is issued there needs to be an escalation procedure executed which informs global security control center (GSC2) of an ongoing attack. After gaining back complete control of the system team has to investigate how attackers got into the system and report it to GSC2. With this information system needs to be secured and security holes need to be patched. Also this process needs to be reported to GSC2 in order to secure other similar system that may be possible targets.

Type 3 trainings take place in systems that have already been hacked. Their main objective is to analyze system state and logs and reconstruct the actions that attackers did. This can help to secure the system as well as give some information to offensive warfare teams how to perform similar attacks. Another objective is to detect what has been changed in the system to preven further damage or fraud.

Offensive Training

It is difficult to train something not very specific that varies every moment. Offensive cyberwarfare is a set of tools and technologies based on security holes in various software. These holes get fixed very quickly and training how to misuse the would become obsolete after several days. Offensive training should be therefore based on general technologies rather than on specific tools.

Training Objectives:

- Psychological fitness (working under time pressure)
- Technological understanding (general concepts of systems and networks)
- Operational procedures and policies understanding
- State/government/army functionality understanding (information flow, command structure)

In order to meet these objectives there should be a training plan set to meet the army needs.

Psychological Fitness

To succeed in cyber battlefield soldier needs to be able to work under pressure and make correct decisions very fast. Just like in convetional warfare a hole or a window in enemy's defence is opened for limited ammount of time. Strike team needs to use this window and every second counts that they can gain with good preparation and training. Stress is not only a side-effect when working under pressure but also a key factor for success. Training should be done just in a same way as conventional trainings by learning procedures in order to minimize the reaction time in between.

Technological Understanding

In conventional warfare it is necessary to know how weapons work in order to use them properly. This same concept is necessary for cyber-warfare. The level of detail must be sufficient to guarantee understanding of what happened, is happening or is expected to happen.

By knowing the technologies a cyberwarior is able to make decisions and predict the enemy move as human interactions are very rare to happen. Understanding of networking and operation systems technology should not be underestimated and should be the main objective of cyberwarior's training.

Operational Procedures and Policies

Technological protection is very limited thanks to opennes of every system. Protective measures don't affect required functionality of a system and therefore can't be expected to be the only defense of a target. By logical security there is also organizational security that comprises of procedures and policies. These are usually deployed in order to strengthen the defences up to a maximum. Due to the human nature they are not as quick and precise as technological means, but they are not very visible and can't be easily predicted.

A s an example if the target follows government cybersecurity standard and has already detected a breach it needs around 10 minutes to report an incident and ask for help. This external help requires at least 30 minutes to analyze the environment and assess the indicators of the breach. All this time can be used for achieving the objectives and covering tracks by cyberattack team. By knowing standard procedures employend in specific industry a cyberwarior is able to predict the human response and assess the actions necessary to take or the remaining time he has to achieve his objectives.

General Target's Functionality

Learning about counterforce functionality and structure helps to choose the correct targets as well as make quick decisions about tactics to be used in specific attack. By hitting correct targets it is possible to achieve expected effect as well as create sufficient confusion and distraction to enlarge the attact window or leave the attacked system unnoticed. Although it is not very usefull for execution cyberforce but it is surely valuable for target choosing or tactics planning,

As an example US government initiated cyber-defence strategy which requires central emergency center. Information about the incident should be sent to the experts there but if the path is disabled and cyberattack team takes over the communication target may be gained easier under control.

Or by estimating time of response from the target knowing of existance of such center can increase the time delay of such response as target is expected to wait until the decision from such center.

CONCLUSION

Gaining importance of information systems in today's warfare shows that information security is being a key to success of a conflict or even a war. Cyber warfare is becoming more and more powerful on today's battlefield and affects development of armies in many countries as well as development of weapon technologies. It's use should not be underestimated as it is highly flexible and hard to detect.

Its costs allow any country to train or hire a team capable of doing more than a complete army. Effective use of such teams can gain dominance on battlefield or force the enemy to retreat by shutting down its command infrastructure or communication network. Value of cyberwarfare is growing and with digitization of conventional warfare technologies as well as using more complex devices creates risks and weaknesses that allow cyberwarfare units to do more damage than they could in past.

Information age is taking over conventional industries and with growing needs for automation and digitization nations realize lack of skilled people able to control them. Governments realize that this problem is slowing economy but they don't realize that it also creates risks and holes in national security strategy. Shuting down nuclear powerplants may destroy the whole economy in a mattter of minutes; opening water dams may kill thousands of people or releasing poisonous chemicals destroy country's nature.

Cyberwarfare units have a important mission to ensure country's survivability, prosperity and stability. They need to ensure national security and in worst case help with disaster recovery.In past countries relied on strength of convetional military units but now future of a country may depend on how well trained cyberwarfare units are and how much practice they have.

Enemy is already there and getting stronger every moment. We must make sure we can keep him from destroying our values we've been creating so hardly.

2

The Evolution of Cyber Warfare

INTRODUCTION

In the spring of 2007, when Estonian authorities moved a monument to the Red Army from the center of its capital city, Tallinn, to the outskirts of town, a diplomatic row erupted with neighboring Russia. Estonian nationalists regard the army as occupiers and oppressors, a sentiment that dates to the long period of Soviet rule following the Second World War, when the Soviet Union absorbed all three Baltic states. Ethnic Russians, who make up about a quarter of Estonia's 1.3 million people, were nonetheless incensed by the statue's treatment and took to the streets in protest. Estonia later blamed Moscow for orchestrating the unrest; order was restored only after U.S. and European diplomatic interventions.

But the story of the "Bronze Statue" did not end there. Days after the riots the computerized infrastructure of Estonia's high-tech government began to fray, victimized by what experts in cybersecurity termed a coordinated "denial of service" attack. A flood of bogus requests for information from computers around the world conspired to cripple (Wired) the websites of Estonian banks, media outlets, and ministries for days. Estonia denounced the attacks as an unprovoked act of aggression from a regional foe (though experts still disagree on who perpetrated it—Moscow has denied any knowledge). Experts in cybersecurity went one step further: They called it the future of warfare.

Cyber Warfare: The New Frontier

The attack on Estonia's "paperless government" (BBC) was one of the most publicized hacks in recent computing history. But it wasn't the first case of cyber espionage, nor the most egregious. It's the "tip of the iceberg of the quantity and quality of attacks that are going on," says O. Sami Saydjari, president of the Cyber Defense Agency, a security consultant, and a former Pentagon computer security expert. Israel, India, Pakistan, and the United States have all been accused of launching similar attacks on adversaries.

China, however, may be the most active. Washington has accused the Chinese of hacking into government computer networks at the U.S. Departments of State, Commerce, and Defense—in some instances making off with data. But accusations of Chinese cyber-meddling reached a crescendo in June 2007, when, according to the Financial Times, hackers broke into a Pentagon network that serves the Office of the Secretary of Defense, briefly shutting it down.

Chinese electronic espionage has also been suspected against British companies (Rolls Royce is one example), as well as government agencies in France, Germany, South Korea, and Taiwan. "Chinese capabilities in this area have evolved from defending networks from attack to offensive operations against adversary networks," Deputy Undersecretary for Defense Richard P. Lawless told a House committee in June 2007. China, like Russia, denies the accusations. Both countries argue any attacks originating from IP addresses inside their countries have been directed by rogue citizens, not their governments. Western targets, however, continue to accuse the Chinese of ratcheting up their cyber attack capabilities.

U.S. CYBER WARFARE ON THE OFFENSIVE

The United States, of course, is no innocent bystander. William M. Arkin, a defense analyst who writes the Early Warning blog for the Washington Post, says "our ability to penetrate into enemy computer networks, our ability to exploit communication networks, to manipulate digital information, is real," but little is known about the precise nature of Washington's offensive capabilities. Some details, however, have leaked. For instance, in March 2004 the Pentagon announced the formation of an Information Operations team—the Network Attack Support Staff—to streamline the military's cyber attack capabilities. The aim, senior military officials said at the time, was to create an "interface between the combatant commanders and the intelligence community."

> " Our information infrastructure ...increasingly is being targeted for exploitation and potentially for disruption or destruction by a growing array of state and non-state adversaries." –Director of National Intelligence Michael McConnell

Arkin, who has reported on cybersecurity issues for over two decades, says the U.S. military also has technologies capable of penetrating and jamming enemy networks, including the classified "Suter" system of airborne technology. According to Aviation Week, Suter has been integrated into unmanned aircraft and "allows users to invade communications networks, see what enemy sensors see, and even take over as systems administrator so sensors can be manipulated into positions so that approaching aircraft can't be seen." Some speculate the Israeli military used the capability during its air raid on a Syrian construction site in September 2007. The United States made use of nascent capabilities in the 1999 Kosovo War (MSNBC.com), and built on those lessons in Iraq (Wired).

CYBER-WARFARE TACTICS

Other cyber tactics are less sophisticated. The attack that temporarily brought down Estonian networks began with a flood of bogus messages targeting government servers, called a "denial of service" attack. The approach harnesses "botnets"—massive networks of interconnected computers—to bombard targeted networks with information requests while masking the location of the primary attacker. James Lewis, a security expert with the Center for Strategic and International Studies (CSIS), says hackers in the Estonia example likely took control of tens of thousands of computers around the world without the knowledge of their owners and directed them at the government's servers. The result, he says, was a relatively minor attack that was nearly impossible to trace.

Another technique is the use of "malware," "spyware," and other malicious programs imbedded into computer systems to steal information without user knowledge. The software is designed to hide undetected and siphon information from its host—everything from secrets stored on personal computers to Pentagon military mainframes. A December 2007 analysis of U.S. Air Force cyber vulnerabilities notes much of the Pentagon's operating systems are off-the-shelf components manufactured overseas, due to cheaper costs. But pinching pennies has potentially opened U.S. military networks to intrusion. "Foreign countries could place hidden components inside the computers, making the computers vulnerable for attack and/or spying," the analysis concludes.

> "Our ability to penetrate into enemy computer networks, our ability to exploit communication networks, to manipulate digital information, is real." –Defense Analyst William M. Arkin

Less common but far more worrisome are cyber attacks aimed at critical infrastructure—like nuclear-power-plant control systems, banks, or subways. In March 2007 the Department of Energy's Idaho Lab conducted an experiment to determine whether a power plant could be compromised by hacking alone. The result—a smoking, self-combusting diesel generator incapacitated by nothing more than keystrokes—sent shivers (CNN) through the private sector. The worries were apparently well-founded.

In January 2008 a CIA analyst told U.S. utilities that hackers had succeeded in infiltrating electric companies in undisclosed locations outside the United States and, it at least one instance, shut off power to multiple cities. The hackers then demanded money (AP). "The [U.S.] government is scrambling to try and protect its own systems, to try and check the Chinese from reading government email," says economist Scott Borg, director of the U.S. Cyber Consequences Unit, a nonprofit research institute that studies cyber threats. "But the focus probably needs to be critical infrastructure. That's what we need to defend."

PATCHING THE HOLES

On paper the U.S. government appears to agree. For over a decade government-sanctioned studies have delved into the subject; the Pentagon published a report on "Information Warfare-Defense" (PDF) in 1996, when public use of the Internet was still in its infancy. Saydjari says all of these studies reached the same conclusion: "The threat and vulnerabilities to our national infrastructure is serious, it's getting worse, and it's getting worse at an increasingly fast rate."

But only recently has the concern been a constant focus of attention for the security and intelligence communities. Part of the attention deficit lies with the difficulty in defining the cyber threat. A 2006 Air Force task force termed cyberspace "a warfighting domain bounded by the electromagnetic spectrum," but air force officials acknowledge "a full understanding of the domain is years away."

What is understood is how potentially devastating the loss of cyberspace dominance could be to U.S. interests. In his annual threat assessment to Congress delivered in February 2008, Director of National Intelligence Michael McConnell discussed "cyber threats" before talking about the war in Afghanistan.

"Our information infrastructure ...increasingly is being targeted for exploitation and potentially for disruption or destruction by a growing array of state and non-state adversaries," McConnell said. "We assess that nations, including Russia and China, have the technical capabilities to target and disrupt" the United States' information infrastructure.

> "Chinese [cyber warfare] capabilities have evolved from defending networks from attack to offensive operations against adversary networks." –U.S. Deputy Under Secretary for Defense Richard P. Lawless

The Pentagon, too, has acknowledged the threat to its infrastructure. The Defense Department is considering banning nonofficial traffic (Federal Computer Week) from its servers, and the U.S. Air Force is creating a Cyber Command to defend Pentagon networks. "When we talk about the speed range and flexibility of air power, the thing that enables this for us is the fact of our cyber-dominance," Air Force Gen. Robert Elder told United Press International.

The recent flurry of high-level pronouncements also comes amid a renewed funding commitment from Washington. In November 2007 the Bush administration called on the National Security Agency to coordinate with the Department of Homeland Security to protect government and civilian communication networks from hackers. The $144 million plan, unveiled quietly in White House budget documents (PDF), aims to enhance "civilian agency cybersecurity and strengthen defenses to combat terrorism."

In January 2008 President George W. Bush signed two presidential directives calling for the creation of a comprehensive national cybersecurity initiative. According to an article by the Wall Street Journal, the White House's 2009 budget request takes the program exponentially further, with an estimated $6 billion request to build a secretive system to protect U.S. communications networks. Details of the proposed program remain classified, angering some civil libertarians who fear monitoring of civilian networks could infringe on privacy rights. Rep. Bennie G. Thompson (D-MS), chairman of the House Homeland Security Committee, has called for the program to be put on hold (PDF) until Congress can adequately review it.

MEASURING THE THREAT

Cyber experts don't dispute that electronic espionage is a vexing problem, or that the United States is a prime target. But they do disagree on how pervasive such attacks are, who is behind them, and how disruptive they may prove to be.

According to a tally by the Heritage Foundation, a conservative Washington think tank, the hackers may already be winning: In 2007 the Department of Homeland Security logged an estimated 37,000 attempted breaches of private and government computer systems, and over 80,000 attacks on Pentagon systems. Some hacks "reduced the U.S. military's operational capabilities," the report says.

Economist Borg says the biggest threat from cyber attacks may be economic. He estimates a shutdown of electric power to any sizable region for more than ten days would stop over 70 percent of all economic activity in that region. "If you can do that with a pure cyber attack on only one critical infrastructure, why would you bother with any traditional military attack?" CSIS' Lewis takes a less alarmist view.

"The U.S. is a very big set of targets, and some of our important networks are very secure. So you could inflict damage on the U.S. but it wouldn't be crippling or decisive," he says. "I've seen people who say a cyber attack could turn the United States into a third-world nation in a matter of minutes. That's silly. We have to be realistic about this."

3

Cyber Warfare and Present Strategies

Crime is a social and economic phenomenon and is as old as the human society. As, Life is about a mix of good and evil, so is the Internet. For all the good it does to us, cyberspace has its dark sides too. The Internet is undeniably open to exploitation. Known as cyber crimes, these activities involve the use of computers, the Internet, cyberspace and the World Wide Web. Cyber crime is the latest and perhaps the most complicated problem in the cyber world.

Cyber crime is an evil having its origin in the growing dependence on computers in modern life. In a day and age when everything from microwave ovens and refrigerators to nuclear power plants is being run on computers, cyber crime has assumed rather sinister implications.

While the worldwide scenario on cyber crime looks bleak, the situation in India isn't any better. Cyber crimes in India are slowly evolving from a simple e-mail crime to more serious crimes like hacking and source code theft. Cases of spam, hacking, cyber stalking and email fraud are rampant despite the enactment of the Information Technology Act, 2000, the India's Cyber Law and setting up of cyber crimes cells in major cities. The problem is that most cases remain unreported due to a lack of awareness.

So, the need of the hour is to make the masses aware of the Cyber Crime itself and their rights and duties in relation to Cyber Crime. As, it is only then can this growing menace be checked.

So, in the present report an attempt has been made to describe the various types of cyber crimes and the present scenario on the cyber crime and the preventive measures that should be taken up to protect ourselves.

The word CYBER SPACE was coined by Willliam Gibson in the science fiction NEUROMANCER, in the year 1984. It is used as a means of denoting the apparent or virtual location within which electronic activities take place. Of late, the word Cyber has become a loose synonym for electronics. Cyber Space therefore is a place where people meet not physically but virtually and communicate with each other electronically. Cyber Space is the aggregate of Intranets, Internet and World Wide Web.

The Internet has opened up a whole new virtual heaven for the people both good and bad, cleaver and naïve to enter and interact with a lot of diverse cultures and subcultures, geography and demographics being no bar. The rise of the Internet as one of the most significant communication and business platforms of this century has come with its own set of issues and concerns. While the Net has brought a host of benefits to the common person and to enterprises, it is also having to grapple with major challenges, primary among them security.

The very same virtues of Internet when gone in wrong hands or when exploited by people with dirty minds and malicious intentions make it virtual hell. Due to popularity of Internet, hacking or breaking into somebody into else's computer is more popular and automated than ever.

There are various frauds of computer and internet related crimes. The most common is the use of viruses to corrupt and destroy data stored in computer systems. The forms of crimes like impersonation, theft of credit card information, e-gambling, espionage, harassment, pornography are on a rise due to the growth of the medium.

CRIME CYBER

Cyber crime consists of specific crimes dealing with computers and networks (such as hacking) and the facilitation of traditional crime through the use of computers.

According to US Department of Justice and the council of Europe, the term Cyber Crime refers to "wide range of crimes that involve computers and networks".

In additional to cyber crime, there is also "computer-supported crime" which covers the use of computers by criminals for communication, documentation or data storage.The computer may be used as a tool in the following kinds of activity- financial crimes, sale of illegal articles, pornography, online gambling, intellectual property crime, e-mail spoofing, forgery, cyber defamation, cyber stalking.

The computer may however be target for unlawful acts in the following cases- unauthorized access to computer/ computer system/ computer networks, theft of information contained in the electronic form, e-mail bombing, data didling, salami attacks, logic bombs, Trojan attacks, internet time thefts, web jacking, theft of computer system, physically damaging the computer system.

CYBER CRIMINALS

The cyber criminals constitute of various groups/ category.

- Some cyber criminals are techie mavericks who take pleasure in writing and releasing destructive viruses.
- Others are suit-wearing professionals who steal copies of their employers' customer databases to take with them when they quit.
- Some are con artists with plans to scam personal information from consumers and use it for financial gain.
- Some are there just for fun

The cyber criminals can be distinguished on the basis of their skill levels and motivations:

Novice

They have limited computer and programming skills. And rely on toolkits to conduct their attacks. Can cause extensive damage to systems since they don't understand how the attack works. Usually looking for media attention.

Cyber-punks

They are capable of writing their own software and have an understanding of the systems they are attacking. Many are engaged in credit card number theft and telecommunications fraud. Have a tendency to brag about their exploits.

Internals

a) Disgruntled employees or ex-employees

These may be involved in technology-related jobs, usually aided by privileges they have or had been assigned as part of their job function.

They pose largest security problem. This group include those people who have been either sacked by their employer or are dissatisfied with their employer. To avenge they normally hack the system of their employee

b) Petty thieves

These Include employees, contractors, consultants who are Computer literate and opportunistic (take advantage of poor internal security). Usually motivated by greed or necessity to pay off other habits, such as drugs or gambling.

Coders

These Act as mentors to the newbie's. Write the scripts and automated tools that others use. Mostly motivated by a sense of power and prestige these are very dangerous have hidden agendas use Trojan horses.

Old Guard Hackers

They don't have any criminal intent but have alarming disrespect for personal property.

Professional Criminals

These basically specialize in corporate espionage. These are guns for hire, are highly motivated, highly trained, have access to state-of-the-art equipment.

Information Warriors/cyber-terrorists

Increase in activity since the fall of many Eastern Bloc intelligence agencies. They are well funded and mix political rhetoric with criminal activity.

Types of Threats

There are basically two types of threats :

1) Directly targeting the computer :

- Privacy invasions & Identity theft
- Hacking and Cracking
- Spam & Phishing
- Web Site Defacements
- Malicious Code
- Denial of Service
- Bot infected computers, etc.

2) Directly have a bearing on the individual or it can be said that these are traditional crimes which use computer as a tool for commission of crime, like;

- Stalking and Sex-related offences
- Vandalism, Conspiracy, Gambling
- Extortion, Smuggling, Hate Crimes
- Copyright infringement, recording and software piracy
- Currency and Document counterfeiting
- Stock market manipulations
- Theft and Fraud

These types of crimes are on a rise due to the growth of the medium itself. So, greater the spread of internet greater will be the increase in the cyber crime incidents.

THREATS DIRECTLY TARGETING THE COMPUTER:

1) Privacy invasions & Identity theft

Privacy can be invaded online in several ways. For example, it can happen when a person:

- fills out forms and enter contests on commercial Web sites
- provides information when registering for Internet services or software (i.e. file-sharing, instant messaging, e-mail)
- completes a personal profile for an e-mail or social networking sites or instant messaging account
- gives personal information to strangers in chat rooms or through instant messaging

Identity Theft

It's the process of wrongfully obtaining and using this personal data for fraud or deception for economic gains. Identity theft is a high-profile security issue, particularly for organizations that store and manage large amounts of personal information, like, government organizations, education sector, health care sector, financial sector, etc.

Not only can compromises that result in the loss of personal data undermine customer and institutional confidence and result in costly damage to an organization's reputation, but data breaches can also be financially costly to organizations: the average cost per incident of a data breach in the United States was $6.3 million and lost business amounted to an average of $4.1 million.11 Also, organizations can be held liable for breaches and losses, which may result in fines or litigation.

In the last six months of 2007, the education sector represented the highest number of known data breaches that could lead to identity theft, accounting for 24 percent of the total (figure1). Despite the high number of data breaches that occurred in the education sector during the last six months of 2007, it only accounted for one percent of all identities exposed during the period, however the government sector ranked second and accounted for 20 percent of data breaches that could lead to identity theft, moreover the government sector had the highest overall number of identities exposed during the period, accounting for 60 percent of the total. There were a number of high profile data loss incidents during the period.

One incident involved Her Majesty's Revenue and Customs (HMRC) in the United Kingdom, when two unencrypted disks containing personal records on 25 million people were lost during transfer from HMRC to the National Audit Office

Hacking and Cracking

Hacking is much of an art, a way of thinking as it is a science.

Hacking means an illegal intrusion into a computer system and/network. Using one's own programming abilities as also various programmes with malicious intent to gain unauthorized access to a computer or network are very serious crimes. There is an equivalent term to hacking i.e. cracking, but the Indian law does not distinguish between the two.

Hacker

This is someone that seeks to understand computer, phone or other systems strictly for the satisfaction of having that knowledge. Hackers wonder how things work, and have an incredible curiosity. Hackers will sometimes do questionable legal things, such as breaking into systems, but they generally will not cause harm once they break in.

Cracker

This is the common term used to describe a malicious hacker. Crackers get into all kinds of mischief, including breaking or "cracking" copy protection on software programs, breaking into systems and causing harm, changing data, or stealing. Hackers regard crackers as a less educated group of individuals that cannot truly create their own work, and simply steal other people's work to cause mischief, or for personal gain."

As per IT act 2000 all kinds of hacking is a punishable offence with imprisonment up to three years or fine up to two lakh or both.

Phishing

Phishing is an attempt by a third party to solicit confidential information from an individual, group, or organization by mimicking, or spoofing, a specific, usually well-known brand, usually for financial gain.

Phishers attempt to trick users into disclosing personal data, such as credit card numbers, online banking credentials, and other sensitive information, which they may then use to commit fraudulent acts. In a typical phishing scam, phishers send out e-mails which appear to come from a legitimate company, in an attempt to scam users into Providing private information that will be used for identity theft. Phishers use a variety of sophisticated devices to steal information—including pop-up windows, URL masks which simulate real Web addresses, and keystroke loggers that capture what you type, such as account names and passwords.

Phishing can be described in two ways: phishing attempts and phishing messages. A phishing attempt can be defined as an instance of phishing message being sent to a single user. Extending the phishing analogy, a phishing attempt can be considered a single cast of the lure (the phishing message) to try to catch a target. A single phishing message can be used in numerous distinct phishing attempts, usually targeting different end users.

A phishing Web site is a site that is designed to mimic the legitimate Web site of the organization whose brand is being spoofed. In many cases, it is set up by the attacker to capture a victim's authentication information or other personal identification information, which can then be used in identity theft or other fraudulent activity.

In the last six months of 2007, the majority of brands used in phishing attacks were in the financial services sector, accounting for 80 percent. The financial services sector also accounted for the highest volume of phishing Websites during this period, at 66 percent. Since most phishing activity pursues financial gain, successful attacks using brands in this sector are most likely to yield profitable data, such as bank account credentials, making this sector an obvious focus for attacks.

Internet service providers (ISPs) were ranked second in unique brands used in phishing attacks during this period, at eight percent. The ISP sector also accounted for the second highest volume of phishing attacks during the period, accounting for 18 percent.

ISP accounts can be valuable targets for phishers because people frequently use the same authentication credentials (such as usernames and passwords) for multiple accounts, including email accounts.

Besides this other forms of phishing is also becoming popular:

Pharming

It's an attempt to defraud Internet surfers by hijacking a Web site's domain name, or URL, and redirecting users to an imposture Web site where fraudulent requests for information are made.

SMiShing

It refers to a phishing attack sent via Short Message Service on cell phones. Cell phone users are sent text messages containing a Web site link which, when visited, could download a Trojan horse, that could allow a Web-enabled phone to be controlled by hackers. SMiShing is another example of how hackers are injecting cell phones and other mobile devices with malware and viruses which could penetrate enterprise networks, according to Rayhawk.

Vishing

Its Just as Internet surfers have gotten wise to the fine art of phishing, along comes a new scam utilizing a new technology. Creative thieves are now switching their efforts to "vishing," which uses Voice over Internet Protocol (VoIP) phones instead of a misdirected Web link to steal user information.

Spear Phishing

It is any highly targeted phishing attack. Spear phishers send e-mail that appears genuine to all the employees or members within a certain company, government agency, organization, or group. The message might look like it comes from your employer, or from a colleague who might send an e-mail message to everyone in the company, such as the head of human resources or the person who manages the computer systems, and could include requests for user names or passwords. The truth is that the e-mail sender information has been faked or "spoofed." Whereas traditional phishing scams are designed to steal information from individuals, spear phishing scams work to gain access to a company's entire computer system. If you respond with a user name or password, or if you click links or open attachments in a spear phishing e-mail, pop-up window, or Web site, you might become a victim of identity theft and you might put your employer or group at risk. Spear phishing also describes scams that target people who use a certain product or Web site

According to annual report for 2007 of CERT (Computer Emergency Response Team), the apex cyber security division under the ministry of information technology of India, there was 392 incidents of phishing in India in the year 2007.

UNDERGROUND ECONOMY SERVERS

Underground economy servers are black market forums used by criminals and criminal organizations to advertise and trade stolen information and services typically for use in identity theft. This information can include government-issued identification numbers such as Social Security numbers, credit cards, credit verification values, debit cards, personal identification numbers (PIN s), user accounts, email address lists, and bank accounts. Services include cashiers, scam page hosting, and job advertisements Such as for scam developers or phishing partners.

The geographic locations of underground economy servers are constantly changing due to the nature of these servers, which are often hosted as channels on public IRC servers. Once a fraud-related IRC channel becomes popular, it is often either shut down by the IRC server administrators or abandoned by its users due to legal liability and the increased possibility of being caught. As such, the location of an underground economy server is primarily driven by convenience and the lifespan of a server may be short. Furthermore, the geographic location of the server is typically not of any consequence to those involved because users of underground economy servers do most of their business electronically.

Criminals advertise their goods and services on IRC servers by listing available items and their prices. Potential buyers will privately contact the sellers to make the deal and finalize payment. Payment options for these goods are either conducted through online currency exchange services or exchange of goods. Unwilling to risk exposure, many purchasers will use the services of cashiers who will convert the information for a fee into true currency, either in the form of online currency accounts or through money transfers. In exchange for the service, cashiers will take a percentage of the cash-out amount.26 Members of underground economy servers are usually self-policing, reporting rippers27 to the administrators of the IRC servers, and also broadcasting this information to warn each other. Often, repeat rippers will be kicked off and banned from the servers.

During the second half of 2007, bank account credentials, including account numbers and authentication information, were the most frequently advertised item observed on underground economy servers, making up 22 percent of all goods.

The advertised price for bank account credentials varied as widely as from $10 to $1,000 USD, depending on the amount of funds available and the location of the account.

Bank accounts that included higher balances, such as business accounts, and EU accounts, were advertised for considerably more. Furthermore, bank accounts that bundled in personal information such as names, addresses and dates of birth were advertised at higher prices.

Current Rank	Previous Rank	Goods and Services	Current Percentage	Previous Percentage	Range of Prices
1	2	Bank accounts	22%	21%	$10–$1000
2	1	Credit cards	13%	22%	$0.40–$20
3	7	Full identities	9%	6%	$1–$15
4	N/A	Online auction site accounts	7%	N/A	$1–$8
5	8	Scams	7%	6%	$2.50/week–$50/week for hosting, $25 for design
6	4	Mailers	6%	8%	$1–$10
7	5	Email addresses	5%	6%	$0.83/MB–$10/MB
8	3	Email passwords	5%	8%	$4–$30
9	N/A	Drop (request or offer)	5%	N/A	10%–50% of total drop amount
10	6	Proxies	5%	6%	$1.50–$30

Table. Breakdown of goods and services available for sale on underground economy servers

Credit cards were the second most commonly advertised item on underground economy servers during this reporting period, accounting for 13 percent of all advertised goods. Full identities were the third most common item advertised for sale on underground economy servers, making up nine percent of all advertised goods.

The popularity of full identities may be due to their versatility and ease of use. With a full identity, a criminal can easily obtain government issued documents, commit credit card fraud, open bank accounts, obtain credit, purchase and/or steal homes, 32 or even evade arrest by masquerading as someone else.

In one case, the CEO of an identity theft prevention company was a victim of identity theft when someone used his social security number, which was prominently displayed on the company's Web site, to obtain $500 loan.

Website Defacement

Website defacement is an attack on a website that changes the visual appearance of the site. These are typically the work of system crackers, who break into a web server and replace the hosted website with one of their own.

Sometimes the Defacer makes fun of the system administrator for failing to maintain server security. Most times the defacement is harmless; however, it can sometimes be used as a distraction to cover up more sinister actions such as uploading malware. High-profile website defacement was carried out on the website of the company SCO Group following its assertion that Linux contained stolen code. The title of the page was changed from "Red Hat vs. SCO" to "SCO vs. World," with various satirical content.

Web site defacement is very common, much more common that webmasters and system administrators would like to admit. The number of defacements is on the rise, especially those done for a political message.

Following its yearly assessment, the CERT (Computer Emergency Response Team), the apex cyber security division under the ministry of information technology of India, found 5,863 Indian Websites underwent defacement by global hackers in 2007.

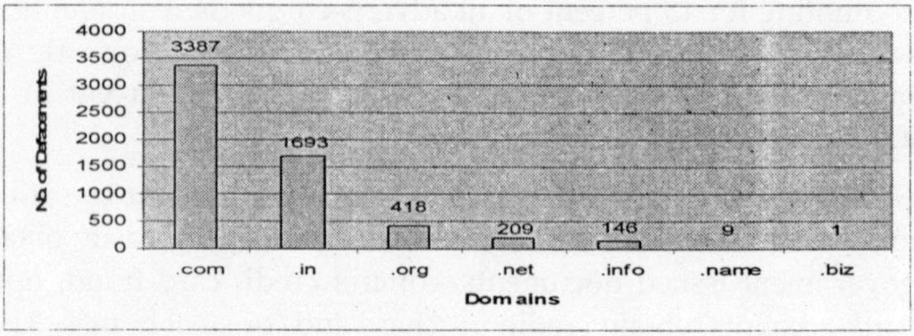

Figure: Number of Indian Websites defaced in 2007

Malicious Software or Malware

These are small programmes or fragments of programmes which cause the malfunctioning/ damage to the system. These are:

Back Door

A programme that opens up access (login, dialup, network) to a machine from the outside to allow an intruder into the machine. Back doors, can give a remote attacker complete control over a compromised computer.

Logic Bomb or Time Bomb

It is a computer programme within another programme and performs destructive acts on the basis of trigger mechanism.

Trojan Horse

It simply a spy programme, disguised as another programme, usually malicious one. It enters into the target computer system hidden in some another programme usually games or some downloaded files.

Trojan is capable of downloading and installing other threats onto the compromised computer. Trojans are also frequently used to steal information that an attacker can sell or profit from in other ways.

During the current reporting period, Trojans made up 71 percent of the volume of the top 50 potential malicious code infections (figure5).

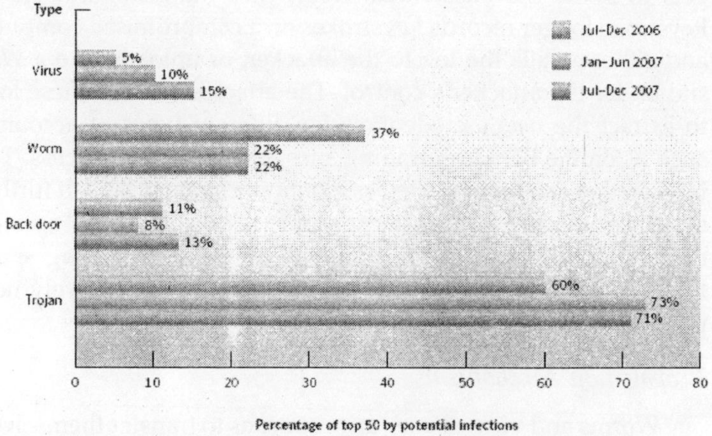

Figure: Malicious code types by potential infections

Worm

It is a programme which propagates itself (without external help) from one computer to another across a data network. a worm usually is a stand alone – not attached to another programme. The first sign of computer worm activity dates back to1982, the first being Elk Cloner followed by Morris worm. Worms made up 22 percent of the volume of the top 50 potential malicious code infections in the last six months of 2007.

Virus

It is a programme that replicates itself. Parasitic, it usually attaches itself to, overwrites or replaces a part of another programme (the host) to spread. Major virus types are:

Boot Sector, Companion virus, Dropper, Stealth virus, File Infector, Polymorphic virus, etc.

Viruses made up 15 percent of the volume of the top 50 potential malicious code infections in the last six months of 2007

Keystroke – logging

It is a programme which records all the keys typed by the user and transmits this information to the attacker who in turn easily gets to know the passwords, credit card numbers, and etc. A keystroke logger records keystrokes on a compromised computer and either emails the log to the attacker, or uploads it to a Web site under the attacker's control. The attacker can use these logs to extract the user's credentials for different types of accounts, such as online banking, trading sites, or ISP account access. The information can then be used as a stepping stone to launch further attacks. For example, the attacker could use the stolen ISP account credentials to set up a phishing site on the free hosting space typically included with these accounts. This is a relatively new phenomenon.

Propagation Mechanisms

Worms and viruses use various means to transfer themselves, or propagate, from one computer to another. These means are collectively referred to as propagation mechanisms, some malicious code samples use more than one mechanism to propagate. The most common methods of propagation include, shared executable files, email attachments. And removable drives, shared network drive. Forty percent of malicious code that propagated did so through executable file sharing.

Threats to Confidential Information

Some malicious code programs are designed specifically to expose confidential information that is stored on an infected computer. These threats may expose sensitive data such as system information, confidential files and documents, or logon credentials. Some malicious code threats, such as Threats to confidential information are a particular concern because of their potential for use in criminal activities. With the widespread use of online shopping and Internet banking, compromises of this nature can result in significant financial loss, particularly if credit card information or banking details are exposed.

Within the enterprise, exposure of confidential information can lead to significant data leakage. If it involves customer-related data—such as credit card information—customer confidence in the enterprise can be severely undermined. Moreover, it can also violate local laws. Sensitive corporate information, including financial details, business plans, and proprietary technologies, could also be leaked from compromised computers.

Threats to confidential information made up 68 percent of the volume of the top 50 potential malicious code infections in the last six months of 2007, causing potential infections Malicious code can expose confidential information in a variety of ways. The most common method is by allowing remote access to the compromised computer through a back door. Remote access component such as a back door accounted for 86 percent of the threats to the confidential information in the last half of 2006.

It is more popular than other techniques. This is because remote access, , gives the attacker extensive control over the compromised computer, allowing for the theft of any information on the computer, the installation of other threats, or the use of the computer for other purposes, such as relaying spam or hosting a phishing Web site. Confidential information threats with keystroke logging capability made up 76 percent of threats to confidential information, last six months of 2007

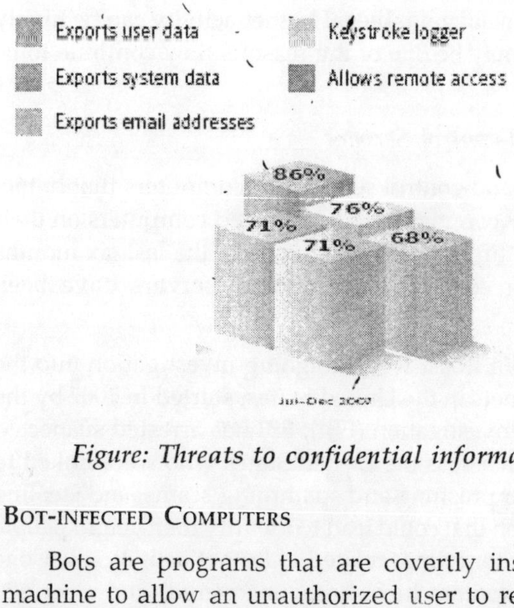

Figure: Threats to confidential information by type

Bot-infected Computers

Bots are programs that are covertly installed on a user's machine to allow an unauthorized user to remotely control the targeted system through a communication channel, such as IRC, peer-to-peer (P2P), or HTTP. These channels allow the remote attacker to control a large number of compromised computers in a botnet, which can then be used to launch coordinated attacks. Bots allow for a wide range of functionality and most can be updated to assume new functionality by downloading new code and features.

Attackers can use bots to perform a variety of tasks, such as setting up DoS attacks against an organization's Web site, distributing spam and phishing attacks, distributing spyware and adware, propagating malicious code, and harvesting confidential information that may be used in identity theft; all of which can have serious financial and legal consequences.

Attackers may favor bot-infected computers because they are able to perform a wide range of functions, are effective in the attacks they mount, and are relatively easy and inexpensive to propagate.

They are also difficult to disable with a decentralized command-and-control model, and most importantly, can be used for substantial financial gain. Illegal botnet activity can be highly lucrative and this may be one of the reasons they continue to be so popular.

Bot Command-and-control Servers

Bot command-and-control servers are computers that botnet owners use to relay commands to botinfected computers on their networks, usually through IR C channels. In the last six months of 2007, 4,091 bot command-and-control servers have been identified.

In Operation Bot Roast II , an ongoing investigation into the criminal use of botnets in the United States, started in 2007 by the Federal Bureau of Investigation (FBI), FBI has arrested suspected botnet owners from across the United States who were linked to multi-million dollar phishing and spamming scams, and stealing personal information that could lead to identity theft., eight people have been indicted for crimes related to botnet activity, over one million victim computers have been uncovered, and over $20 million in economic losses have been reported.

SPAM

Spam is usually defined as junk or unsolicited email sent by a third party. While it is certainly an annoyance to users and administrators, spam is also a serious security concern as it can be used to deliver Trojans, viruses, and phishing attempts. It could also cause a loss of service or degradation in the performance of network resources and email gateways.

Between July 1 and December 31, 2007, spam made up 71 percent of all email traffic monitored at the gateway. Eighty percent of all spam detected during this period was composed in English. Also, 42 percent of all spam detected worldwide originated in the United States. The United States hosts the most spam zombies of any country, with 10 percent of the worldwide total.

Current Rank	Previous Rank	Country/Region	Current Percentage	Previous Percentage
1	1	United States	42%	50%
2	3	United Kingdom	5%	4%
3	14	Russia	4%	2%
4	2	China	4%	4%
5	7	Poland	3%	3%
6	6	Taiwan	3%	3%
7	4	Japan	3%	4%
8	8	Germany	3%	2%
9	5	South Korea	3%	3%
10	15	Spain	2%	1%

Table 3 top ten countries of spam origin

The most common type of spam detected in the first half of 2007 was related to commercial products, which made up 27 percent of all spam detected. Commercial products spam usually consists of advertisements for commercial goods and services.

It is frequently used to sell designer goods, such as watches, handbags, and sunglasses, the profits from which can be substantial given that the goods sold are often cheaply made counterfeits. In other cases the spammers may simply be attempting to collect credit card and personal information for use in identity theft.

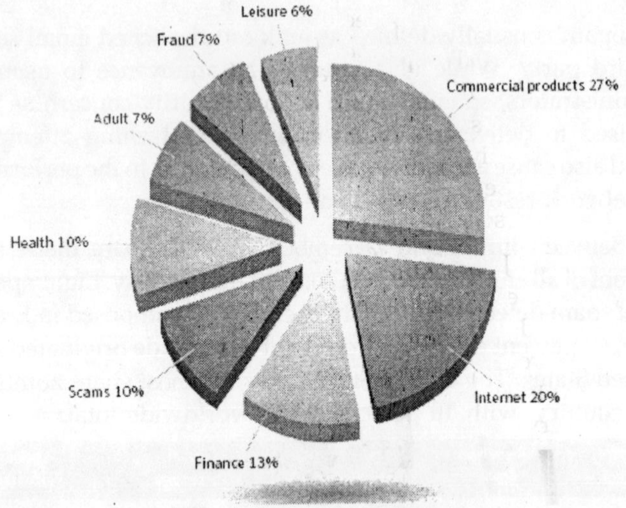

Figure: Top spam categories

Twenty percent of the spam was Internet-related. This type of spam is typically used to promote Web hosting and design, as well as other online commodities like phishing and spam toolkits. Since phishing and spam toolkits cannot typically be advertised by legitimate means, such as through banner ads on Web sites, spam tends to be the only way to promote them.

Spam related to financial services made up 13 percent of all spam detected in the last six months of 2007, making it the third most common type of spam during this period.

Denial of Services

A purely malicious attack with the purpose of disabling access or availability of a resource. The main objective of this type of attack is to prevent the legitimate users of a service from using it. It is often abbreviated as DoS.

A DoS attack may come in variety of flavors. Attacks may flood a network with large amount of data or deliberately consume a scarce or limited resource, there by blocking the entire flow of information by attacking the medium through which the data must travel.

Scanning or Probing

It is basically testing a networked computer for vulnerabilities (typically vulnerable services, but also checking for vulnerable accounts and passwords), remotely via the network. Scanning is normally conducted as a prelude to a more directed attack on systems that the intruder has found to be vulnerable.

Theft of Service

An attack with the purpose of obtaining unauthorized access to a resource (computing cycles, network bandwidth, disk space, etc). In some cases the motive behind the theft is to avoid paying (for information, internet access, etc): in other cases the motive is to obtain access to a resource that is restricted or denied to the perpetrator. Some times certain unscrupulous elements somehow get hold of others passwords and use the internet services free of cost, with the knowledge of account holder. In February 2000, the economic offences Wing of Delhi Police registered and investigated a case of theft of 107 hours of Internet time. They traced the culprit and booked him under section 307 of IPC, the culprit was a computer engineer. This was stated to be the first instance of an arrest in a cyber crime case in Delhi.

4

Trends in Cyber Attacks

These types of crimes are on a rise due to the growth of the medium itself. So, greater the spread of internet greater will be the increase in the cyber crime incidents.

As, per the Symantec Global Internet Security Threat Report, April 2008, Volume XII:

- The United States accounted for 31 percent of all malicious activity.
- The United States was the top country of attack origin in the second half of 2007, accounting for 24 percent of worldwide activity,

Current Rank	Previous Rank	Country	Current Percentage	Previous Percentage	Bot Rank	Command-and-Control Server Rank	Phishing Web Sites Host Rank	Malicious Code Rank	Spam Zombies Rank	Attack Origin. Rank
1	1	United States	31%	30%	1	1	1	1	1	1
2	2	China	7%	10%	3	5	2	2	4	2
3	3	Germany	7%	7%	2	2	3	7	2	3
4	4	United Kingdom	4%	4%	9	6	7	3	12	5
5	7	Spain	4%	3%	4	19	15	9	9	4
6	5	France	4%	4%	8	13	6	11	7	6
7	6	Canada	3%	4%	13	3	5	4	35	7
8	8	Italy	3%	3%	5	10	11	10	6	8
9	12	Brazil	3%	2%	6	7	13	21	3	9
10	9	South Korea	2%	3%	15	4	9	14	13	10

Table: Malicious activity by country

It is clearly evident that the United States had the most malicious activity, this is because it has the most established broadband infrastructure in the world: 94 percent of U.S. households have access to available broadband connections, and its 65.5 million broadband subscribers represent 20 percent of the world's total, more than any other country.

China had the second highest amount of worldwide malicious activity during the last six months of 2007, accounting for seven percent, since China has the second highest number of broadband subscribers in the world, with 19 percent of the worldwide broadband total.

But the situation is no better in India with the cyber crime cases increasing at a fast rate.

TRENDS IN INDIA IN 2007

Following its yearly assessment, the CERT (Computer Emergency Response Team), the apex cyber security division under the ministry of information technology of India, found that cyber crime in the country has accelerated about 50 times since 2004.

CERT's report tries to say that the highest growth has occurred in computer related crimes that attack e-commerce businesses and financial service on the Net.

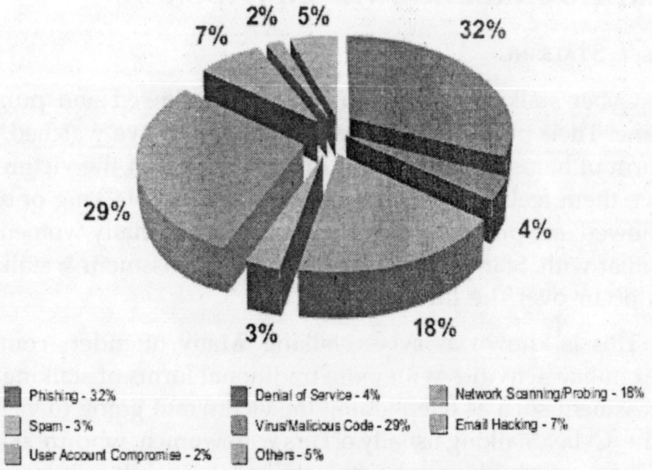

Figure: Security incidents reported during 2007

The agency recorded just 23 cyber crime incidents in 2004 in contrast to a huge 1,237 in 2007. These primarily included phishing attacks, distribution of viruses/malicious code and illegal infiltration to computer networks.

Further, according to annual report for 2007 of CERT, there were 392 incidents of phishing, accounting to 32% of all the incidents,358 cases of virus proliferation (accounting to 29%) and 223 cases of network infiltration (accounting to 18%) recorded in 2007. Compared to this, there were only 3 phishing attacks, 5 cases of virus proliferation and 11 incidents of network infiltration reported in 2004.

CERT, found 5,863 Indian Websites that underwent mutilation or defacement by global hackers in 2007. The government agency also tracked 1,805 'open proxy' servers that allow anonymous browsing. It also detected more than 25,000 bot-infected computers. Furthermore, a data of the government revealed that in January 2008, 87 security related incidents were recorded in contrast to 45 in December 2007. Of these, 47% involved phishing, 25% related to worm/virus under the malware category, 21% to unauthorized scanning, and 7% to technical help under separate categories.

THREATS TARGETING THE INDIVIDUALS

Cyber Stalking

Cyber stalking is when a person is followed and pursued online. Their privacy is invaded, their every move watched. It is a form of harassment, and can disrupt the life of the victim and leave them feeling very afraid and threatened Stalking or being 'followed' are problems that many people, especially women, are familiar with. Sometimes these problems (harassment & stalking) can occur over the Internet.

This is known as cyber stalking. Many offenders combine their online activities with more traditional forms of stalking and harassment such as telephoning the victim and going to victim's home. Cyber Stalking usually occurs with women, who are stalked by men, or children who are stalked by adult predators or pedophiles. A cyber stalker does not have to leave his home to find, or harass his targets, and has no fear of physical violence since he believes he cannot be physically touched in cyberspace. He maybe may be on the other side of the earth or a neighbour or even a relative. And a stalker could be of either sex.

Typically, the cyber stalker's victim is new on the web, and inexperienced with the rules of netiquette & internet safety. Users that are especially vulnerable to being targeted are those in:

1. Live Chat or Internet Relay Chat
2. Message Boards and Newsgroups
3. Social Networking Sites

The main targets are the mostly females, children, emotionally weak or unstable, etc. It is believed that Over 75% of the victims are female, but sometimes men are also stalked.

The main motives of cyber stalkers are:

Sexual Harassment

This should not surprise anyone, especially women, since sexual harassment is also a very common experience offline. The internet reflects real life & consists of real people. It's not a separate, regulated or sanctified world. The very nature of anonymous communications also makes it easier to be a stalker on the internet than a stalker offline

Obsession for Love

This could begin from an online romance, where one person halts the romance and the rejected lover cannot accept the end of the relationship. It could also be an online romance that moves to real life, only to break-up once the persons really meet. Then one person again cannot accept the NO. Sometimes, this obsession stalking can even start from real life and then move over to cyberspace. One of the problems with obsession stalking is that since it often starts as real romance, much personal information is shared between persons involved.

This makes it easy for the cyber stalker to harass their victim. Sometimes, an obsession can also be a fixation by a stranger on another user for no valid reason. Since these obsession stalkers live in a dream world, it is not always necessary for the target to have done anything to attract her (or his) attention in the first place. Obsession stalkers are usually jealous and possessive people. Death threats via email or through live chat messages are a manifestation of obsession stalking.

Revenge & Hate

This could be an argument that has gone out of hand, leading eventually to a hate & revenge relationship. Revenge vendettas are often the result of something you may have said or done online which may have offended someone. Vendettas often begin with arguments where you may have been rude to another user.

Sometimes, hate cyber stalking is for no reason at all (out of the blue)- you will not know why you have been targeted nor what you have done, and you may not even know who it is who is doing this to you & even the cyber stalker does not know you. In fact you have NOT been individually targeted at all - you have been chosen as a random target by someone who does not know you! This stalker may be using the net to let out his frustrations online.

Ego & Power Trips

These are harassers or stalkers online showing off their skills to themselves and their friends. They do not have any grudge against you - they are rather using you to 'show-off' their power to their friends or doing it just for fun and you have been unlucky enough to have been chosen.

Most people who receive threats online imagine their harasser to be large and powerful. But in fact the threat may come from a child who does not really have any means of carrying out the physical threats made. It is estimated that there are about 2, 00,000 real-life stalkers in America today. Roughly one in 1,250 persons is a stalker.

Cyber stalking is very much prevalent in India also. In India's first case of cyber stalking, Manish Kathuria was recently arrested by the New Delhi Police. He was stalking an Indian lady, Ms Ritu Kohli by illegally chatting on the Web site MIRC using her name.

He used obscene and obnoxious language, and distributed her residence telephone number, inviting people to chat with her on the phone. As a result of which, Ritu kept getting obscene calls from everywhere, and people promptly talked dirty with her. In a state of shock, she called the Delhi police and reported the matter. For once, the police department did not waste time swinging into action, traced the culprit and slammed a case under Section 509 of the Indian Penal Code for outraging the modesty of Ritu Kohli.

In a more recent case in Kolkata, A senior official who allegedly sent obscene e-mails from a fictitious ID, created in the name of a woman subordinate has landed himself in jail. The man used to visit chat rooms on the Net and give the phone number and details of the woman and even invited them to her home. The woman then complained to the CID, upon examining her e-mails, It was revealed that the computer from where the mails were sent was in the woman's office.

Finally, the computer of the woman's boss was identified and the man was arrested. The man has been booked under the Information Technology Act.

Cyber sex/ Cyber porn Addiction

The expansion of computer databases on the Internet has provided the greatest access yet to sexually explicit images access by both adults and children. Cyber porn is more than naked women. Demand for images goes far beyond what can be found in a bookstore magazine rack. Pedophilia, bestiality, bondage, and sadomasochism make up a majority of the images. These are images, movies, and online chat that used to be only available on the bad side of town but which can now be obtained in the privacy of one's home. Home computers have become the "ultimate brown wrapper" for pornography.

Cybersex/Pornography Addiction is a specific sub-type of Internet addiction. Estimates suggest that 1 in 5 Internet addicts are engaged in some form of online sexual activity (primarily viewing cyber porn and/or engaging in cybersex). Studies show that men are more likely to view cyber porn, while women are more likely to engage in erotic chat. People who suffer from low self-esteem, a distorted body image, untreated sexual dysfunction, or a prior sexual addiction are more at risk to develop cybersex/ cyber porn addictions. In particular, sex addicts often turn to the Internet as a new and safe sexual outlet to fulfill their underlying compulsive habit.

Online pornography is popular. Sexually explicit forums are the most popular areas on computer online services online porn is big business. Nearly three fourths (71%) of the sexually explicit images surveyed originate from adult bulletin- board systems (BBS) attempting to lure customers to additional collections of cyber porn. There they can charge monthly fees and take credit card numbers for individual images. The five largest adult BBS systems have annual revenues in excess of $1 million.

On of the most important cases related to cyber porn in India was when Indian police in December2004 arrested a top boss of an Indian subsidiary of the Internet auction house eBay for allegedly Web hosting the sale of a porn clip that was said to show two teenage classmates engaged in oral sex at a prominent high school in the Indian capital In a recent case(Feb. 2008) Chennai's Fast Track Court (FTC) sentenced medical practitioner L. Prakash, the first accused in a cyber-porn case, to life imprisonment and fine of Rs.1.27 lakh.

Three other accused were sentenced to seven years rigorous imprisonment (RI) and a fine of Rs.2, 500 each. The doctor, who was running a clinic, used a farmhouse at Kalanchikuppam near Ennore and a guesthouse at Valasaravakkam to detain girls and sexually exploit them with the help of the other accused.

The accused took pictures and uploaded them on the internet. Besides this, child pornography is also increasing on the net the Internet. In this case_(1997) a 47-year-old Ohio man posing as a 15-year-old communicated through computer messages with a 14-year-old girl and was able to convince her to send him sexually explicit photographs and videotapes of herself performing sexual acts.

The cyber relationship went on for 18 months, since the girl was 12. The offender pled guilty to one charge of inducing a minor to produce child pornography Children are not the only victims of sexual assault involving the Internet.

In England, Christopher Graham Elliott was sentenced to 7 years in prison for raping and inflicting actual bodily harm on a woman he met online

CREDIT CARD AND ATM RELATED FRAUDS

Internet banking frauds and credit card frauds are growing in India. Of late, we are witnessing a trend of credit card frauds and ATM frauds in India as well. The Cyber Law of India, as contained in the Information Technology Act, 2000 (IT Act, 2000), is also silent on this aspect.

Thus, Internet banking frauds and credit card frauds are growing in India. Although credit card fraud is certainly on the rise — and credit card fraud on the Internet is rising even more dramatically — But, as consumers graduate to the shop-easy internet and pay with their cards, instances of fraud are bound to rise. Equally disturbing are crimes affecting online banking, which until recently, because of security concerns, was the fastest growing activity on the Internet, with three quarters of Europeans banking online and 38 percent of U.S. adults.

The increase in Internet fraud could be expected when we look at how many more businesses are accepting online transactions. Twenty-five million people in Britain alone now shop online. The problem is that the criminals are targeting the customers more than the technology. It is not about hacking into computers as much as it is about tricking users into revealing their card or account details. Fraud is increasing in e-ticketing, e-shopping and the service sectors, where no physical delivery of goods is involved.

According to ICICI Bank 60% of online card fraud occurs only while buying an air tickets. Indian Airlines, for instance, asks for 'a' particular proof of identity, which a consumer mentions in the online form, such as a driving license or a passport. So till ID becomes mandatory across all airlines, a consumer could as well be prepared to notice an inflated card statement despite going strictly by the rulebook.

In April 2006, a 26-year-old Mumbai executive keyed in her credit card number and the three-digit security code on the e-booking site of an airline. She bought a ticket for Bangalore. In July, she was shocked to find an Rs 20,000 additional credit drawn from her account. "Two tickets from the same airline were booked on two different days in June using her card.

The first was a Dwarka-Mumbai ticket for Rs 6,000, and the other, a Delhi-Dubai one for Rs 14,000. She did not get a response from her card company till August. "Then she approached the cyber crime cell and lodged the complaint.

So, for safer transactions, an advanced card such as Verified by Visa (VbV) and MasterCard Secure Code comes in handy. Here, a consumer requires a password during a transaction to validate his identity. ATM frauds are more common than credit card fraud in India. All the ATM's of a bank are connected through a dedicated computer network and hence are more vulnerable to fraudulent access. Many frauds have been reported at Delhi, Chandigarh and Mumbai, where large amount of money was withdrawn by unscrupulous elements through ATM's. in most of the cases the PIN was obtained by hacking the database of the concerned banks and also by phishing.

Cyber Laundering

Money laundering is said to be the "process by which one conceals the *existence*, illegal source, or illegal application of income, and then disguises that income to make it appear legitimate" As money technology has evolved, methods of payment have also changed, but cash still often remains a preferred method of payment by many people. Over the past few decades various media and industry experts have predicted the demise of cash and the advent of the "cashless" society.

Since, money in a modern economy exists chiefly in the form of electronic entries in computerized recordkeeping systems or data bases so conventional laundering has paved way for cyber laundering comprising the use of internet. One of its potential key features is anonymity. The proceeds of crime that are in the form of e-money could therefore be used, for example, to buy foreign currency and high value goods to be resold. E-money may therefore be used to place dirty money without having to smuggle cash or conduct face to face transactions.

The money launderer can control transactions from his PC. He can transfer money virtually instantaneously and thereby build up an extensive audit trail in a short space of time. The transfers can be made through many jurisdictions making it harder for prosecutors from one jurisdiction to follow the audit trail.

Therefore the features of the Internet that makes it ideal for commerce also make it ideal for money laundering:

- Speed
- Access
- Anonymity
- Capacity to extend beyond national border

As a result cyber-launderers benefit for the following reasons:

- Inability to identify and authenticate parties.
- Lack or inadequacy of audit trails, record keeping or suspicious transaction reporting by the technology provider.
- Use of higher level encryption to block out law enforcement.
- Transactions that fall outside the existing regulatory definitions.

Intellectual Property crimes / Distribution of Pirated Software

Intellectual property consists of a bundle of rights. Any unlawful act by which the owner is deprived completely or partially of his rights is an offence. This is the traditional type of intellectual property theft where one producer copies material or process from another for profit. The common form of IPR violation may be said to be software piracy, copyright infringement, trademark and service mark violation, theft of computer source code, etc. The Hyderabad Court has in a land mark judgement has convicted three people and sentenced them to six months imprisonment and fine of 50,000 each for unauthorized copying and sell of pirated software.

Defamation

It is an act of imputing any person with intent to lower the person in the estimation of the right-thinking members of society generally or to cause him to be shunned or avoided or to expose him to hatred, contempt or ridicule. Cyber defamation is not different from conventional defamation except the involvement of a virtual medium.

Netspionage

Unscrupulous companies have always been delighted to take advantage of new opportunities to sabotage or steal from a dangerous competitor. The development of information networks and vulnerable points of attack merely emphasizes this and increases the opportunities. Netspionage is where confidential information is stolen by hackers, to sell to a competitor or for the use of individuals business exploits. Espionage was originally limited to governments, but with the information age, the rise of corporate espionage has been rapid. One tool used to steal secrets is TEMPEST (Transient Electromagnetic Pulse Emanation Surveillance Technology) that allows a scanner to read the output from a computer up to a kilometer away. It is non-invasive and virtually undetectable.

According to recent surveys, worldwide losses suffered through misappropriation of computerized intellectual property cost copyright owners close to $20 billion last year.

One of the most recent and publicized cases is where hackers broke into Microsoft's computer system and allegedly had access to source codes behind Microsoft's software for some considerable time and could have stolen blue prints of the firm's window and office products. Microsoft commented that "this is a deplorable act of industrial espionage".

In a recent case involving two major stockbrokers and a large European Bank, one of the brokers decided to set up a system dealing in government bonds and began building a network across Europe, which meant placing servers in all of the major banks to transfer information to the dealing rooms. The network manager was known to many of the banks because he had once worked for a rival, and he was given access to top-security computer rooms. In one of the banks, the space allocated for the server was next to one of its rivals, which already had a government bond operation. After a quiet chat with his boss, the network manager was given a discreet nod and told to lose? 10,000 on expenses to place a connection from the rival's server to his company's server. Because of his time at the rival he was able to decipher the code, and thus gave his company real time access to its rival's buy and sell prices, allowing it to undercut and make a killing.

In China, the government is so concerned with the threat of the Internet as a vehicle for Netspionage that it shut down 127 net cafes, to curb the spread of online information, and to halt the spread of state secrets.

SOCIAL NETWORKING SITES AND CYBER CRIME

The majority of adults who use of social networking sites like MySpace and Face Book engage in dangerous behavior that exposes them to cyber crime.

It is not just the average net user who is a fan of social network sites, so are hi-tech criminals.

The quasi-intimate nature of the sites makes people share information readily leaving them open to all kinds of other attacks, warn security firms. Detailed information gathered via the sites will also help tune spam runs or make phishing e-mail more convincing. Cyber criminals are getting personal, aiming malicious attacks at social networking sites – targeting them as honey pots of confidential personal data, instead of targeting more traditional financial-based websites with phishing scams, e-criminals are now more frequently looking to source a wide range of consumer data by compromising social networking accounts. In addition, by targeting sites that consumers trust, these criminals are cleverly increasing the chances that their schemes will be successful and consumers will accidentally hand over personal information.

Social Networking Sites Top Targets for Identity Theft

About 74 percent of adults who use social networking sites have given out personal information like an e-mail address, birthday or social security number. Giving out a social security number, paired with a birthday and name could provide enough ammunition for criminals to hack into financial records and compromise users' personal information, besides compromising their personal information adults are also leaving their computers vulnerable to attacks by downloading files from other profiles.

And it isn't only personal computer networks at risk, as many of the people visit social networking sites when they're at work - jeopardizing business networks. This data can give criminals knowledge about the names of employees at a company, insight in its managerial make-up or information about its processes to lend credibility to other attacks.

This information could help attackers embarking on social engineering attacks which attempt to con employees by posing as another worker or a business partner.

Already at the end of 2007 Brazilian users of Google's Orkut were subject to an attack by a worm that tried to steal bank account details. The malicious program, which also tried to hijack compromised computers, propagated via booby-trapped links placed on the personal page of Orkut users.

With the growth of social networking sites, blogging, chat rooms, or instant messaging, children today are more in danger. Over 50 percent of teenagers in USA visit social networking sites and most of them do so on a daily basis!

Indian children are catching the social networking bug too. Some children visit these sites to increase their friend's circle, some to keep in touch with friends they cannot meet, and to make plans, socialize, or share information. Unfortunately, most children reveal a lot of personal details on their profiles which can easily be misused and their personal details can harm them even.

On the one hand where they increase a person's friend circle, they can also increase exposure to people who could be dangerous and many a times this type of information has lead to dire consequences when people have been stalked and in extreme cases murders have also been committed. The orkut angle in the kidnapping and murder of Adnan Patrawla, is an example of how dangerous it can become to befriend a stanger and then going out to meet them even more dangerous.

We need to understand that coming across even one wrong person in our entire life can have serious implications. There are certain norms that we need to adhere to both in our personal as well as social lives and if we breach them by ourselves, the consequences can affect all those around us. Social networking sites are all over the internet and a number of youngsters tend to be misled. But one cannot blame the internet or these sites for individual actions. It is important for us to be alert and take care about the information we are passing on to others. As a ground rule one must never pass on information without knowing anything about the other person. One can ask for the other person's phone number or address in order to get to know them better. It is better to build upon healthy contacts rather than falling in wrong hands.

One needs to take several things in account while interacting with people on social networking sites:

- Do not reveal confidential information on the site.
- Never agree to meet a stranger all by yourself.
- If at all, you have to go, then, do take someone along.
- Trust your instincts. If you get the slightest hint of getting threatened or feel uncomfortable, confide in an adult, report to the police and to the social networking site.
- Do not flirt on the site as people have fake identities.
- Remember that once you post information, you cannot delete it as older versions exist on other people's computers.
- Try not to post your photo as it can be altered and transmitted in various unethical ways
- Before you try to meet someone, try to gather as much information about him/her as possible. Meet the stranger only when you are satisfied that you know enough about him/her.

5

Cyber Terrorism

There is the need to distinguish between cyber terrorism and cyber crime. Both are criminal acts. However there is a compelling need to distinguish between both these crimes. A cyber crime is generally a domestic issue, which may have international consequences; however cyber terrorism is a global concern, which has domestic as well as international consequences. The common form of these terrorist attacks on the Internet is by distributed denial of service attacks, hate websites and hate emails, attacks on sensitive computer networks, etc.

Technology savvy terrorists are using 512-bit encryption, which is next to impossible to decrypt. The recent example may be cited of – Osama Bin Laden, the LTTE, and attack on America's army deployment system during Iraq war. Cyber terrorism may be defined to be " the premeditated use of disruptive activities, or the threat thereof, in cyber space, with the intention to further social, ideological, religious, political or similar objectives, or to intimidate any person in furtherance of such objectives" Another definition that covers within its ambit every act of cyber terrorism is:

A terrorist means a person who indulges in wanton killing of persons or in violence or in disruption of services or means of communications essential to the community or in damaging property with the view to –

(1) Putting the public or any section of the public in fear; or

(2) Affecting adversely the harmony between different religious, racial, language or regional groups or castes or communities; or

(3) Coercing or overawing the government established by law; or

(4) Endangering the sovereignty and integrity of the nation

And a cyber terrorist is the person who uses the computer system as a means or ends to achieve the above objectives. Every act done in pursuance thereof is an act of cyber terrorism.

PROVISIONS LAID BY INDIAN LAW AGAINST CYBER CRIME

The Indian parliament considered it necessary to give effect to the resolution by which the General Assembly adopted Model Law on Electronic Commerce adopted by the United Nations Commission on Trade Law. As a consequence of which the Information Technology Act 2000 was passed and enforced on 17th May 2000.The preamble of this Act states its objective to legalise e-commerce and further amend the Indian Penal Code 1860, the Indian Evidence Act 1872, the Banker's Book Evidence Act1891 and the Reserve Bank of India Act 1934. The basic purpose to incorporate the changes in these Acts is to make them compatible with the Act of 2000. So that they may regulate and control the affairs of the cyber world in an effective manner.

Moreover cyber crime cells have come up in cities such as Bangalore, New Delhi and Mumbai, where cyber crime cells do exist, there is potential for improvement. Any and every incident of cyber crime involving a computer or electronic network can be reported to a police station, irrespective of whether it maintains a separate cell or not, Or the crime can be directly be reported to The SP. But in many areas the police officials are themselves not aware of what cyber crime is. So, it is evident that the Law enforcement agencies are not well-equipped and oriented about cyber crime yet. There is an immense need for training, and more cities need to have such cells. We need to create special tribunals headed by trained individuals to deal solely with cyber crimes, but with powers to levy heavier penalties in exceptional cases.

Unless there is solid deterrence, cyber crime will rise steeply. There is also a need for IT-savvy lawyers and judges, as well as training for government agencies and professionals in computer.

PREVENTION OF CYBER CRIME

Prevention is always better than cure. It is always better to take certain precaution while operating the net. The 5P mantra for online security is Precaution, Prevention, Protection, Preservation and Perseverance.

The following things should always be kept in mind:

As an Enterprise

- Employ defense-in-depth strategies, which emphasize multiple, overlapping, and mutually supportive defensive systems to guard against single-point failures in any specific technology or protection method. This should include the deployment of regularly updated antivirus, firewalls, intrusion detection, and intrusion protection systems on client systems.
- Turn off and remove services that are not needed.
- If malicious code or some other threat exploits one or more network services, disable or block access to those services until a patch is applied.
- Consider implementing network compliance solutions that will help keep infected mobile users out of the network.
- Enforce an effective password policy.
- Configure mail servers to block or remove email that contains file attachments that are commonly used to spread viruses, such as .VBS, .BAT, .EXE, .PI F, and .SCR files.
- Isolate infected computers quickly to prevent the risk of further infection within the organization.
- Perform a forensic analysis and restore the computers using trusted media.
- Train employees to not open attachments unless they are expected and come from a known and trusted source, and to not execute software that is downloaded from the Internet unless it has been scanned for viruses.
- Ensure that emergency response procedures are in place. This includes having a backup-and-restore solution in place in order to restore lost or compromised data in the event of successful attack or catastrophic data loss.

- Educate management on security budgeting needs.
- Test security to ensure that adequate controls are in place.
- Be aware that security risks may be automatically installed on computers with the installation of file sharing programs, free downloads, and freeware and shareware versions of software. Clicking on links and/or attachments in email messages may also expose computers to unnecessary risks. Ensure that only applications approved by the organization are deployed on desktop computers.

As a Consumer

- Consumers should use an Internet security solution that combines antivirus, firewall, intrusion detection, and vulnerability management for maximum protection against malicious code and other threats.
- Consumers should ensure that security patches are up to date and that they are applied to all vulnerable applications in a timely manner.
- Consumers should ensure that passwords are a mix of letters and numbers, and should change them often. Passwords should not consist of words from the dictionary.
- Consumers should never view, open, or execute any email attachment unless the attachment is expected and the purpose of the attachment is known.
- Consumers should keep virus definitions updated regularly. By deploying the latest virus definitions, consumers can protect their computers against the latest viruses known to be spreading in the wild.
- Consumers should deploy an anti phishing solution. They should never disclose any confidential personal or financial information unless and until they can confirm that any request for such information is legitimate.
- Consumers should be aware that security risks may be automatically installed on computers with the installation of file-sharing programs, free downloads, and freeware and shareware versions of software. Clicking on links and/or attachments in email messages (or IM messages)

may also expose computers to unnecessary risks. Ensure that only applications approved by the organization are deployed on desktop computers.

- Some security risks can be installed after an end user has accepted the end-user license agreement (EULA), or as a consequence of that acceptance. Consumers should read EULAs carefully and understand all terms before agreeing to them.
- Consumers should be aware of programs that flash ads in the user interface. Many spy ware programs track how users respond to these ads, and their presence is a red flag. When users see ads in a program's user interface, they may be looking at a piece of spy ware.

CONCLUSION

We all must remember that Cyberspace is a common heritage of ours which we have inherited in our life times from the benefits of ever growing technologies. Capacity of human mind is unfathomable. It is not possible to eliminate cyber crime from the cyber space. It is quite possible to check them. History is the witness that no legislation has succeeded in totally eliminating crime from the globe. The only possible step is to make people aware of their rights and duties (to report crime as a collective duty towards the society) and further making the application of the laws more stringent to check crime. Undoubtedly the Information Technology Act 2000 is a historical step in the cyber world. But there is a need to bring changes in the Information Technology Act to make it more effective to combat cyber crime. It should be kept in mind that the provisions of the cyber law are not made so stringent that it may retard the growth of the industry and prove to be counter-productive.

This Cyberspace is the lifeline of the entire universe and given its irreversible position today, it is the duty of every citizen to contribute toward making the said cyberspace free of any trouble or cyber crime.

6

Cyber-Defense

The Internet is insecure to a degree which threatens national security. This paper presents a strategic approach to this problem, based on fundamental causes, rather than a tactical approach based on specific vulnerabilities and enforcement techniques. The fundamental weakness of the Internet is identified as resulting from a common historical tendency for new technologies to favor convenience over safety.

For reasons specific to the nature of the Internet, this "convenience overshoot" has reached quite dangerous proportions. Systematic steps need to be taken to correct this convenience overshoot by all of Internet end-users; Internet-related manufacturers; and government. Within this framework, a set of recommendations is provided.

INTRODUCTION

It is clear to those who have studied the problem that the United States (and other technologically advanced nations) faces a dangerous, sustained, and increasingly effective attack on its critical information infrastructure. This paper differs from many others in presenting a strategic approach to boosting the inherent security of the Internet and related infrastructure, rather than a series of tactical responses to known weaknesses and threats.

The Internet is the Great Facilitator. The coupling of data communication and high-speed computers unifies things which were formerly disparate. The Internet unifies geography, extending our reach instantly around the world. And it unifies information, allowing data formerly scattered in numerous sources to be easily combined. The Internet aids communication, collaboration and exchange. While generally beneficial, new risks arise when these increased capabilities are used by our attackers.

We have often likened the Internet to a highway. Another analogy is to compare the Internet to the oceans. Prior to the development of modern roads, water transport was even more important than it is today. Much as the Internet today is a medium for attacking us, the oceans made the British Isles a constant and pleasing target for invaders. Britain, having a long and easily reached coastline, was the target of numerous invasions in historical times from the Romans through the Normans, and no doubt extending back indefinitely through prehistory.

Something quite different, however, has happened in the last one thousand years. Britain holds the unique distinction among major powers of not having been successfully invaded since the year 1066. The reason is largely the development of the British navy. The British navy had the effect of converting the oceans from a highway for invaders into a powerful defensive moat. In essence, the British found a strategic solution to a structural problem.

It is worth noting some of the things which the British did not do (or which were not effective), as they have some bearing on the discussion of Internet security today. British security did not rely primarily on tracking all possible invasion plans; on intercepting all suspicious communication; on a system of rapid response to landings; on massive retaliation; on seizure of suspicious Scandinavian fishing boats; or on keeping a low international profile to avoid threats. Nor is it likely that any of these approaches, by themselves, would have been effective, regardless of how Draconian they were in implementation. Instead, the British simply held control of the seas, which stopped all potential invasions, known or otherwise.

The approach taken here is similarly based on a strategic solution to the structural weaknesses of the Internet. In the short-term, it complements tactical responses such as surveillance and expanded enforcement. In the long-term, it renders tactical response less necessary, and thus acts to further secure our civil liberties. The advantage of a strategic approach is that it increases our actual security, while reducing our need to develop a fortress mentality.

THE EXTENT OF THE THREAT

There is no serious question that the United States currently has an extremely dangerous vulnerability to attacks on its information infrastructure. This vulnerability has been extensively documented elsewhere: see, for instance, *Critical Foundations: Protecting America's Infrastructure.* Numerous specific instances have also been reported in the popular press. It is worth, however, briefly summarizing the nature and extent of the threat as a basis for the discussion in subsequent sections.

Cyber-attacks based on viruses (embedded code fragments) and worms (standalone programs) have already cost us well into the tens of billions of dollars in quantifiable damage and lost productivity. Lloyds of London, which has an institutional interest in accurate cost estimates, puts the worldwide cost of the LoveBug virus alone at over $15 billion (mostly uninsured). A separate estimate by the firm Computer Economics puts the worldwide cost of virus and worm attacks on information systems at $10.7 billion for 2001 through August; $17.1 billion for all of 2000; and $12.1 billion in 1999.

Quantifiable damage, however, is only part of the problem. For instance, the Sircam worm, which infects all versions of Microsoft Windows, was discovered on July 17th of this year. Aside from sometimes filling all unused memory or deleting all files, Sircam e-mails out files from an infected computer's hard disk. To the extent that this compromises medical, financial or trade-secret information, the cost can not be quantified.

Besides Sircam, recent months have seen several potent new worms, including Code Red, Code Red II, and Nimda, all of which exploit vulnerabilities in Microsoft's IIS server software. Nimda, for instance, infects computers running Microsoft Windows 95, 98, ME, NT and 2000; uses multiple infections routes, including e-mail, browsers, open network shares and vulnerabilities left behind by other viruses; and has the effect of leaving infected computers open to intruders. In addition to direct damage to infected computers themselves, once an intruder has control of your computer it can be used as a base to infect other computers, or to launch "denial-of-service" (DoS) attacks against major sites. In one kind of a DoS attack, the target site is bombarded with spurious information requests which prevent its normal operation. The most famous such attacks occurred during February of 2000, when major sites such as Amazon.com, Buy.com, CNN and eBay were disrupted.

As another example, on July 19th, 2001 the White House was the target of a DoS attack made possible by the Code Red worm. Current trends suggest that things are getting worse, rather than better. It is expected that over 2,000 new software vulnerabilities will be discovered this year. This is about twice the 1,090 from last year, which in turn is more than twice the number from the year before. At the same time, the sophistication and damage caused by computer worms is also rapidly increasing. Nimda propagates with unprecedented speed. Some researchers predict new classes of "flash worms" which could spread in minutes or seconds, leaving little time to react.

We should also note that criminal groups have been moving aggressively online. The FBI estimates that electronic crime costs about $10 billion per year, and that organized crime groups based in Eastern Europe have stolen over 1 million credit card numbers from web sites in the U.S., making use of vulnerabilities in Microsoft Windows NT. An estimate by the Director of the Privacy Rights Clearinghouse puts the cost from the fraudulent use of credit cards at $4 billion per year. Aside from the substantial disturbance to the lives of those directly victimized, the cost of credit card fraud is passed on to businesses and consumers in the form of higher credit card fees and interest rates, and to law enforcement in terms of a higher case load.

Theft of credit card information is one example of the more general problem of identity theft, in which one person uses the identifying information of another. Identify theft is useful to criminals both as a means to misappropriate the assets of the victim, and as a way to camouflage the origin of criminal activity. Identity theft is also of use to terrorists. Testimony before the U.S. Senate Judiciary Subcommittee on Technology, Terrorism, and Government Information estimated 500,000 to 700,000 victims of identity theft in the year 2000.

Victims are often unaware that their identity has been stolen until years afterwards, when they discover damage to their credit rating or criminal charges on their record, affecting their purchase or employment opportunities and possibly landing them in jail. Clearing the record is difficult and time-consuming, and by one victim's estimate can easily generate costs of $10,000-$15,000. Consider, too, the hidden cost on the legal system of dealing with this volume of crime. Identity theft is facilitated by the existence of personal information on poorly-secured web sites (although more traditional means of obtaining personal information are of course also widely used, such as retrieving discarded, unsolicited credit card offers). The range of sites which have been shown to be vulnerable to computer intruders is quite comprehensive. Some examples:

- Almost all of the Fortune 500 corporations have been successfully penetrated.
- One pre-approved test attack in 1996 demonstrated the ability to completely take over the information systems of a major metropolitan police force, including the ability to monitor and alter dispatches and court records. While that particular police force has since taken substantial steps to improve its security, there is little doubt that vulnerabilities remain both there and across the country.
- Public statements in November, 1997 by the U.S. Senate Judiciary Subcommittee on Technology, Terrorism and Government Information concerning the "Eligible Receiver" exercises include the following findings: 62-65% of all Federal Computer Systems have known security holes which can be exploited; between 250 and 600 DoD systems were broken into in 1996; and more than 120 countries or foreign organizations have or are developing formal programs that can be used to attack and disrupt critical Information Systems Technology (IST) used by the

U.S. "While much of the [Eligible Receiver] exercise remains classified, I believe it is fair to say that it revealed some serious vulnerabilities in government information systems that must be corrected."

- According to an April 16th, 1998 report in the Washington Times on the Eligible Receiver exercise, "Using software obtained easily from hacker sites on the Internet, a group of National Security Agency officials could have shut down the U.S. electric-power grid within days and rendered impotent the command-and-control elements of the U.S. Pacific Command, said officials familiar with the war game."
- An actual penetration of a computer system controlling the California power grid, undetected for 17 days, occurred this year. (Different views are given concerning how close the attackers came to being able to affect the power supply.)
- The FBI recently issued a list of the top 20 Internet vulnerabilities, stating that "the Internet wouldn't be able to withstand a major attack."
- Comments by senior Bush advisor Karl Rove to the New York Times shortly after the September 11th tragedies suggest that the attackers had access to White House codes. According to one report, those responsible for the September 11th, 2001 attack on the World Trade Center were in possession of the top-secret White House code words; of the code groups of the NSA; and of all or part of the codes used by the Drug Enforcement Administration, the National Reconnaissance Office, Air Force Intelligence, Army Intelligence, Naval Intelligence, Marine Corps Intelligence and the intelligence offices of the State Department and Department of Energy. They had also allegedly penetrated the NSA's electronic surveillance system.
- "Information warfare specialists at the Pentagon estimate that a properly prepared and well-coordinated attack by fewer than 30 computer virtuosos strategically located around the world, with a budget of less than $10 million, could bring the United States to its knees."

The Cisco routers which direct the vast majority of traffic on the Internet are also known to have vulnerabilities.

Based on prior experience, we can expect an increase in cyber-attacks in the wake of the September 11th tragedies. It may or may not be coincidental that the dangerous Nimda worm was first detected exactly one week after the World Trade Center attack.

The consensus of the information security community appears to be that our systems are becoming less secure, rather than more secure, over time. For one report on the current state of cyber-security, see the recent Congressional testimony by Jeff Carpenter, Manager of the CERT/CC. For a discussion of current weaknesses in governmental cyber-security, see the September 26th, 2001 Washington Post article "Key U.S. computer systems called vulnerable to attack".

It is not clear that it is currently possible, with the tools in common use, to guarantee the protection of sensitive information which is accessible via the Internet.

Why is our information infrastructure sustaining such large (and growing) damage? The structural weaknesses of the Internet, and the means to strengthen it, will be discussed below. Put simply, however, the Internet was built out of straw. And the world is full of wolves.

THE ROOTS OF THE INTERNET SECURITY PROBLEM

> "For Zeus, who guided men to think, has laid it down
> That wisdom comes alone through suffering." —
> Aeschylus, *Agamemnon*

There are technical approaches to securing the Internet which will be discussed below. However, these technical approaches are secondary. They can only be effective to the extent that we first reduce a bias against strong Internet security. The poor state of Internet security (as documented above) is an extreme case of a general pattern. We invent technologies to provide convenience. However, any powerful tool may also create new problems, which it may take years to fully understand and control. This delayed response between embracing the convenience of a new technology, and responding to its safety concerns, might be termed "the convenience overshoot". For instance, the modern automobile industry can be dated to the introduction of the Ford Model T in 1909, or to its moving assembly line production in 1913. However, it was only in the 1930's that some physicians began self-installing lap belts, and not until 1956 that Ford introduced lap belts as an option for some models.

Similarly, while the first steam powered locomotive was operating in 1804, it was not until the 1870's that a safe and effective braking system came into use, based on the ideas of George Westinghouse. One interpretation of the convenience overshoot is that it results simply from the time to grasp the safety issues for a new technology, followed by the time to overcome inertia sufficiently to address them. A somewhat a deeper analysis may be useful, however.

There is a fundamental trade-off between convenience and safety. Safety does not come for free. Putting a lock on a door, for instance, increases safety while increasing the price of the door and making it slightly more time-consuming for authorized people to enter. The convenience of successful technologies is readily apparent and easily marketed. A constituency for safety develops only over time, and requires a concerted effort by customers, manufacturers, and perhaps government to carry the day.

For the Internet, the convenience vs. safety trade-off occurs at three layers.

Layer 1: *Data communication* between different sites on the Internet.

Layer 2: *Operating systems* controlling computers.

Layer 3: *Software applications* running on top of operating systems.

In all three cases, there has existed a strong bias in favor of convenience, rather than security, to the detriment of both individual and collective safety. Let us first outline the form of this bias for each layer, followed by more general discussion.

At Layer 1, the underlying data communication protocol standard for most of the Internet is Internet Protocol Version 4, or IPv4, whose origins trace back to the mid-1970's. Descended from a time when the precursor of the Internet was a relatively small, closed network of trusted sites, IPv4 established a simple, open protocol lacking built-in security against malicious uses such as IP spoofing, in which one site masquerades as another for purposes of intrusion or data theft. Despite the radical change in the character of the Internet over the last 25 years, we are only now making the transition from IPv4 to a more secure (and robust) IPv6 data communication protocol.

At Layer 2, one form that the convenience bias takes is the presence of a high number of (at least theoretically) useful operating system features. Any powerful feature is potentially a weapon which can be used by intruders. By default, operating systems tend to ship with a multitude of features turned on. It is then up to end-users, many of them with insufficient computer training, to figure out how to turn off potentially insecure features. In a recent FBI list of the top 20 Internet security flaws, this practice of shipping software with all features turned on is listed first.

At Layer 3, we again have the problem of a bias towards convenient but dangerous features. An additional risk at the application level is poor integration between the application and the operating system, or between different applications. Poor integration may lead to "chinks in the armor", creating vulnerabilities.

While the Internet convenience overshoot outlined above is typical in form to other new technologies, the magnitude of the problem has now risen to constitute a national security threat. This level of severity is due to three factors. The first factor is the incredible power of software, to both help and threaten. Software is limited primarily by ideas, not by the properties of materials. It is thus the closest that engineering has come to magic. Networking extends this power immensely, and the misuse of its capabilities makes cyber-attacks possible.

The second factor is the speed with which the Internet has developed. We have had very little time, by historical standards, to respond to the Internet convenience overshoot. The Internet, as a platform for commerce and use by the general public, is less than 10 years old and continues to grow exponentially. We do not have 40 years to wait for the Internet equivalent of a seat belt to reach the market, nor 70 years for the equivalent of the locomotive pneumatic brake. The third factor is that software security problems are invisible to the naked eye. We do not see software vulnerabilities with the same ease that we notice an unlocked door. Even security experts may not be aware of security flaws in new software until well after it has been released and installed on millions of computers.

As yet, market pressures have not worked strongly in the direction of producing secure software. For the above reasons, customers have had difficulty evaluating their risk, and making a corresponding vote in the market place. Software manufacturers have therefore lacked strong pressure from their customers to produce secure software. A further factor is that software manufacturers in general do not bear the costs associated with security flaws in their products.

Because security costs are not yet accurately reflected in purchase decisions, competitive pressures make it difficult for software manufacturers to provide a high level of security. Any "good Samaritan" company which does aim for high security is placed at a competitive disadvantage. Its products will be slower to market; may have less features; and will have higher development costs. This analysis may help to explain why the number of new software security vulnerabilities discovered has doubled in each of the last two years. According to the CERT/CC (a major reporting center for Internet security problems):

"There is little evidence of improvement in the security of most products; developers are not devoting sufficient effort to applying lessons learned about the sources of vulnerabilities. The CERT/CC routinely receives reports of new vulnerabilities.

We continue to see the same types of vulnerabilities in newer versions of products that we saw in earlier versions. Technology evolves so rapidly that vendors concentrate on time to market, often minimizing that time by placing a low priority on the security of their products. Until customers demand products that are more secure or there are legal or liability changes, the situation is unlikely to change."

Yet a further impediment to Internet security is the distributed nature of the problem. A cup that leaks in one spot leaks in its entirety.

While subnets can be and are protected separately, the presence of vulnerable computers on the Internet poses some degree of threat to everyone else on the Internet. For example, in a denial-of-service (DoS) attack, huge numbers of infected computers may be used to bombard a major site. Owners of computers contributing to the attack are often unaware of their role, or even that their computer has been infected.

The protection of the private data which forms the basis for identity theft is similarly a distributed problem. Our private data is held in the databases of myriad institutions, in many cases without our knowledge. Penetration of any one of these databases as the result of a cyber-attack is just as damaging as penetrating all of them. The chain hangs by its weakest link.

SPECIFIC RECOMMENDATIONS

> "For a successful technology, reality must take precedence over public relations, for nature can not be fooled." — Richard Feynman, Physics Nobel Laureate, in his report on the Challenger Space Shuttle disaster.

This section provides specific recommendations to secure the Internet. The essence of the approach is not to focus primarily on the tactics of fixing specific security problems (although that is necessary as well), but rather to correct the structural deficiencies which have consistently produced these problems for many years. A two-level hierarchy of actions is required. The first, and most important, is to correct the Internet convenience overshoot: that is, to speed up the natural process whereby the market place will increasingly reflect true safety costs. The second level has to do with software development and usage.

Level 1: Correcting the Internet Convenience Overshoot

As discussed earlier, there is a fundamental trade-off between convenience and safety. Early in a technology's history, there is a tendency to focus on the conveniences which it can provide.

Over time, we become wiser and make safety adjustments where necessary. The Internet is currently in the midst of this transition. We have created a tool of great convenience. Unfortunately, it has left us unsafe from acts of malice. In the natural unfolding of events, Internet security will be enhanced.

However, we do not have time for this natural process to pursue its stately trajectory. The degree to which the Internet is now vulnerable constitutes a national security threat. It is encumbant on users of the Internet; on manufacturers; and on government to act in such a way as to reduce this threat.

The first requirement is one of education, so that the market place will better reflect true security costs. We need to make generally known the extent of the threat, both individual and collective; the dangers of specific products, as well as the degree to which they have been tested by independent third parties; and the steps which can be taken to reduce security threats, as outlined below.

The second requirement is organization. Organization in terms of both people and standards. Groups provide a forum to identify problems, disseminate possible solutions, and agitate for change. Standards are a organized means by which to judge the practical world. One security standard, Common Criteria certification, is described below.

The third requirement (the necessity of which one hopes will be eliminated or reduced by the first two) is regulation. We do not allow convenience vs. safety issues for new medical drugs to be arbitrated in the market place. We require that new medical drugs be proven safe before they are made available to the public. This limitation to free markets is justified by the extreme danger of acting otherwise. If less drastic measures are unsuccessful, the same may be judged true of Internet products.

Level 2: Software Development and Usage

The Level 1 discussion above was concerned with reducing the bias against Internet security. Level 2 is concerned with implementation steps to strengthen Internet security as rapidly as possible.

Recommendation: Ship Software with Most Features Turned Off

In October, 2001, the FBI and the SANS Institute jointly released the "Twenty Most Critical Internet Security Vulnerabilities." In their opinion, the majority of successful attacks via the Internet can be traced to these twenty problems. Number one on the list, affecting all systems, is that most software manufacturers by default enable too many functions, some with security holes.

"The vendor philosophy is that it is better to enable functions that are not needed, than to make the user install additional functions when they are needed. This approach, although convenient for the user, creates many of the most dangerous security vulnerabilities because users do not actively maintain and patch software components they don't use. Furthermore, many users fail to realize what is actually installed, leaving dangerous samples on a system simply because users do not know they are there."

The software necessary to perform common end-user tasks such as browsing the web, sending e-mail and word processing is not inherently more complex than a Volvo. There is no reason why it should not be similarly robust and secure.

Consumers have a reasonable expectation that a software product, installed straight out of the box in accordance with the manufacturer's directions, is safe to use. Currently, this is far from being the case.

PromoteTrusted Operating Systems

Current Internet practice notwithstanding, it is in fact possible to create highly secure operating systems. And they do in fact exist. For instance, in January, 2001 a $50,000 prize was offered to any hacker able to break into a test ecommerce site protected by the Argus Pitbull software product. Despite more than 5 million attacks from an estimated 100,000 to 200,000 would-be intruders, the prize went unclaimed. Similarly, Pitbull stood up to all attacks at a recent hackers' convention in Las Vegas.

Pitbull makes use of "trusted operating system" techniques. The essential idea behind trusted operating systems, which goes back to the 1980's, is compartmentalization. Users and processes are limited to the specific information and capabilities needed to carry out their tasks.

The various approaches to operating system security can be understood by analogy to the problem of designing ships that are less likely to sink. Software firewalls are roughly equivalent to wrapping a strong hull around a leaky ship. This approach can work reasonably well but is prone to catastrophic failure. A single puncture in the hull, either through an accident or deliberate malice by an insider, will sink the ship. The common software practice of opening ports through the firewall (to support, for instance, e-mail, web services, or Internet chats) is roughly equivalent to deliberately dynamiting a doorway in a ship's hull in order to facilitate loading and unloading goods. It works well until such time as the ship sinks.

Trusted operating system techniques are equivalent to creating separate, watertight compartments in a ship, so that even if one (or more) compartment develops a leak the ship will stay afloat. Why, despite a history dating back to the early 1980's, are trusted operating systems not in widespread use?

The answer goes back to the discussion in Section 3 of the bias towards convenience over safety. Just as watertight compartments in a ship add to design and development costs, as well as reducing ease-of-motion for passengers and crew, similar inconveniences affect trusted operating systems. Trusted operating systems cost more to develop and administer, as well as reducing ease-of-use.

Never-the-less, trusted operating systems should be promoted, perhaps legislatively, for the same safety reasons that we promote compartmentalized ship design. Perhaps more so: a sinking ship is an isolated event; an operating system that is taken over by an intruder is a platform for attacking other sites. A trend towards trusted operating systems will occur naturally as Internet security problems begin to be addressed.

However, the need to secure our information infrastructure is sufficiently compelling that additional steps should be considered. These steps might include requiring trusted operating systems for critical government (and possibly commercial) sites at some point in the future; taxing sites based on the security level of their operating system; or supporting research and training in the use of trusted operating systems.

In view of the cost of identity theft, securing private data about individuals is a long-term goal of considerable importance. One possible approach is to require that institutions holding private data either protect it behind a trusted operating system or else keep it unconnected to the Internet.

Promote Open-Source Software

Traditionally, commercial software products have been distributed as "machine code" (readable by computers), but without the "source code", which is the human-readable version. Source code is something like the blueprint for a building. You can learn a lot by examining a completed skyscraper. But you can learn a lot more (such as how to upgrade the wiring or whether the plumbing was set up correctly) if you also have the blueprint.

"Open source" software products comes with source code available, and generally (although not necessarily for this discussion) with rights to redistribution. The emergence of open source software is interesting economically and socially. However, it is also important from a security perspective.

One's first instinct might be that having software source code widely available decreases security. After all, if the source code is available, does this not make it easier to plan an attack? Somewhat surprisingly, the truth is quite the opposite. Hiding the source code can only improve "accidental" security: security which arises simply because a particular vulnerability has not yet been discovered. Accidental security is a disaster waiting to happen. What we want instead is "intrinsic" security: software products which can stand up to any possible attack. Intrinsic security is enhanced by having as many people as possible examine the source code. Insurance premiums are beginning to support this argument.

Having source code available reduces the security risk associated with poor software engineering. Open source code also reduces the risk of deliberately inserted backdoors for intruders. The European Parliament recognized this point in a resolution favoring open source software passed in September, 2001. Under the Clinton Administration, the President's Information Technology Advisory Committee (PITAC) endorsed open-scurce software as the new model for high-end computing needs.

It is in our security interests that the software defending our online sites have been read and tested by as many people as possible. For this reason, government procurement policy should favor the acquisition of products which use open source software.

Open source need not imply the absence of a commercial organization supporting the software. It does, however tend towards a service model (in which a company contracts to support certain capabilities using an available body of open source software) rather than towards a manufacturing model (in which a company sells software as a finished good).

Upgrade the Internet Data Communication Protocol to IPv6

The dominant Internet protocol for data communications is still IPv4, with a design that is over 20 years old. IPv4 is vulnerable to "IP spoofing", in which one site pretends to be another for purposes of intrusion. IPv4 also.lacks a built-in way to protect the confidentially of data at the level of individual information packets sent across the Internet.

The transition to the more secure IPv6 protocol is under way. This transistion should be encouraged. The European Union has called for the rapid adoption of IPv6 as a data security measure.

Encourage Diverse Software Platforms

Widespread standardization on the same software tools reduces development, purchase, maintenance, training and usage costs. It also magnifies the destruction if a weakness is found in these tools. "Government systems are often bought in bulk and installed to the same recipe. Finding a flaw and taking over one allows you to take over others easily."

Similarly, the speed with which Internet worms can travel, and the systematic damage which they can cause, is related to the fact that a small number of weaknesses will get them into a very large number of computers. Such systematic software vulnerabilities are akin to the weakness of monocultures in biology. It is known that plant disease epidemics tend to move more rapidly through a "monoculture" (population of one species) than a mixed population. An efficiency is gained by only growing the most productive grains available; but the entire crop can be lost if a pest specific to that particular plant arises.

The convenience of standardization comes at the risk of epidemic. It is hard to know what advice to give on this knowledge; except to be aware that standardization is not an unmitigated good.

A diverse software environment may tend to arise naturally as Internet security problems are taken more seriously. For instance, banks and other institutions may have the incentive to create special-purpose software tools for their customer's online transactions. These tools will provide limited functionality specific to that institution, highly tested for security. More inconvenient than current practice? Most certainly. But that is the cost of safety. The Internet was created with a decentralized design in order to prevent a single hardware point-of-failure from bringing the entire system down. However, using the same software everywhere, with the same vulnerabilities, comes close to creating a single software point-of-failure. The degree to which it holds a software monoculture goes some way towards explaining why the Internet is now much more vulnerable to attacks on its software than on its hardware.

Promote Use of the Common Criteria Framework

The Common Criteria (CC) for Information Technology Security Evaluation is a framework for tackling information security problems.68 It provides concepts and principles of IT security. It also provides constructs for expressing IT security objectives; for selecting and defining IT security requirements; and for writing high-level specifications for products and systems.

The CC is an international standard aimed at a wide audience. It is intended to provide a shared security language for consumers, developers, vendors, evaluators, certifiers, validators, overseers, accreditors and approvers. Product developers can seek CC certification from independent evaluation facilities as an indication of the product's level of security. The CC is also useful for organizations developing their own internal security policies.

The most important thing about the CC is simply to know that it exists, what it means, and that it holds the respect of security professionals. Over time, checking CC certification should be a part of the decision-making process in acquiring new products.

Promote Internet Immune Response

When a new security weakness is found, the health of the Internet depends on how quickly defensive patches propagate, compared to the speed with which new attacks appear. If a new attack exploiting a weakness appears before computers on the Internet have been patched, the result is an epidemic of invaded computers.

The Internet footrace between the defense and the attackers is currently being won easily by the attackers. For instance, as of March, 2001 computer criminals were still making use of vulnerabilities in Microsoft Windows NT for which free security patches were available in 1998. Even if security patches have been downloaded, steps may not have been taken to remove the effects of previous infections. It is estimated that 430,000 Microsoft servers currently have back-door programs installed which allow sensitive data (such as credit card numbers) to be stolen.

Unless the supply of new Internet vulnerabilities drops considerably, the health of the Internet will essentially depend on the relative speed with which the defense and attackers respond to newly-discovered weaknesses. As discussed above, Internet security is a distributed problem: all computers on the Internet, even those properly secured, are threatened by infected computers. It should therefore be a matter of policy to try to speed up the Internet "immune response": the speed with which all computers on the Internet are protected against newly discovered weaknesses.

Methods for doing so include:

1. Supporting and publicizing services to check computers for the currentness of their security patches, and for installed back-door programs.

2. Refusing to accept communication from computers which are not up-to-date on their security patches, instead refering them to the appropriate site to improve their security.

Promote the Use of Integrity Filters

Many "data" files sent around the Internet contain powerful "macros" (software fragments) to execute certain functions. XML and Microsoft Word, for instance, support this capability. The convenience which these macros may provide comes with the risk that their power will be used maliciously. One does not want to ban such macros, as they are often useful. One would, however, like to know whether they are present and make an informed decision about one's level of risk.

A possibility is to systematically develop the use of "integrity filters". The idea would be that files could be developed using integrity filters which monitor the use of macros. Using cryptographic techniques, the integrity filter could certify that the file was created using the filter, and report on the level to which macros are present in the file.

Anyone receiving the file could then use automated tools to check the macro report from the integrity filter, and make an informed decision about whether to accept the file.

Note that the use of integrity filters need not be in any sense mandatory. They would provide an optional added level of security to those who wanted it.

Promote Gradations of Software Capabilities

The discussion indicated that small number of people using easily available software have the capability to cause enormous damage on an international scale. From this viewpoint, a modern personal computer connected to the Internet comes reasonably under the definition of a munition. It is both futile and undesirable to attempt to limit the availability of powerful software on personal computers connected to the Internet. However, making available computer operating systems with different levels of capability would be of assistance to the defense. Currently, it is standard practice to ship operating systems to all customers which have the full feature set needed by the most sophisticated users. Refering back to the discussion of convenience vs. safety, this means that all operating systems shipped are maximally dangerous.

A safer approach might be to provide most users with stripped down operating systems supporting only the most common functionality. These operating systems would contain less code, would change less often, and would be heavily tested for security problems. State-of-the-art operating systems would be aimed only at the most sophisticated users with a need for their capabilities. There would be nothing to prevent any user from acquiring a high-end, state-of the art operating system. However, sites might chose to reduce their security risk by not accepting communication from high-end operating systems; or only accepting communication if the owners of such systems are technically certified as being able to operate them safely.

One might see the Internet as evolving into an environment in which most endusers have relatively simple operating systems which lack dangerous features and have been carefully tested for security problems. Those with technical sophistication would continue to use current operating systems. And sensitive government or e-commerce sites would use trusted operating systems, which are more expensive and time-consuming to maintain, but which provide both a high degree of functionality and a high degree of security.

CONCLUSION

> "You may know in future, and tell other people, how greatly better good deeds prosper than evil ones." — Homer, Odyssey

Fundamental problems require fundamental solutions. The perilously insecure state of the Internet is not inevitable, nor is it the result of a series of arbitrary technical problems with particular products. It is rather the result of a common historical trend which in this case has gotten dangerously out of control: the tendency of new technologies to favor convenience over safety. In consequence, we now find ourselves dependent on the mercy of those who have none. If the fundamental problem is a "convenience overshoot", the fundamental solution must be to actively promote safety. This must happen on the part of all of Internet end-users; Internet-related industries; and the government. Specific recommendations for steps to be taken were given above.

Security is a distributed problem. We are all at risk for so long as there are significant pockets of insecure computers on the Internet. In view of this, we must work together as a community for both individual and collective safety. In Benjamin Franklin's apt phrase, "we must all hang together, or most assuredly we will all hang separately."

ENCRYPTION

The body of this chapter, though dealing with information security, has made no mention of encryption. This is not because encryption is unimportant! Quite the contrary. It is rather because encryption is of tactical importance, and this paper has dealt with strategy. Encryption is a particular tool to be used as needed within a security framework. We have dealt here with that framework. The solution to information vulnerabilities is not simply to "encrypt everything". However, one can not close without mentioning the current pressure for legislation to weaken publicly-available encryption. The motivation for this drive is understandable (the desire to prevent our enemies from communicating in secret). However, this type of legislation should be opposed for three reasons.

1. It is incapable of achieving its stated objective.
2. It has the potential to greatly weaken our information infrastructure.
3. From a civil rights point-of-view, it violates the fairness principle that the privacy rights accorded to a conversation should not depend on the distance over which the conversation takes place.

Let us detail these reasons in turn.

1. It is incapable of achieving its stated objective.

Restrictions on strong encryption can not be effective in limiting the ability of those who wish to communicate in secret over the

Internet. This is partly because encryption algorithms are simple to program and easily available. It is also because of the sheer volume of the information ocean in which we are now afloat. The amount of information traffic on the Internet is growing faster than ever, currently doubling every 6 months. Internet traffic is expected to reach 15 million terabytes per month by 2003. Attempting to intercept communications, in this context, is a matter of searching for an ever more easily hidden needle in an exponentially growing haystack.

Further complicating the intercept problem is the online development of "steganography" (literally, "covered writing"), the ancient technique of hiding a message in other data. One modern application of steganography is to the hiding of messages in the video and audio data files which slosh around the Internet in prodigious quantities. Data file steganography defeats traffic analysis: if posted to an Internet site, a data file may be downloaded by thousands of people, only one of them the intended recipient aware of the secret message. Software supporting data file steganography is readily available in a wide variety of forms.

Steganography poses would-be message interceptors with three problems, all of them insoluble. Firstly, the existence of a secret message embedded in a data file can not be detected. Secondly, if the message is detected, it can not be decrypted. Thirdly, if it is decrypted, the intended recipient of the message will still be unknown, unless named in the message itself.

As one might expect, reports indicate that Osama Bin Laden's Al Qaeda uses steganography. Fundamentally, as mentioned in the introduction, the Internet destroys the importance of geography. Just as we have always had the ability to carry out private conversations within a room, we now have the ability to carry out private conversations over great distances. There is nothing one can do to change this situation, short of turning the Internet off.

The Internet is not an effective tool for intelligence gathering. Effective intelligence gathering will instead have to be based on traditional techniques such as the use of informants, as well as wire-tapping prior to encryption at the suspect's keyboard, or with video cameras aimed at the suspect's screen.

2. *It has the potential to greatly weaken our information infrastructure.*

Any restriction on cryptography weakens the defense of critical infrastructure, thus making us more vulnerable to cyber-attack. Particularly dangerous are "key recovery" schemes, in which the government would keep "back door" access to all encrypted communication.

Key recovery systems would increase the cost and difficulty of encryption, thereby slowing its development and leaving our infrastructure more poorly defended; introduce more complexity into the encryption process, and therefore more risk of technical failure; and give more people access to decryption keys, therefore increasing the risk of lost security through corruption.

Additionally, key recovery implies that the master keys have to be stored somewhere, presumably in one or more government databases. To the extent that government sites are known to be vulnerable to attack, this creates the risk of an "encryption Chernobyl", in which all encrypted information nationwide becomes simultaneously available to hostile forces. Encryption is useful as a defensive weapon. Attempts to restrict encryption are not useful as an offensive weapon.

3. *From a civil rights point-of-view, it violates the fairness principle that the privacy rights accorded to a conversation should not depend on the distance over which the conversation takes place.*

As mentioned before, the effect of the Internet is to destroy the importance of geography. We can carry on a conversation almost as easily across the country as across a room. Why should the two types of conversation be accorded different levels of privacy protection? Legal restrictions on encryption have the effect of reducing the privacy of remote communication for those who abide by the law. The equivalent of encryption restrictions for local communication would be to demand that the government be allowed to install microphones in all rooms. To the extent that the latter violates Fourth Amendment rights, so does the former.

7

Methodology of Studying Cyber Crime

We are detecting, with increasing frequency, the appearance of doctrine and dedicated offensive cyber warfare programs in other countries. We have identified several, based on all-source intelligence information, that are pursuing government-sponsored offensive cyber programs. Foreign nations have begun to include information warfare in their military doctrine, as well as their war college curricula, with respect to both defensive and offensive applications. They are developing strategies and tools to conduct information attacks.

John A. Serabian, Jr., Information Operations Issue Manager, Central Intelligence Agency, before the Joint Economic Committee on Cyber Threats and the U.S. Economy, February 23, 2000.

Foreign governments pose a serious and structured threat because they not only have access to the appropriate technology, but also are able to enhance the effectiveness of this technology through the use of the all source intelligence support, extensive funding, and organized professional support. In addition, government agencies may be able to conduct more extensive programs because of their willingness to invest in longer term goals and objectives.

The Electronic Intrusion Threat to National Security and Emergency Preparedness (NS/EP) Internet Communications, Office of the Manager, National Communications System, December 2000, p. ES-2. While we have not seen such attacks from a nation state, that is solely because no state or non-nation state actor has yet seen sufficient strategic advantage to be gained by doing so, and this condition will not last indefinitely.

Dr. Daniel T. Kuehl, National Defense University, before the Joint Economic Committee, U.S. Congress, February 23, 2000

THE ARGUMENT

Critical infrastructure protection became a veritable watchword in local and national security policy circles, even before the 9/11 terrorist attack and the establishment of the Department of Homeland Security. The success of the 9/11 conspiracy has been attributed in part to a "failure of imagination" on the part of the U.S. defense and intelligence community. This, in turn, has spawned reactive, "worst case" predictions, along the lines that, "the attack the experts say cannot happen or that terrorists are not interested in pursuing is simply an attack that hasn't happened yet." Seasoned observers, such as military analyst Anthony H. Cordesman writing on cyber warfare and related matters, point out the need for calm reflection and accurate calibration of the problem before allocating scarce tax dollars to critical infrastructure protection. With respect to cyber warfare, Cordesman observed in December 2000:

"There is a flood of uncertain and poorly defined data on the threat, much of which is highly anecdotal. Incidents tend to be exaggerated while the overall pattern in the threat may be understated or missed altogether. Cost and risk estimates are issued that are little more than guesstimates, often using ridiculous methods and data. There is a critical lack of technological net assessment of the trends in offense and defense..."

Among the recommendations that Cordesman offers for consideration is the suggestion that the U.S. should identify and assess its "real vulnerabilities" and avoid extending the federal role in critical infrastructure protection at random—an effort that may only create false and inappropriate priorities.

The purpose of this report is to provide a frank and dispassionate assessment of the degree of vulnerability of information technology networks in the United States to "through the wires" attacks by selected foreign nation-states. Although our research has inherent limitations (for example we rely exclusively on published sources), we trust that publication of our findings will serve as a primer on cyber warfare matters, accessible to expert and nonprofessional alike. We address both external threats and internal U.S. vulnerabilities. Our goal is to pierce some of the myths and exaggerations related to cyber warfare. In our concluding chapter, we couple our assessment with recommendations to local and national policy makers.

Some experts maintain that cyber attacks with potential strategic national security effects, often referred to as an "electronic Pearl Harbor," are impossible. Others proclaim they are inevitable. Contemporary predictions on these matters run from the benign to the apocalyptic. Experts toward the benign end of the spectrum often cite the robustness, resiliency, and redundancy of the Internet as inherent characteristics of a system that would prevent a cyber attack from producing catastrophic results.4 James Lewis of the Center for Strategic and International Studies (CSIS), for example, argues that:

"Some people actually believe that this stuff here that they're playing with is equal, if not a bigger threat, than a dirty bomb... Nobody argues — or at least no sane person argues — that a cyber attack could lead to mass casualties. It's not in any way comparable to weapons of mass destruction. In fact, what a lot of people call them is 'weapons of mass annoyance.' If your power goes out for a couple hours, if somebody draws a mustache on Attorney General Ashcroft's face on his Web site, it's annoying. It's irritating. But it's not a weapon of mass destruction. The same is true for this."

On the other hand, experts with access to classified sources point out that the growing tendency in advanced industrial economies to link internal business management tools and administrative controls to the Internet could be catastrophic for overall U.S. security. Former White House Cyber Security advisor, Richard Clarke, for example, observes:

"We, as a country, have put all of our eggs in one basket. The reason that we're successfully dominating the world economically and militarily is because of systems that we have designed, and rely upon, which are cyber-based. It's our Achilles heel. It's an overused phrase, but it's absolutely true. It could be that, in the future, people will look back on the American empire, the economic empire and the military empire, and say, "They didn't realize that they were building their whole empire on a fragile base. They had changed that base from brick and mortar to bits and bytes, and they never fortified it. Therefore, some enemy some day was able to come around and knock the whole empire over."

A third set of observers maintains that the truth lies somewhere in between, and that it is best to be vigilant. They argue for a new way of approaching electronic defenses. One of the main proponents of this middle course is Bruce Berkowitz. In 1995, he wrote that cyber attacks could degrade both civilian and military networks. He emphasized the importance of mounting an information warfare "civil defense" because:

"Civilian information systems are prime candidates for attack...Just as cities are targeted in strategic bombing, in future wars we can expect civilian information systems to be hacked, tapped, penetrated, bugged, and infected with computer viruses."

In 1996, a RAND research group observed that:

"Civilian data encryption and system protection are rudimentary. Talented computer hackers in distant countries may be able to gain access to large portions of the information infrastructure underlying both U.S. economic wellbeing and defense logistics and communications."

Moreover, in 2001, a CSIS conference of Homeland Security experts concluded:

"We've known for at least a decade that the country's critical infrastructure depends on computer systems and

> information networks that are subject to debilitating cyberattacks. But until now, network attacks have been more burdensome than anything, and costly for only a handful."

BACKGROUND

There exists the possibility that foreign nation-states—not only the U.S.—could mount and finance a well-organized cyber warfare program. This would allow them to utilize a cyber attack capability against an adversary. A multi-faceted cyber attack employing various techniques could be highly disruptive if the United States and its allies were unprepared for it.

A cyber attack by nation-states targeting the transportation, communications, or banking sector computer systems in the United States would, at a minimum, entail significant economic costs that would affect jobs and growth. Cyber attacks could also indirectly lead to disruptions in daily civilian life that go beyond the level of temporary nuisance to inflict sustained uncertainty, confusion, and even chaos across significant elements of the population.

In the most extreme of cases, these disruptions could cause human casualties. Cyber attacks occur on a frequent basis and in a near-instantaneous manner; as the world becomes more connected, more machines and more people will be affected by an attack. In the months and years to come, cyber attack techniques will evolve even further, exposing various— and possibly critical—vulnerabilities that have not yet been identified by computer security experts. Moreover, such attacks could also be coordinated to coincide with physical assaults, in order to maximize the impact of both.

> During the past five years, the world has witnessed an escalation in the number of cyber attacks involving hackers attacking and counterattacking in the context of regional or local disputes.
>
> When peacekeeping operations began in Kosovo, NATO and Serbian hackers attacked back and forth attempting to control each other's electronic resources.12 The same

has occurred during the Palestinian-Israeli conflict,13 the India-Pakistan disagreement over Kashmir,14 and between Chinese and American hackers during the accidental bombing of the Chinese Embassy in Belgrade in 1999 and the May 2001 downed spy-plane incident.15 A cyber war between Chechen and Russian hackers has also taken place during the conflict between the Russian military and Chechen fighters. These cyber wars coincided with actual physical conflicts but intrusions, in one form or another, also have taken place in isolation.

In recent years, the scope and sophistication of cyber attacks have also expanded. Whereas antecedent attacks were relatively benign, more recent intrusions have compromised vital communications and critical infrastructure systems, such as public utilities connected to the Net. The Slammer worm, for example, exploited a vulnerability in Microsoft's SQL database software that led to cascading effects in our electronic infrastructure that were certainly not predicted beforehand. Airline booking systems and bank Automated Teller Machines (ATMs) were among other systems impacted by Slammer infections. The Slammer worm also significantly degraded computer systems that control monitoring capabilities at the Davis-Besse nuclear power plant in Ohio.

As of this writing, the Department of Homeland Security (DHS) is dedicating significant resources to detecting, protecting against, and responding to cyber attacks.18 Most recently, the NCSD announced the creation of a national cyber alert system aimed at "home users and technical experts in businesses and government agencies." In the view of Department of Homeland Security officials, the danger of cyber attacks requires that immediate action be taken to protect the networks critical to our function as a society. However, these actions may not be enough to change a culture of lax cyber security standards, an apathetic attitude possessed by computer expert and novice alike.

ROOT OF THE PROBLEM

Most networks and therefore most computers are connected to each other in some way, be it sharing the same access provider, central server, or accessing the same set of computers. This connectivity is rapidly increasing because of the free market development of central network hubs, a point that is discussed later in the chapter.

Although a completely accurate map of the overall Net has not been produced, it is logical to reason that the 95% of privately owned networks are connected to each other in some way. Indeed most computers share the same operating system software and communicate with all other computers using the standard set of TCP/IP protocols. The interoperability benefits of standardized protocols and the spread of recently devised worms and viruses such as Nimda and Sasser are testament to the links between these networks.

At the beginning of the transformation of society in the mid-1990s through the introduction of applications connected by networks and the Internet, profit-oriented, entrepreneurial programmers focused on creating massively used network-based utilities. These network-based utilities, such as search engines (significantly reducing information costs), automated clearing house transactions seamlessly linking consumers with financial institutions (increasing efficiency and accuracy of transactions), and near instantaneous communications capabilities (voice over internet protocol or VoIP, instant messaging, e-mail) have become the applications that many in business and daily-life take for granted.

Some of these utilities run on the Internet backbone; others run on private networks with links to other networks through the Internet. The quest in the United States for economic efficiency (i.e., through reduction in the cost of information acquisition) has produced an almost unparalleled state of dependency. Our adversaries no doubt have already observed this dependency.

The pervasiveness of IT networks in the United States is rapidly evolving into what military writers call a strategic center of gravity, especially because of the myriad, often unaccounted for, links to the electric power grid and other elements of the critical infrastructure. As CIA analyst John Serabian testified in early 2000, "We have spent years building an information infrastructure that is interoperable, easy to access, and easy to use. Attributes like openness and ease of connectivity which promote efficiency and expeditious customer service are the same ones that now make the system vulnerable to attacks against automated information systems."

As with any new technological advance, inventors and consumers in the computer and IT sectors seek to optimize the cost-reducing effects of technology. In the rush to maximize economic efficiency, safety and security concerns are often set aside and have only recently been noticed by people from software engineers to the home computer user.

> American institutions, government, media, military, and other organizations rely in large measure on trust in both the utilities that allow them to function as well as the integrity of the information residing in databases. Integrity in the market place formerly was centered on people-to-people handshakes. Today computer-to-computer handshakes often take precedence.
>
> Information technologies pervade daily life, with much of today's medical and scientific community and financial markets relying on electronic databases and communications, without which neither could function. The electronic news media, broadcasting in its 24-hour format and worldwide scope, also could not perform in the absence of networked technology and computeraided dissemination. Compromising the electronic systems, even today when the technological revolution is in its infancy, would cause a significant drop in the confidence in these systems. As Stephen E. Flynn, a senior fellow at the Council of Foreign Relations points out, "the main benefit of attacks on critical infrastructure is not the immediate damage they inflict, but the collateral consequences of eroding the public's trust in services on which it depends." Even after a cyber attack is halted or discontinued, the issue of data

corruption, sorting out what information remains reliable and what has been irreparably harmed is an issue that insidiously undermines trust.

Cyber Warfare Defined

In our research, we found that experts employ diverse definitions of cyber warfare, depending on the weight or emphasis accorded to various actions, actors, and intent. We attempted to minimize the all-encompassing and academically confusing expression "information warfare" to describe electronic attacks.

In this document, we also eschew other terms, such as information operations, electronic warfare, "hacktivism", information disruption, or cyber terrorism. In each of these terms there exists a common link to cyber activities, yet each term is different enough to not entirely capture or mostly miss the definition of cyber warfare. As stated at the outset, cyber warfare, involves units organized along nation-state boundaries, in offensive and defensive operations, using computers to attack other computers or networks through electronic means. In the future, if not already common practice, individual cyber warfare units will likely execute through the wires attacks against targets in a cooperative and simultaneous manner. The overall intent is to seek advantage over an adversary by compromising the integrity, confidentiality, or availability of a computing device.

CRITICAL NETWORKS ARE TARGETS

The most likely targets of cyber warfare are critical networks. Critical networks are those that if interrupted for significant portions of time (several days or several weeks or indefinitely) or perform erratically or intermittently (i.e., accessible only Tuesdays and Thursdays) would disrupt daily life. Networks can be large or small, and are often integrated with other architectures in a redundant chain. But there are those systems that do not have built-in redundancy and whose disruption would halt all activities associated with the network.

For example, the news media disseminate information on the Internet. CNN's website is a popular news source, as is the

New York Times electronic edition. However, if access to the Internet were suddenly disrupted for several weeks, consumers of these news sources would turn to alternatives such as print media and television. CNN's website could itself have a backup server, which would prevent a cyber attack from significantly limiting its customers' access to electronic news.

Other networks, such as the 911 emergency system, medical information systems controlling sensitive data such as dosage requirements and patient records, and the automated-clearinghouse functions of major banks, the Federal Reserve, credit card companies and other financial institutions, would suffer from disruption or denial as well as disinformation. In July of 2000, Japanese cell phone users with Internet capability had their telephones hijacked by lines of code contained in e-mails directing their telephones to dial 110, the country's 911 network, tying up emergency lines.

According to FBI reports, a witness in a criminal case was nearly murdered when the criminal he was about to testify against broke into a hospital network and increased the dosage of his medication until it amounted to a lethal amount if administered. The information presented thus far underscores the dynamic growth, rapidly changing technologies, and simultaneous complexity and vulnerability assocated with the cyber warfare domain.

In general, compromises at the national level that undermined popular confidence and day-to-day trust or resulted in damage to key national or multinational economic sectors would likely be more disruptive than local events. But the scope, direction, duration, and intent of observed attacks are hard to pinpoint. It is often difficult to disentangle the various threads of cause and effect. An adversary may employ digital laundering techniques to mask the source of the action, complicating traceability.

MOTIVATION: FOILING THE TARGET PROVIDES THE INCENTIVE

To recapitulate, the U.S. economy is becoming networked in a spiraling, complex fashion. This means that an adversary can obtain advantage by remotely accessing such networks through electronic means, compromising data integrity and undermining trust. In addition, according to security experts, trends in both dependency and connectivity overlap; convergence has made U.S. national information networks more vulnerable and therefore more attractive as targets of cyber attack. As retired Colonel Marvin Leibstone of the Computer Security and Technological Studies Project aptly puts it, "the more content there is on the Internet, and thus more valuable the contents, the more incentive there is to crack it to dominate it. And, thus, the need grows for additional protective layers and for organizations to work alongside one another." And the U.S. National Intelligence Officer for Science and Technology observed in 2001:

- The growing connectivity among secure and insecure networks creates new opportunities for unauthorized intrusions into sensitive proprietary computer systems within critical U.S. infrastructures such as the nation's telephone system.
- The complexity of computer networks is growing faster than the ability to understand and protect them by identifying critical nodes, verifying security, and monitoring activity.
- Firms are dedicating growing, but still insufficient, resources to the defense of U.S. infrastructures against foreign cyber attack—perceived as a low likelihood threat compared to routine disruptions such as accidental damage to telecommunications lines. Adversaries that cannot match U.S. conventional military strength have an incentive to employ asymmetric strategies to exploit our vulnerabilities. Different adversaries will have different goals in scouting our communications nodes and compromising our IT systems. Among these are: intelligence gathering, software theft, compromising systems or data integrity, and perception management.

As CIA analyst John Serabian stated in Feburary 2000:

- "There are any number of incentives to use cyber attacks, including economic, industrial, and military rationales. By way of example:

- Trillions of dollars in financial transactions and commerce move over a medium with minimal protection and only sporadic law enforcement—a structure the most complex the world has ever known.
- Increasing quantities of intellectual property reside on networked systems; and
- Opportunities abound to disrupt military effectiveness and public safety while maintaining the elements of surprise and anonymity."

Years from now when historians look back upon the bridging years between the end of the 20th and beginning of 21st centuries, they will likely note the defining constructs of this time to be the socioeconomic phenomenon known as globalization and the evolution of the beginnings of the Information Age. One expert predicts that in the near future, in "as little as 3-5 years, the I&T sector [information and telecommunications] will host the complete convergence of telephone, data and video networks into a single, packet-based architecture – a unified next generation network (NGN)." In the midst of the all-pervasive revolution in information processing, sharing, and communication, cyber warfare—the employment of computer-to-computer attack strategies constituting offensive and defensive operations—is no longer a leap of imagination or the work of science fiction authors.

STUDY METHODOLOGY

As stated at the outset, this study is concerned with a realistic assessment of cyber attack capabilities of various nation-states, such as Russia, China, North Korea, and Iran. It rests on an interdisciplinary approach blending strategic, technological, and political analysis. In compiling this primer on cyber attack capabilities and threats, our overall approach is to disaggregate complicated technical matters to assess the true nature of the challenge. Our goal is to avoid erecting policy prescriptions on a false or misleading foundation. We first define the issues involved in offensive cyber warfare.

In the next section, the country studies, we evaluate the research and investments in the field of cyber warfare by selected nation-states. In the conclusion, we identify and characterize information network vulnerabilities in the United States. We derive findings and recommendations by comparing and balancing potential threat capabilities against broadly understood vulnerabilities.

Using Open Source Literature

Building on previous research, and relying exclusively on open source data, we collected information on and analyzed the cyber attack capabilities, means, and motivations of several foreign countries. Our current assessment of the available open source evidence leads us to believe that several nation- states are developing such capabilities as part of an offensive cyber warfare program.

This is neither a deterministic piece nor a predictive piece on the course of action of cyber attack-capable nation-states. It also does not detail the possible events to follow a coordinated, deliberate cyber attack. Our approach is to define more systematically:

(1) external nation-state capability and intent to engage the U.S. asymmetrically through these means; and

(2) key factors that make the U.S. an especially inviting target. Our conclusions are also compared to known cyber events that have already taken place in the hope of leading the analysis to a more balanced result.

While some might question the validity of findings such as ours derived exclusively from open sources, we believe that our use of published materials bolsters our assessments. Assuming it is unlikely that classified information leaks into the open source arena, if such restricted information identifying and characterizing foreign cyber capabilities is generally on the mark, it would suggest a systematic bias in this report toward *understating* the threat.

Research and Works Consulted

During the formative stage of this investigation, a review was undertaken to identify relevant studies and reports. In addition to general works on cyber warfare issues by noted authorities, our review identified several articles focusing on cyber developments in single countries. For example, retired Lieutenant Colonel (U.S. Army ret.) Timothy L. Thomas has written on cyber warfare developments China and Russia.38 Other experts, such as Grey E. Burkhart, have researched Iran and India.39 In the course of our investigation, we did not encounter any comprehensive reports analyzing the cyber warfare capabilities of several nation-states using an analytical framework similar to ours.

To assess the general nature of cyber warfare, we consulted several standard reference works such as Greg Rattray, *Strategic Warfare in Cyberspace* (2001); Dorothy E. Denning, *Information Warfare and Security* (1999); John Arquilla and David Ronfeldt, *Cyber war is Coming!* (1993); and Dan Verton, *Black Ice: The Invisible Threat of Cyber Terrorism* (2003). We also consulted several U.S. government publications (civilian and military), and specialized defense publications such as *Jane's Intelligence Review*. To develop a preliminary list of countries relevant to our proposed inquiry, we examined published Congressional testimony by government officials and academic experts; academic journals focusing on strategic warfare, non-conventional weapons, and national security issues; and publications of the U.S. Department of Defense.

To collect military and civilian IT-related information pertaining to the individual countries examined in this report, we reviewed foreign language resources, including selected government publications and websites, academic journals, and on-line news sites. We also relied heavily on standard media publications and "grey" source websites. The statistical data presented in this study is synthesized from a variety of sources including the CIA's *World Fact Book*.

Country Selection

The research team accorded priority to nation-states previously identified in the review and other open sources as seeking to develop a cyber attack capability. The countries in this category are Russia, China, North Korea, and Iran. We then selected for study additional countries that did not appear consistently in all the assessments provided but for which we had identified some interest in expert publications and professional social science journals. Two of the countries in this category are India and Pakistan, selected because of their intrinsic interest and reported propensity to use cyber attacks in regional disputes. Resource and time constraints did not permit addressing several additional nation-states of potential interest, such as Israel, Syria, and the former Yugoslavia.

Collection Plan

In reviewing each country, the research team used the topic headings to structure the overall information collection. To acquire the necessary background, between October 2002 and September 2003 the team surveyed the extensive body of reports on the dependence of U.S. critical infrastructure on computer controls and the related vulnerability of the U.S. to cyber attack. Between September 2003 and September 2004, periodic updates and revisions to the country studies were performed as more incidents and data appeared in the open source realm. Building on this survey of expert reports, academic research, and engineering panel findings we then began research on the specific countries listed above. We collected data within the various topic areas in the above table.

Analysis

Beyond the collection framework, our overall analytical approach towards development of cyber attack capability measurement was shaped by the work of Professor Dorothy E. Denning, among others. Professor Denning argues that cyber threats are a function of three factors: Intent; Capability; and Opportunity. To simplify our work, we equated the well-publicized vulnerabilities in the U.S. electronic infrastructure with "opportunity." With regard to the intent, we assumed that any credible official documents or published statements by a foreign government or its military leaders concerning adoption of an offensive cyber warfare program (or doctrine) were sufficient to imply motivation to at least develop a cyber attack capability.

The ubiquity of computer and other information technologies plus the portability of knowledge enables sub-national elements, such as terrorist cells, to launch cyber attacks. With respect to technical and institutional capabilities, nation-states—because of resource and other endowments—often possess the means to enhance the effectiveness of malicious intrusions.

Cyber attacks, if applied on a massive scale by a nation-state intelligence service, for example, could yield important strategic effects. The broad spectrum of both possible attack sources and degrees of disruptiveness is addressed in the concluding chapter of this report. Many of the countries proved difficult to evaluate through open sources.

Closed societies, such as the state of North Korea, present difficult problems for researchers. First, the amount of official information available is very limited. Second, sources from rival states such as South Korea that may give clues into North Korea's cyber capabilities are often unreliable due to bias among other factors. For example, the South Korean Central Intelligence Agency (KCIA) often publishes reports that contain factual errors to represent North Korea in a negative light. Lastly, translating foreign languages often results in subtle interpretational differences that may lead to differing analytical conclusions.

To recapitulate, the present report focuses on topic areas that may reveal a nation-state's means and motivations to launch cyber attacks. The following categorization of evidence specifies the topic areas and some detail on their indicators and related measurement criteria.

Category One Evidence

Direct links to a foreign cyber warfare capability

1) U.S. Government Reports and Foreign Official Statements
   - This evidence is the aggregate of U.S. Department of Defense assessments on a state's cyber warfare capability and that state's own official guidelines (doctrine) for waging cyber conflict.
2) Foreign Military and Intelligence Agency Research
   - This area embraces multiple domains including military IT projects, equipment acquisition, active cyber warfare units, computer security, and specialized training.

Category Two Evidence

Circumstantial links indicating a baseline information technology infrastructure necessary to support a cyber warfare operation

3) Information Technology Investment

- This area embraces domains such as industrial electronics, information technology research and development efforts, network infrastructure investment, advanced university engineering curricula, software development, and state-to-state information technology initiatives, including technical assistance and training programs. To summarize, the purpose of this report is to provide a rigorous analysis of the cyber warfare capabilities and intentions of foreign countries that is accessible to professional and nonprofessional readers. Cyber warfare is attractive to our adversaries because unprotected computer networks—frequently cited as America's Achilles heel—create a simultaneous dependency and vulnerbility.45 Although we have benefited from the insights of previous research, public discourse, in many cases resting on anecdotal evidence, often inhibits understanding. We hope to raise awareness and add value to the debate through a more systematic treatment of the issues.

8

Scenario in the China

WELTON CHANG

> Our warfare methods must adapt to the needs of information warfare. We must use all types, forms, and methods of force, and especially make more use of nonlinear warfare and many types of information warfare methods which combine native and Western elements to use our strengths in order to attack the enemy's weaknesses, avoid being reactive, and strive for being active. In this way, it will be entirely possible for China to achieve comprehensive victory over the enemy even under the conditions of inferiority in information technology.
>
> Major General Wang Pufeng
>
> *China Military Science*, Spring 1995
>
> "I asked why the Chinese talk in terms of "three represents," "four looks," and other such phraseology. All of you understand this, but I had to find out. Then I asked myself how those historic stratagems and sayings imbedded in Chinese culture, and the Chinese understanding of military science, affect Chinese thinking in the information age. And I was surprised to find that few had given this area as much thought as I assumed they would have. Analysts appeared more consumed with what China was doing today than how China would use its past or its tradition of military science to shape the present. Undoubtedly, a few historic Chinese phrases are

> thrown around when attempting to "get close" to the Chinese mentality in official speeches and even during an analysis of strategy and tactics, but I found precious few analysts had applied those strategies and concepts to electrons. Maybe that is because it is more difficult to measure the intent of an electron than it is to measure the intent of a tank."
>
> Lieutenant Colonel (ret.) Timothy Thomas, U.S. Army
>
> *Testimony before the US-China Commission*, August 3, 2001

By the early 1990s, China's military recognized that a revolution in military affairs was developing that came about as a result of the new possibilities opened up by information technologies. China's military began exploring cyber attacks as an asymmetric means of countering a technologically superior adversary on, as well as off, the battlefield. With the support of an integrated national plan, the People's Liberation Army (PLA) has developed cyber warfare doctrine, implemented basic cyber warfare training for its officers, and conducted cyber warfare exercises.

China claims to be developing a unique model for employing cyber attacks, though upon closer scrutiny much of what is claimed to be unique parallels similar research done by American experts working on cyber warfare. A number of events provide some evidence the government of China condones and may even sponsor computer hacking. Beijing's foreign and internal intelligence services continue their systematic collection of science and technology information to support national goals, showing both an interest in the material collected and the high-tech collection methods. China also seeks commercial information technology products manufactured internally to meet its technology needs. While military cooperation with Russia, a country that may have developed a substantial cyber warfare program, continues, China may be developing its own models for military information collection and for the use of cyber attack technologies.

BACKGROUND

China is working diligently to sustain its rise in the world's geopolitical order. Events such as China's first manned space flight and a successful bid to host the 2008 Summer Olympic Games highlight some recent national achievements. China plans to build the world's largest dam, longest bridge, fastest train, and highest-capacity railroad. Beijing has crafted and implemented a multifaceted strategy by integrating its foreign, domestic, military, and economic policies in order to achieve its national objectives. Edward Sobiesk writes that a cyber warfare strategy would be a logical answer to the Chinese government's current objectives of increasing "national power." A cyber warfare strategy would help to realign the international system and balance of power to one that would be more conducive to the increase of this theoretical "national power."

In the short term, China's primary foreign relations issue is the question of an independent Taiwan. However, some experts believe it is unlikely that China would launch a full-scale war over the island. China considers the island a renegade province and is hostile to any moves Taiwan makes towards independence. Recent news reports as well as the official military publication titled *China's National Defense in 2002* outline force projection capabilities (primarily focusing on China's medium and long-range missile assets) and reaffirm Beijing's hard-line stance regarding Taiwan's independence. According to this publication, "China's armed forces will unswervingly defend the country's sovereignty and unity, and have the resolve as well as the capability to check any separatist act." Another issue of national importance is security relations with India as border and other disputes continue to strain relations between the two countries.

China maintains secrecy concerning its military and intelligence activities as well as for all other matters of national security. Significantly, both the 2000 *Report to Congress on Implementation of the Taiwan Relations Act* and the 2003 *Annual Report on the Military Power of the People's Republic of China* note U.S. intelligence community knowledge-gaps in significant aspects of Chinese military power. American military analysts suggest that public documents, such as *China's National Defense in 2002*, may be calculated attempts to appear to be providing open information while actually keeping significant developments secret or hiding important military deficiencies.

At the operational level, there is little concrete evidence in open source materials describing the implementation of the new directives released in 1999 by the People's Liberation Army (PLA) Academy of Military Science. What Chinese military experts state as fact concerning supposed cyber warfare developments may not actually reflect real actions taken by the PLA.

U.S. GOVERNMENT REPORTS AND FOREIGN OFFICIAL STATEMENTS

United States government officials have been reporting on China's development of cyber attack capabilities since the late 1990s. China allegedly sees cyber attacks as a component of an integrated strategy to defeat a technologically and numerically superior enemy military force. The rapidly growing Chinese economy supports the ability of the PLA to test and adopt new information technologies as a component of its modernization plans. In his 1998 testimony before the Senate Committee on Government Affairs, former CIA Director George Tenet said, "We know with specificity of several nations that are working on developing an information warfare capability."

Commenting on a Department of Defense assessment, Tenet said that the Chinese are attempting to "leapfrog" American military technology advances by using asymmetric means of implementing "Information Warfare" capabilities. Michael Pillsbury, a research fellow at National Defense University, observed in 1997 that Beijing had the world's largest program of its type. "Judging by their military writings, they are saying that information warfare is the core of what they want to do," he said. "This way they can leap over the obsolescence of their tanks, ships, and aircraft and focus on the vulnerability of high-tech forces" like those of the United States and Taiwan. The PLA has recognized the U.S. military dependence on technology in not only command and control, but intelligence gathering and precision strikes as well.

CIA Information Operations Issue Manager, John Serabian, testified before the Joint Economic Committee in February 2000 concerning China's cyber capabilities. Mr. Serabian commented that cyber warfare is becoming a possible strategic alternative for countries "that realize that, in conventional military confrontation with the United States, they will not prevail." The CIA official quoted the remarks of an unidentified Chinese general: "We can make the enemy's command centers not work by changing their data system.

We can cause the enemy's headquarters to make incorrect judgment(s) by sending disinformation. We can dominate the enemy's banking system and even its entire social order." Cyber attacks represent a viable strategy for countries that are "out-gunned" in conventional warfare, Serabian testified. "These countries perceive that cyberattacks, launched from within or outside the U.S., represent the kind of asymmetric option they will need to level the playing field during an armed crisis against the U.S."

The PLA has made significant strides in using information technologies to support its military objectives. The U.S. Defense Intelligence Agency Director, Vice Admiral Lowell E. Jacoby, noted in 2003 "our greatest concern is China's military buildup. Last year marked new high points for unit training and weapons integration—all sharply focused on the Taiwan mission and on increasing the costs for any who might intervene in a regional Chinese operation. We anticipate no slowdown in the coming year." Command, Control, Communications, Computers, and Intelligence (C4I) modernization and automation efforts are ongoing. China maintains separate civilian and military communication networks.

Programs to support C4I are greatly enhanced by commercial information technologies now readily available in China. In examining the dual use of technologies, China is reported to have placed considerable emphasis on protecting its own C4I networks from computer attacks including viruses.

The U.S. Department of Defense (DoD) reports that a Chinese strategic and tactical military revolution is underway. In the 2003 DoD *Annual Report on the Military Power of the People's Republic of China*, the authors write, "the relative technological inferiority of the PLA has led to the exploration of asymmetric methods of enabling 'the inferior to defeat the superior'." Despite the statements in the DoD report, Charles Bacon believes that "China lags behind the U.S. in the development of Information Warfare capability and will probably remain behind for some time."

Evolution of Chinese Views on Cyber Warfare

In July of 2004, Jiang Zemin, who has remained the Central Military Commission Chairman, "called on Chinese military forces to be equipped with information technology for the strategic goal of winning information warfare." The development of Chinese strategy in the domain of cyber warfare can be traced to the early 1990s. Following the conclusion of the first Gulf War in 1991, the Chinese government and PLA doctrinal thinkers began to analyze the U.S. military victory.

American and Coalition military forces used joint operations coordinated by electronic means in order to defeat the Iraqi military. In the initial salvo of U.S. missiles, most of Iraq's command and control capabilities, as well as its information gathering radar sites were destroyed. Beijing, and many other world powers, viewed the overwhelming victory combining information technologies and conventional power as a Revolution in Military Affairs (RMA). Throughout the reports and statements China has released and published on cyber warfare, two main lines of thought stand out.

First, cyber warfare strategy (as does conventional warfare strategy) in Chinese literature makes references to Sun Tzu in nearly every written document. While the actual effect of Sun Tzu's strategic principles of warfare on the modern Chinese variety is hard to discern, it is clear that Sun Tzu is a great influence, at the minimum, on Chinese doctrinal writing.

Second, cyber warfare strategy is in keeping with national goals because it is a cost-effective way of conducting asymmetric operations against an adversary.

The Beginnings of Doctrinal Research

In one of the first papers written on Chinese cyber warfare doctrine, Shen Weiguang wrote:

> "Those who take part in information war are not all soldiers. Anybody who understands computers may

> become a 'fighter' in the network. Think tanks composed of non-governmental experts may take part in decision-making; rapid mobilization will not just be directed to young people; information-related industries and domains will be the first to be mobilized and enter the war..."

Shen, now a purported expert in cyber warfare, described the "concept of 'take-home' battle" in which the Chinese would conduct a different and personal type of People's War with computers. The evolution from the People's War strategy to the adoption of information technologies to defeat superior enemies may be seen as an integral component of a Chinese plan to become a world leader without having to spend an inordinate percentage of its GDP in a military build-up. The development of a cyber warfare arsenal is referred to by U.S. expert Lieutenant Colonel (rct.) Thomas as "adding wings to a tiger," i.e., giving increased capabilities to a foreign military largely considered to be the only power in the world that can, in the future, rival the American military. The Chinese military is attempting to produce its own specific type of "Chinese" cyber warfare strategy, much like the attempt to form socialism and communism into ideas that can be applied specifically to the Chinese people.

Several researchers at the Chinese Academy of Military Science, China's National Defense University, and the Wuhan Communications Command Academy have published books concerning the usage of cyber warfare. Further data for analysis can be gleaned through an examination of the development of unique Chinese cyber warfare strategies.

The U.S. tends to focus on the computer network attack aspects of cyber warfare but China's cyber warfare focuses more on psychological operations and denial and deception of military data. In times of war, Chinese cyber warfare doctrine focuses on defeating the enemy before stepping into battle; meaning that Chinese forces should have a signficant information advantage in future battles so that the outcome of engagement should be largely predetermined. PLA senior Colonel Wang Baocun, a Chinese cyber warfare strategy expert, states that cyber warfare strategy reinforces the notion of Sun Tzu's "subduing the enemy without battle."

He states that the purpose of cyber warfare is to "force the enemy side to regard their goal as our goal," to "force the opponent to give up the will to resist and end the confrontation and stop fighting by attacking an enemy's perception and belief via information energy." Apparently unique Chinese elements can be found in other writings as well. Senior Colonel Wang, in his article *The Current Revolution in Military Affairs and its Impact on Asia-Pacific Security*, defines cyber warfare as "a form of combat actions which attacks the information and information systems of the enemy while protecting the information and information systems on one's own side." Furthermore, Colonel Wang states that "the key elements of cyber warfare are military security, military deception, physical attack, electronic warfare, and net warfare, and its basic purpose is to seize and maintain information dominance."

In 1999, two other PLA senior Colonels, Wang Xiangsui and Qiao Liang published, *Unrestricted Warfare* [Chao Xian Zhan], a widely referenced work on the advantages of asymmetry in the contemporary Information Age. The work drew its conclusions from analyzing both the weaknesses and strengths of the U.S. conventional military prowess. *Unrestricted Warfare's* main thrust was an argument that those who saw that the root of global hegemony was an overpowering force on the battlefield would be surpassed by those who saw that the lines between economic, political, and military warfare were disappearing.

Qiao and Liang argued that in the future, raw military power will neither be the only or main way for a nation to spread its influence nor the most cost-effective way to cause harm to an adversary. A key point of *Unrestricted Warfare* stems from the idea of "build[ing] the weapons that fit the fight" instead of "fighting the fight that fit one's weapons." Wang and Qiao's ideas seem to have affected the PLA's thinking on how to better use its resources and military investment, leading to a reduction of the active military forces and an increase in military information technology.

Because the PLA lacks the conventional strength to defeat superior adversaries, Chinese strategists believe that innovative cyber warfare strategies can play a key role in an asymmetric victory. Major General Dai Qingmin's article on cyber warfare titled *Innovating and Developing Views on Information Operations* reasons that China's technological deficiencies can be overcome by developing good cyber warfare strategies.

Among these strategies are "jamming or sabotaging an enemy's information or information system, giving an enemy a false impression and launching a surprise information attack on him at the same time, causing an enemy to make a wrong judgment or take wrong action, etc." The primary conclusion of the author (Dai Qingmin) is that Chinese warfare strategies have undergone a transformation. Concentrations of forces (mass armies that characterized the Chinese military) will be replaced by new and more efficient strategies using information technology, effectively blurring the front and rear lines of combat.

FOREIGN MILITARY AND INTELLIGENCE AGENCY RESEARCH

China continues to maintain the largest conventional military forces in the world. Despite this fact, the PLA recognizes its limited effectiveness due to its inability to project force as well as to fight an all-out conventional war with the United States. The DoD estimated in March 2002 that publicly reported Chinese military spending totals $20 billion. However, much of the PLA's spending, such as foreign weapon purchases and research and development, is not reported. Although estimates vary, the PLA budget could total as much as $65 billion.

Further, most force modernization costs are outside the publicly available spending figures. Relevant to this study, the recently released PLA budget shows a change in the priorities of the PLA: a 9.6% budget boost targeted improvements in "rapid-response and IT warfare" and preparation for emergencies. PLA General Guo Boxiong emphasized that the Chinese military must improve its ability to win high tech warfare.

The Chinese military is clearly pursuing cyber warfare to counter the widely acknowledged dominance of the American conventional military. The Chinese have termed this research approach "acupuncture warfare." Acupuncture warfare has been defined as "paralyzing the enemy by attacking the weak link of his command, control, communications and information as if hitting his acupuncture point in kung fu combat."

A component of this strategy, discussed further in the Information Technology Investment section of this report, is the use of civilian hackers. According to senior Colonel Wang, the civilian apparatus can be made to cooperate with the military cyber warfare forces to strengthen cyber attack operations. Senior Colonel Wang emphasizes that anyone with a computer can join in the fight against an opposing force acting as a force multiplier. To this end, there is some evidence that officially condoned hacking occurred following the mid-air collision between an American surveillance plane and a Chinese fighter aircraft on April 1, 2001.

In a *Jane's Intelligence Review* article published in 2002, U.S. Army Lieutenant Colonel (ret.) Thomas finds that the PLA divides Chinese cyber warfare strategy into three parts: surveillance, attack, and protection. Network and electromagnetic surveillance allows the PLA to collect information on potential targets and develop an attack plan against critical infrastructure. Computer information attack refers to "operations to disrupt, sabotage and destroy information in enemy computer network systems using specialized equipment, software or firepower." Protection refers to prevention of enemy surveillance and attack options against friendly computer systems.

Strategic targets of Chinese cyber warfare may include computer networking systems linking "political, economic and military installations of a country as well as society in general." According to Lieutenant Colonel (ret.) Thomas, many Chinese theorists have proposed organizing "network special warfare detachments and computer experts to form a shock brigade of 'network warriors' to accomplish these tasks."

Training for future cyber attack operations is of primary importance to the PLA. Among the PLA's cyber warfare training centers are the Communications Command Academy in Wuhan, the Information Engineering University in Zhengzhou, the Science and Engineering University, and the National Defense Science and Technology University in Changsha. All of these centers maintain professors and experts on cyber warfare to train PLA soldiers.

PLA officer course curriculum includes: basic theory, including computer basics and applications; communications network technology; the information highway; units connected by IT; electronic countermeasures; radar technology; cyber warfare rules and regulations; cyber warfare strategy and tactics; theater and strategic cyber warfare; information systems, including gathering, handling, disseminating and using information and combat command, monitoring, decisionmaking, and control systems. Other formal training for PLA officers includes the usage of information weapons, simulated cyber warfare, protection of information systems, computer virus attacks and counterattacks, and jamming and counter-jamming of communications networks.

Military exercises conducted by the PLA also involve cyber wafare. For example, the first "special" (meaning cyber warfare) PLA battle took place in October 1997. In the Shenyang Military Region, a Group Army (GA) underwent a computer attack that paralyzed its systems. The GA countered with virus-killing software, and the exercise was termed an "invasion and anti-invasion" event. This exercise involved the deployment of ground, logistics, medical, and air force units. The second occurred in October 1998, when the Chinese military staged an integrated high-technology exercise that united several military regions around the country.

The center of gravity of the exercise was the Beijing Military Region, where a joint defense warfare drill used a "military information superhighway" for the first time. Another exercise took place in October 1999 when the PLA conducted another cyber warfare simulation. Two army groups of the Beijing Military Region gamed a "confrontation" campaign against computer networks. Reconnaissance and counter reconnaissance, interference and counter-interference, blocking and counter-blocking, and air strikes and counter air strikes were among some of the high-tech tactics practiced during the exercise. Finally, in July of 2000, the Chengdu Military Region conducted a confrontational campaign exercise on the Internet.

The Chinese military is growing not only in its understanding of and competence in cyber warfare, but also in its development of cyber warfare-related technologies. Moreover, the PLA is increasing the number and training of organizations involved with cyber warfare.

Chinese Major General Dai writes that not only has the Chinese military made leaps and bounds in strategy, they have also put the theories to test with their cyber warfare divisions acting as operational forces against each other. Ten strategies that were employed in these exercises include "planting information mines, conducting information reconnaissance, changing network data, releasing information bombs, dumping information garbage, disseminating propaganda, applying information deception, releasing clone information, organizing information defense, and establishing network spy stations."

China is developing a strategy for integrating the country's civilian computer experts in military reserve units within the PLA. The PLA has developed recruiting programs for technical experts possibly in order to develop their cyber warfare assets. Military reserve units specializing in cyber warfare are in development in several cities. As Wang Xiaodong, an officer in the PLA stated, "the Chinese population numbers in the billions. If one or two per cent of any population has an IQ over 139, as studies predict, then China must have tens of millions of people in this category.

The problem is how to find more information space and equipment for all of these people." This serves the dual purpose of fulfilling the Maoist concept of a People's War and creates a large electronic army. James Mulvenon, in writing for RAND, imagines the possible usage of such a People's War against an adversary:

> "When one imagines scenarios in which the PLA would be concerned with preemptively striking U.S. forces during the deployment phase for early strategic victory, it is difficult to avoid the obvious conclusion that the author is discussing a Taiwan conflict. For the PLA, using IW against U.S. information systems to degrade or even delay

> a deployment of forces to Taiwan offers an attractive asymmetric strategy. American forces are highly informationdependent, and rely heavily on precisely coordinated logistics networks . . . If PLA information operators using PCs were able to hack or crash these systems, thereby delaying the arrival of a U.S. carrier battle group to the theater, while simultaneously carrying out a coordinated campaign of short-range ballistic missile attacks, "fifth column," and IW attacks against Taiwanese critical infrastructure, then Taipei might be quickly brought to its knees and forced to capitulate to Beijing."

The PLA continues to develop its cyber attack capabilities. Ongoing budget increases, improvements in basic C4I, training, exercises, and new programs to recruit civilian experts are indications of China's plans. In addition to active forces, the PLA maintains reserve units whose sole mission is to perform cyber warfare functions. These units have participated in cyber warfare exercises and simulations.

As of 2003, the Department of Defense reports that "China has the capability to penetrate poorly protected U.S. computer systems and potentially could use computer network attacks to strike specific U.S. civilian and military infrastructures. This antiaccess strategy is centered on targeting operational centers of gravity, including C4I centers, airbases, and aircraft carrier battle groups located around the periphery of China." Despite China's apparent strides in developing cyber warfare, some skeptics see a pattern among Chinese military thinkers as they continually turn to cyber warfare as an apparent cure-all for an increasingly outdated and obsolete military.

They argue the threat from cyber warfare operations is exaggerated because the PLA continues to lack sufficiently modern weapons and equipment to pose a threat to the U.S. military, even if it was able to successfully wage cyber warfare in a military setting. These critics also believe that although the Chinese military has a fully realized doctrinal understanding of cyber warfare, they lack the knowledge and technology to implement it. However, through examination of open source materials, it is evident that

China already is, in practice, a rising force, and a potentially knowledgeable wielder of cyber warfare and cyber war capabilities. China maintains significant foreign and internal intelligence capabilities. Chinese intelligence services have a special interest in espionage pertaining to the information technologies.

> According to the 2003 Department of Defense *Annual Report:* "As of 1991 there were roughly 4,000 individual intelligence organizations operating in China. Many of these organizations are associated with state-owned enterprises, research institutes, and academies affiliated with China's defense industrial base. The collection of technical information probably continues to be orchestrated by the CDSTIC, which now is subordinate to the PLA's General Equipment Department (GED). The GED reportedly oversees a complex web of factories, institutes, and academies that are subordinate to China's nuclear, aeronautics, electronics, ordnance, shipbuilding, and astronautics industries. Each of these institutions has an import/export corporation to facilitate the import of technology and knowledge."

Rob Koepp, a researcher at the Milken Institute in Santa Monica, argues that China is more than merely interested in catching up to the West in terms of technological development. Mr. Koepp believes that China wants to "bring about fundamentally innovative technology over time" that will set standards for the whole world. According to the Federation of American Scientists, the Ministry of State Services (MSS), a Chinese intelligence organization, may "aggressively target the U.S., placing particular emphasis on the high tech sector heavily concentrated in Southern California, and in the Silicon Valley. Cover for Beijing's espionage in the United States may includes [sic]the 1,500 Chinese diplomats operating out of 70 offices, 15,000 Chinese students who arrive in the U.S. each year, and 10,000 Chinese who travel in some 2,700 visiting delegations each year."

In addition to intelligence activities, open sources almost certainly help Chinese information collection efforts. For example, in 1991 the China Defense Science and Technology Information

Center (CDSTIC) published a science and technology collection manual titled *Sources and Techniques of Obtaining National Defense Science and Technology Intelligence*.

This document "suggested that 80 percent of China's defense S&T needs are met through open and gray source (purchase/ subscription) materials." Further, the guidebook provided detailed information on foreign open sources concerning defense technology. With American information infrastructure vulnerabilities often published in open sources, China's intelligence services may be better positioned to focus their activities on high value targets. Active intelligence programs by China, both internally and externally, are in all likelihood delivering information on new technologies and how they may be used to exploit adversaries' weaknesses. In addition, the proliferation of overseas Chinese diplomats, businessmen, and students may serve as an ongoing network for collecting open source data from a structured set of requirements produced by the Chinese government.

INFORMATION TECHNOLOGY INVESTMENT

China's efforts to acquire and develop information technologies for commercial and military uses are extensive. The CCP fully supports the adoption of efficiency-enhancing information technology. However, the use of the Internet and other technologies for political activities not authorized by Beijing is strictly controlled. According to Lu Chengzhao, deputy director-general of the Office of China National Network and Information Security Coordinating Group, "China's public Internet emergency response system is being constructed and perfected and China is expected to complete the construction of National Network and Information Security System in five years."

China's top leaders, many with advanced degrees in the mechanical sciences, have been supportive of technological infrastructure improvements as a component of overall economic development. China uses various methods—seed funding, tax breaks for information technology research and development, utilization of technology development zones—to attract overseas investment, technical knowledge of advanced technology, and management experience. The Chinese government continues to stress the need to "import technology rather than finished goods, and to renovate factories through selective purchase of key technology rather than through purchase of whole plants." China is actively seeking foreign direct investment, especially for those seeking to develop high-technology products. Recent reports comment that the Chinese government "gives funding to academic institutions and new small companies to commercialize products of academic research."

According to the 2003 DoD *Annual Report,* "thousands of PRC business entities have been established in the United States. The bulk of the business conducted by these entities is probably legitimate, but an undetermined number may target dual-use commodities and controlled technologies restricted from sale to the PRC." The report's authors also note that "authoritative PRC journals have recommended an increase in the use of overseas ethnic-Chinese scientists to transfer foreign technology."

In addition, with increased "out-sourcing" to China in recent years, there is the risk that software companies could deliberately embed back-doors in the programming code which would render the software vulnerable to intrusion. The presence of a software "time bomb" might not be detected until it is too late. China may be using technically capable individuals to engage in hacking activities.

As outlined in the Official Doctrine section of this paper, authors have written about the mass mobilization of the Chinese population for cyber attack operations. It is difficult to ascertain through exclusively open sources the extent of Chinese hackers' involvement with the central government. However, it is clear that hackers have launched cyber attacks following physical incidents. iDefense analysts state that the hackers in China are not actually "state-sponsored"; they place them under a category labeled "state-controlled."

For example, after the May 2000 bombing of the Chinese Embassy in Belgrade, hackers attacked United States political, military, and civilian web sites. The following year, Department of Defense officials warned that reprisal was likely on the anniversary of the 2000 accidental bombing. The Chinese Liberation Army Daily reportedly advocated the recruitment of civilians to aid in the cyber attacks. After major attacks did not happen, Air Force Maj. General John Bradley commented "We expected another series of attacks from Chinese hackers, but actually the government of China asked them not to do that."

Following the collision of an American reconnaissance aircraft and a Chinese fighter plane on April 1, 2001, Chinese hacker groups, such as the Honker Union of China and the Chinese Red Guest Network Security Technology Alliance, organized sustained cyber attacks against American targets. The FBI's National Infrastructure Protection Center (NIPC) issued an advisory warning of "the potential for increased hacker activity directed at U.S. systems during the period of April 30, 2001 and May 7, 2001."

In the 2001 report *Cyber Attacks During the War on Terrorism: A Predictive Analysis*, ISTS reported that "it remains unclear whether the Chinese government sanctioned these attacks, but, in light of the fact that these activities were highly visible and no arrests were made by Chinese officials, it can be assumed that they were at least tolerated, if not directly supported by Chinese authorities." Hacker organizations may also have received help from the Chinese government in developing software, viruses, and methods to attack various computer networks.

A number of recent Internet worms including Lion, Adore, and Code Red are suspected of having originated in China. Keith Rhodes, the Chief Technologist at the U.S. General Accounting Office (GAO), commented that the Code Red worm could be traced to a university in Guangdong, China.

This assertion must be viewed critically since other computer security experts, including the NIPC, have commented that they are unable to ascertain the worm's origin. There have been other incidents in which the Chinese government has been accused of helping hackers execute cyber attacks on foreign targets.

Two Canadian ISPs, BestNet and Nebula Internet service, accused the Chinese government of sponsoring hackers with a political agenda. The crackers launched a denial of service attack at the Internet Service Providers' servers because the two ISPs had been hosting websites for the Falun Gong, a religious group that is outlawed in China. The attacks were traced back to the Beijing Application Institute for Information Technology and the Information Center of Xin An Beijing.

The method of attack began with penetration of the ISPs' servers and then turned to flooding the servers with incomplete information requests that caused the hosted site to crash. Although the methods were unable to bring down BestNet's services, Nebula Internet went offline due to the flood of data.

The U.S. Department of Transportation also contacted Nebula because an IP address involved in a "probe" on the Federal Aviation Administration server was traced back to Nebula's servers. Hypothetically, Chinese government use of hacker organizations appears to fall within the doctrinal themes set out in the cyber warfare iteration of the People's War philosophy.

Further supporting this position are the recruitment programs set up by the PLA to attract technical experts. Long-term priorities to collect science and technology information would seem to suggest the Chinese government pragmatically uses the resources at it disposal to achieve its goals.

Lastly, as demonstrated by the monitoring of political activities in cyber space, the Chinese government controls access to Internet connections and is almost certainly aware of cyber attacks that originate from within its territory. Sponsorship of hacker groups may be costefficient for the Chinese government. In comparison to maintaining large numbers of military cyber warfare specialists, lower-budget hacker groups can support and obfuscate military cyber attack operations, with little outlay of additional government resources.

China continues to procure military and dual-use technologies from Russia and other countries. Russia has a well-documented offensive cyber attack program.109 In addition, China participates in military exchanges with other nations such as Pakistan and North Korea. According to *China's National Defense in 2002* the "PLA's foreign military academic exchanges and technical cooperation have also constantly developed" including "ex-change visits of more than 100 delegations or groups of military experts with several dozen countries." For example, the Chinese President of the University of National Defense Science and Technology, the PLA institution that developed the first Chinese supercomputer, visited Russia on a military exchange in 2002.

Instead of following the traditional methods of purchasing technical assistance, China may be building a network for collecting information that will be utilized in commercial and military development programs.

Media reports indicate that China acquires information technologies illegally. In November of 2003, Gao Zhan, formerly a researcher at American University, pleaded guilty to charges of illegally exporting computer technology to China, some of which may have wound up in the hands of the Chinese military.

A report noted that "among the items sent to China were microprocessors that can be used in digital flight control and weapons systems, including identifying targets. Although these microprocessors also have commercial uses, they cannot be exported without permission of the U.S. government."

In December of 2003, Sun Microsystems was fined $291,000 for allegedly exporting advanced computers to China that were eventually used for military purposes. According to the report, Sun sent a powerful E5000 series server to China back in 1997, more specifically to a company called Automated Systems Ltd. based in Hong Kong. Eventually U.S. federal agents found the machine at the Changsha Institute of Science and Technology, which is in mainland China.

CONCLUSION

The Chinese government has formulated and is implementing an integrated strategy of diplomatic, informational, military, and economic policies to achieve its national objectives. Although open literature strongly suggests that Beijing is pursuing cyber warfare programs, secrecy hampers detailed assessments. The CIA and Department of Defense report that China sees cyber warfare as a viable asymmetric strategy when facing technologically superior adversaries.

Chinese military institutions have published works on cyber warfare. These studies stemmed from evaluations of the revolution in military affairs that was triggered by the United States' overwhelming victory over an adversary with similar conventional military capabilities to that of China in the 1991 Gulf War. Analysis of Chinese studies on cyber warfare indicates that Beijing is developing a distinct model drawing on United States doctrine and ancient Chinese warfare tenets. Overall, the Chinese see cyber attacks as a way to combat and neutralize a superior enemy.

Although China maintains the largest conventional forces in the world, digital Command, Control, Communications, Computers, and Intelligence (C4I) capabilities are lacking. The Chinese military has spent considerable resources upgrading its C4I networks.

These efforts have resulted in what appears to be an appreciation of the potential vulnerability of systems built with commercially available technology, an appreciation that has led to investments in computer network defense especially against viruses.

The Chinese military routinely trains its officers concerning information technology developments. A number of exercises that tightly integrate cyber attacks into conventional scenarios have increased Chinese understanding of the dynamic involved in information operations. The PLA has implemented programs to recruit technical experts to support its cyber attack capabilities.

It is almost certain that Beijing's intelligence services are systematically collecting science and technology information from outside China's borders to support national goals. China has published collection handbooks outlining how open source materials can substantively contribute to China's research and development efforts. In addition to highly publicized international spy cases involving technology and intellectual property theft, China has significant internal security and intelligence services monitoring Internet activity. Implementing many economic reforms, the Chinese government grants a number of incentives to foreign companies and domestic academic research to further national goals. China has targeted dual use technologies for import by Chinese owned businesses around the world.

China may be harnessing the technological skill of its hacker population to support cyber attacks. Media reports support this position, but no conclusive evidence was uncovered during the research for this study. Chinese military purchases of weapons and technology from Moscow coupled with official exchanges with Russia, a country that in all likelihood maintains an offensive cyber attack capability, continue.

9

Scenario in India

The traditional concept of national security has undergone fundamental changes over the years. It is no longer synonymous with sufficient military strength to defend the nation and its interests. In today's world, military might alone does not guarantee either sovereignty or security.

The more realistic and comprehensive approach to national security also includes economic strength, internal cohesion, and technological prowess. The rapid technological developments underway at the same time not only facilitate these events by reducing our reaction time but add entirely new dimensions of threat and challenges, such as the Revolution in Military Affairs (RMA) and offensive/defensive information warfare.

Government of India "Challenges to the Management of National Security"

Report of the Group of Ministers on National Security, February 2001 The defense forces on their part have adopted information warfare doctrines, which include infosec as a vital element.

There is a growing partnership between defense and private industry to evolve IT security solutions for the defense information infrastructure....As defense reliance on commercial off the shelf technology (COTS) grows, the dilemma of selecting an appropriate vendor has been to a large extent addressed by the CII [Confederation of Indian Industry] online defense directory—a web-based listing of Indian software vendors working on defenserelated systems and applications.

Lt. Commander Prashant Bakshi, "Security Implications of a Wired India: Challenges Ahead"

Strategic Analysis, April 2001

The Indian Government's Task Force on Cyber Crime is joining hands with corporate bodies to fight Pakistani net infiltrators. The move came after hackers claiming to belong to a Pakistani organization called G-Force, defaced the home page of the Ministry of External Affairs website. A total of 162 Indian websites have been hacked into and defaced so far this year, a phenomenal increase from 72 last year.

Strategic Affairs Newsbrief, May 2001

BACKGROUND

India has experienced, and continues to undergo, cyber attacks in a variety of forms. On June 7, 1998, for example, an anti-nuclear group "Milw0rm" reportedly hacked into the Bhaba Atomic Research Center (BARC) network to protest India's nuclear tests. In the same time period, Pakistani hacker groups, such as Death to India, Kill India, Dr. Nuker, and G-force Pakistan, openly circulated instructions for attacking Indian computers. According to a 2003 account in *The Hindu*, for more than two years the hacker war between India and Pakistan has been intensifying, leading to the defacement of hundreds of websites on either side.

"Earlier this year, newspaper reports had indicated that an unnamed virus launched by a secretive Indian hacker group had rendered 200 Pakistani websites inaccessible for several days and erased the hard disks of scores of computer [sic] in the Pakistani Government as well as the private sector in that country."

Cyber attacks consequently pose more than a theoretical challenge to the Indian government's day-to-day national security agenda. In response to these attacks, the leaders of India's armed forces have embraced the need for change and have begun to build partnerships with industry intended to transform the military into a technology-focused force. In the late 1990's, New Delhi undertook a review of defense posture in the framework of what strategists call the "Revolution in Military Affairs" (RMA) posed by the application of digital technologies to precision guided weapons, battlefield awareness, and instantaneous communications. In a 2001 report, *Challenges to the Management of National Security*, political leaders focused on addressing military and related threats below the nuclear threshold and highlighted cyber offense and defense:

The emergence of non-state terrorist actors and the rise of their international influence is accelerating. Much of their activity is clandestine and outside the accepted international norms... India is at the receiving end of these violent elements and is likely to remain a target of international terrorism in the future.

Strategies need to be evolved to counter the threat of Weapons of Mass Destruction Terrorism (WMD) as well as cyber terrorism; the latter especially against infrastructural and economic assets such as banking, power, water, and transportation sectors.

> Due to its history, geographic location, and heterogeneous population, India faces a broad and complex range of security threats. On the one hand, there is the *domestic* threat to national unity. The insurgency in Kashmir, actively assisted by Pakistan, is a notable example. Less publicized internal challenges include left wing extremist (e.g., Maoist) violence, illegal migration (from Bangladesh), and "caste, communal and sectarian" unrest often deriving from fundamentalist rivalries and the constraints of traditional religious obligations. As a recent official study puts it: "There is no Indian community which is not a minority in some other parts of the country."
>
> On the other hand, *external* pressures from China, Bangladesh, and particularly Pakistan pose persistent challenges. A few years ago, tensions between India and Pakistan, each armed with nuclear missiles, were higher than at any time in the past decade. India holds enormous conventional military superiority over Pakistan and its defensive posture "is heavily tailored to the problem of potential conflict" with Islamabad. Intended transformation in India's strategic doctrine and military operational art complemented the sweeping changes in

the information technology economy that began in the early 1990's.

Toward the end of that decade, India's IT sector internationalized for example through the U.S. IT industry's joint investment ventures with offshore companies to develop software. Manufacturers in India were logical partners for U.S. companies because the subcontinent offered a supply of well-trained, low-cost labor.

U.S. GOVERNMENT REPORTS AND FOREIGN OFFICIAL STATEMENTS

Military analysts in the U.S. and elsewhere today emphasize a generalized shift in doctrine away from traditional methods of combat toward tactics and weapons designed to produce dominance in the information "battle space." Such dominance could embrace either offensive information operations or steps to protect domestic assets and critical infrastructures against "cyber threats— or both." India represents a relevant case study. India's defense establishment in the late 1990s grasped the importance of the digital revolution and its relevance to the military operational art. The Report of the Group of Ministers on National Security noted in early 2001:

The future battlefield in [the Indian] context is likely to be more digitized and transparent and would experience an exponential increase in the deployment of electronic devices, signaling the growing primacy of the electromagnetic spectrum...Thus while India needs to ensure credible nuclear deterrence...it has to simultaneously maintain adequate and duly modernized conventional forces which are properly managed, led and equipped to take advantage of the RMA and which can take care of any possible conventional conflicts."

The Indian Army formally announced a shift in doctrine in 1998 to embrace electronic warfare and information operations capabilities. This new doctrine, or IT-Roadmap, enumerates ambitious plans up to 2008. These plans encompass hardware, software, and human resource development, with a goal of "enhancing the IT quotient" per soldier. According to one of the architects of the new doctrine, Army Chief of Staff General V.P. Malik, the Roadmap is intended "To establish a strong information technology infrastructure to act as a force multiplier by incorporating fully automated and networked operational and management information system [sic], complemented by fully information technology literate manpower." Assumptions behind this initiative are:

- Software rather than hardware is increasingly critical to adding value in related Industries
- Industry standards are becoming more open and uniform worldwide, allowing easier market entry and innovation
- Global competitiveness and ease of transnational communications translates into faster improvements in products, architecture, and infrastructure.

General Malik has remarked that "computing is about openness, so why build and write code that can be bought off the shelf?" In addition, partnership and networking with industry can produce synergies. "The Army would prefer to enter into a long-term understanding with the information technology industry so that we can work in tandem towards a common goal."

FOREIGN MILITARY AND INTELLIGENCE AGENCY RESEARCH

Contemporaneous with the military's plan to adopt an IT-roadmap, the defense industries production sector in India has instituted parallel reforms. Prior to 2000, military production and procurement were confined to government-owned companies for ideological and security reasons. In recent years, however, the armed forces have become more open to public/private sector collaboration in the defense sector.

The military has learned that technologies developed by private industry (such as encryption) may strengthen security. As an Indian military officer recently commented, "We are heavily into cyber security now and are in the process of creating a security envelope since the most advanced armies in the world face 3,000 to 4,000 attempts to hack their networks." In response to a multi-year campaign waged by the Confederation of Indian Industry

(CII) requesting a share of the contracts previously reserved for public sector firms, the Minister of Defense and the CII's National Committee on Defense decided in 2000 to "establish a strong partnership between defense and industry to enlarge the role and scope of Indian industry in defense."

Accordingly, the Ministry of Defense and the CII formed six Task Forces: Longterm partnership; commercial process; Defense Research and Development Organization (DRDO)-Industry partnership; Defense Public Sector Undertakings-Private Sector complementary; IT for Defense; and Strategy for Defense Exports. In a May 2002 briefing titled "Indian Defense Market: Opportunities for Private Investment", the CII Chairman listed three "modernization thrusts: Information technology and information warfare; electronic warfare and C4I2 [command, control, communications, computer, information, and interoperability] infrastructure; and mobility."

The briefing explains that the government has invited private sector participation because private producers offer modern technologies, efficiency and aftersales service, and lower costs through market competition. In a related statement, the CII Chairman said he expects "a large number of reputed companies to look towards defense not just as a supplier of defense products but as a partner in building a stronger and self-reliant armed force." Reportedly, he went on to suggest that the government, jointly with the industry, should formulate product and supplier development strategies.

TRAINING

The Army's IT roadmap, promulgated in 1998, asserts that all its officers and junior leaders will become computer literate by 2002. In 1999, the Army Institute of Information Technology introduced its first course at its temporary campus in Hyderabad to teach war fighters the rudiments of IT warfare. Simultaneously, three army technology institutes, two in Secunderabad (in Andhra Pradesh) and one in Pune (in Maharashtra state) began to introduce IT as part of their syllabus. The Ministry of Defense in New Delhi is now considering a report, submitted in early 2002, calling for a thorough overhaul of defense management and research, education, and training in India's military services. Reportedly, the linchpin of the recommendations under consideration is the creation of a National Defense University (NDU) in New Delhi.

One of the focal points of the NDU will be information warfare and the digital revolution. According to a journalistic account, "The University will try to change the way our soldiers think and learn. All joint service organizations like the National Defense Academy...the Defense Services Staff College...and the Center for Defense Management...and the National Defense College...will be brought under its purview."

Media reports regarding the recommendations indicate the NDU will house a National Institute of Strategic Studies. Reportedly, the latter Institute will be a "research organization with a futuristic view." It will host a war gaming and simulation department. In addition to the armed services, civilian organizations, including the intelligence services, will be allowed to join the Institute.

According to media reports, the National Defense Academy (NDA) in Pune in June 2002 graduated its first group of students earning the degree of Bachelor of Science in computer science. Media sources say the three-year course is consistent with the latest trends in electronic warfare and growing computerization in the armed forces. A top graduate, Cadet Vishal Jain, told a reporter, "From decoding intercept signals of the enemy to the use of sonars/radars, IT has an important role to play in modern-day warfare."

Jain explained that the "three year course included training in computer architecture, language principles of programming, network, system analysis and database management system. Other NDA cadets, who opt for the regular B.A. degree, reportedly are required to enroll in a three-semester computer course conducted at the Center for Development of Advanced Computing (C-DAC) in Pune. C-DAC's mission, as described on its Website, is to emerge as the premier R&D institution for the "design, development, and deployment of world class IT solutions..." In addition to high performance computing and communications, the Center's areas of interest embrace multilingual technologies, multimedia, education and training, and eGovernance. The Indian military is investing significant resources to develop information technologies and to train technologically capable forces. Private companies have developed programs to integrate their technologies more directly into the defense sector's needs. Further, the Defense Research and Development Organization has initiated several programs for the development of critical technologies and systems under government auspices, including chip development. The National Defense University will centralize information warfare training and simulations for the Armed Forces and the intelligence services.

The Central Bureau of Investigation (CBI) is responsible for criminal and counter intelligence matters. The National Cyber Cop Committee, established by the software industry association in early 2001, includes representative police officials from all states in India, the CBI, and the Ministry of Home Affairs. It conducts workshops for judicial and police officers to explain various Internet-related crimes.

The committee also researches methods and solutions to prevent intrusions into government websites. According to a 2002 report, the Ministry of Technology and the Central Bureau for Investigation have developed a diverse national strategy to protect India's infrastructures. This strategy recommends "involving assistance from software industries" where necessary. In addition, the U.S. and India have set up a Cyber Security Forum to provide a conduit for an exchange of information on cyber threats. The forum fosters bilateral discussions on civilian and military infrastructure protection, legal cooperation and law enforcement, security standards, and research and development. According to a September 2003 report, the CBI and the U.S. Federal Bureau of Investigation completed a joint training course in New Delhi embracing "instruction on advanced cyber techniques used by some terrorist groups..."

OPERATIONS

Pakistani intelligence services are paying Western hackers \$500-\$10,000 to deface Indian websites, according to Ankit Fadia, an Indian computer security consultant. Pakistani hacktivist groups, he says, are defacing at least 60 Indian sites monthly. "Targets include government and business sites, including VSNL, India's oldest and largest Internet Service Provider, and even those of non-government organizations. Those that have been attacked include Infosys and Satyam, Indian headquartered IT companies, an Indian oil company, and the Ministry of Information Technology."

Although computer hacking is considered illegal under Indian jurisprudence, India's computer professionals have nonetheless established hacker groups to defend and retaliate by attacking Pakistani websites. According to a report in the Indian press, Indianspy, a hacker claiming to represent the Indian Hackers Club, defaced 8 Pakistani websites in mid-2003 and posted messages ridiculing pro-Pakistani hackers who have been targeting Indian websites.

Indianspy targeted the website of Comsats, an ISP provider in Pakistan. The National Cyber Cop Committee reportedly receives advice from a group of teen hackers. According to the president of the association, the teens will "tell us where our soft spots are— where government and industry websites are most vulnerable, thus helping strengthen our esecurity."

Recently, India's military intelligence gathering institutions underwent a significant restructuring in response to perceived intelligence failures in connection with the 1999 Kargil intrusions by Pakistan. In early 2002, on the recommendation of a Ministerial-level group under Home Minister Advani, a Defense Intelligence Agency (DIA) was established to coordinate the directorates of Army, Naval, and Air Force intelligence. According to a journalistic account, the DIA will be responsible for executing cross-border operations and collecting tactical intelligence in neighboring states through human sources.

DIA is also being given responsibility for the Signals Intelligence Directorate and the Defense Image Processing and Analysis Center (reconnaissance through satellite imaging). Unconfirmed reports indicate that the armed forces plan to establish an information warfare agency under the tri-service integrated defense staff within the DIA. The new agency, called the Defense

Information Warfare Agency (DIWA), will manage all aspects of IW, such as psychological operations, cyber war, and electromagnetic and sound waves. According to a February 2003 account, "DIWA will be the nodal agency that will make policies for all the three services as well as formulate countermeasures to enemy propaganda."

The Research and Analysis Wing (RAW) is India's civilian foreign intelligence gathering agency. RAW, whose structure and operations are not disclosed to parliament, reportedly reports to the Prime Minister's office and has played a key role in espionage and disinformation campaigns against Pakistan and other neighboring countries.

In early 2003, India's intelligence agencies announced the establishment of a National Technical Intelligence Communications Center (NTICC). The purpose of this body, which is a sub-unit of India's intelligence Research and Analysis Wing, is to provide technical and electronic intelligence to the Intelligence Bureau and the Defense Intelligence Agency. According to Jane's Intelligence Review, the NTICC will focus on intercepting communications among Kashmiri terrorists now employing mobile Thurya handsets. In the future, the communications center plans to develop an interception capability modeled on the Echelon system attributed to the U.S. Department of Defense.

A separate report states that this specialized intelligence gathering agency will act as a "super feeder agency for providing technical intelligence to other agencies on internal and external security...The organization will do hi-tech surveillance jobs, including satellite monitoring, terrestrial monitoring, Internet monitoring, considered vital for the national security apparatus."

INFORMATION TECHNOLOGY INVESTMENT

Overall, as described above, the Indian government has elaborated a comprehensive strategy that integrates information technologies into its military. The armed services have developed IT roadmaps that lay out long-term requirements for new technologies as well as the human resources necessary to employ them. The government has forged new models for public / private sector collaboration. Changes in military thinking and loosening of formal and informal restrictions on joint manufacturing ventures will probably pay off in technological advances in the coming years.

Until recently, India's political establishment appeared mired in a sclerotic business culture resting on government guidance and inefficient defense/public sector undertakings. According to reliable reports, significant change is under way in this sector. Several reports comment on the defense sector's potential to leverage the IT software industry in India. For example, Bharat Electronics Ltd. (BEL), reportedly India's "premier" electronics organization dedicated to the development and manufacture of state-of-the-art electronic equipment for use by the armed forces and paramilitary organizations, inaugurated a military software development center in 2002, initially employing 60 professionals.

By 2003, the number of employees making "embedded software" rose to 100. BEL's website indicates that the firm strives to retain technological leadership through in-house research as well as through collaboration with Defense Labs, foreign companies, universities and research institutes. BEL also plans to increase overseas sales of its products. With respect to private enterprise and India's domestic IT infrastructure, the sub-continent is emerging as one of the principal global players in the Info-Tech sector. Software development is India's fastest-growing foreign exchange earner.

Technical research and education institutions such as Indian Institutes of Technology and the Tata Institute of Fundamental Research are second to none. Leading institutes linked to defense, space, financial, and development projects continue to provide exemplary research.

Historically, India was slower than many countries to embrace the digital era. In 1984, the central government in New Delhi initiated measures to loosen bureaucratic controls and promote private initiative, especially in selected "target" industries such as telecommunications and computers. These actions were taken because official government licensing requirements deterred start-up enterprises. In the early 1990's, regional policy makers at the state level, such as in Andhra Pradesh, boldly embraced the software development sector, yet the central government continued to vacillate. Internet access was extended outside academia through the central government's official telephone monopoly VSNL project and a few public-sector industries adopted information technologies.

However, the central authorities resisted the global trend toward privatizing the telecommunications backbone. While expansion of the IT sector is hampered by such legacies as limited bandwidth, low PC penetration, and relatively low telephone density, considerable improvements have been made recently.

INDIA'S IT INFRASTRUCTURE

India's overall performance in the IT sector is mixed, despite success in software development. This stems primarily from obsolete technical infrastructure and inadequate investment in the communications sector. According to a recent academic analysis, Internet expansion depends upon availability of several factors including the telecommunications infrastructure, networking engineers and end users, networking and end user hardware, and government leadership. The following paragraphs characterize India's IT infrastructure along these four dimensions. Infrastructure: India's telephone network backbone historically has been limited in size and reliability. Although changes are ongoing, the sub-continent continues to lack a fiber optic backbone for high-speed data communications. Moreover, VSNL, the state monopoly in international telephony and domestic Internet service, has inflated the cost of IT services. A report released in 2001 indicates that 500 hours annually of dial-up service can cost $200 for a slow speed connection.

Engineers: The Indian government has a long tradition of support for technical education. The sub-continent is a significant exporter of engineers and scientists. According to one source, Silicon Valley boasts numerous Indian millionaires and American immigration rules have helped Indians disproportionately. Small groups of skilled engineers, working indigenously, are reportedly largely responsible for India's internationally competitive computer software industry.

Networking and end user hardware: Traditionally, IT manufacturing has been a protected industry in India. With respect to computer hardware and peripherals, manufacturing growth in the 1990's was reported to have been limited due partly to minimal growth in the domestic market and partly to the inability of the volume-limited manufacturers to be competitive. When foreign investors attempted to enter the Indian market, New Delhi's lack of intellectual property protection posed problems.

Government leadership: Until the early 1990s, New Delhi's slow moving government bureaucracy and other factors impeded progress in the IT field compared to neighboring countries such as China. Building on India's formidable human resources in the computer and engineering fields, the government in the early 1990s invested in Software Technology Parks and other programs to spur development of the intellectual property. These efforts, supported by reform-minded state governments, introduced a policy environment conducive to growth.

INFORMATION TECHNOLOGY ACTION PLAN...

Recognizing that the country risked falling behind in the global IT race, the Indian Prime Minister convened a National Task Force on Information Technology and Software Development. The Task Force report published in 1999 proposed a three-part program to liberalize the telecommunications industry and transform India into a "global IT superpower."

The three categories for transformation were:

1. Accelerating the creation of an IT infrastructure
2. Establishing policy and regulatory environment to boost software exports to $50 billion by 2008
3. Extending the use of IT to all segments of society.

PROMISES INFRASTRUCTURE IMPROVEMENTS

The Common Action Plan to Promote IT in India, adopted in mid-2000, calls for a national highspeed network backbone, expansion of the Internet, rise in PC-penetration, and "localization" of Indian languages. The government reportedly will allow entry of foreign investors interested in expanding available bandwidth, permit private companies to lay underwater cables for the Internet, and permit ISPs to establish international gateways and lease bandwidth on foreign satellites.

Private industry is also engaged in expanding terrestrial Internet infrastructure. According to a recent study, Reliance Group is laying optical fiber cable in 16 Indian states, linking 115 cities over a length of 60,000 kilometers. BSNL, the large public sector telephone service provider, reportedly has awarded licenses to 14 entities allowing them to provide optical fiber cables, right-of-way towers and infrastructure for end-to-end connectivity throughout the sub-continent.

This embraces public sector companies, such as railways and utilities, enjoying right-of-way for existing infrastructure.

1. *Internet*

Due to low per-capita income, weak telecoms infrastructure, lack of a high-speed backbone, noncompetitive telephone tariff charges and other factors, Internet development is at an early stage in terms of the number of connections and overall use. Nevertheless, in the interval 1999- 2000, the number of ISPs reportedly rose from 15 to 90 (a six-fold increase). Experts predict that most practical communications benefits for the foreseeable future are likely to derive from business—not consumer—use.

In particular:

> "Global connections will be much enhanced by India's liberalized access to international Internet gateways and to privately-provided undersea cable access. This access alone could offer India's companies opportunities that otherwise would flow to other better connected Asian competitors."

2. *Software Development Industry*

India's annual software sales revenues rose dramatically from approximately $1.7 billion in 1996-97 to an estimated $5.7 billion in 1999-2000. The latter figure constitutes about 65 percent of total IT revenues. By contrast, hardware and peripherals account only for about 23 percent.

The share of the total attributable to international sales has risen commensurately. According to the software industry association, in 1999-2000 nearly 70 percent of India's software revenues derived from exports. The U.S. accounts for approximately 60 percent of the software export market.

The spectacular growth of India's software industry stems from a variety of sources, such as IThubs, qualified leadership, and the availability of well-educated labor willing to work for a fraction of the cost similar workers earn in the client's home country.

A study published in the monthly journal of the Institute for Defense Studies and Analyses (IDSA) states that India's software industry has been growing from "strength to strength." Y2K reportedly was a turning point. The run-up to 2000 saw Western nations seeking Indian software professionals to solve anticipated problems. The Indian software industry earned an estimated $2.5 billion from Y2K business (between 1996 and 1999). Key economic indicators are as follows:

- Over the five year period 1996-2000, India's IT industry had a compound annual growth rate averaging 40.5 percent, almost double the growth rate of the industry in many developing countries;
- Software exports in 1999-2000 amounted to $4 billion, accounting for over 10 percent of India's total exports;
- Sales of PC desktop units attained 1 million units in 1999-2000, and the domestic hardware share grew by 58 percent;
- Among the Fortune 500 companies, 185 outsourced their software requirements to India in 1999-2000;
- Among the 23 software companies in the world with Carnegie Mellon Software Engineering Institute certification, 16 are based in India;
- Key software firms, such as Infosys, Wipro, and Satyam Computers, are listed on the NASDAQ.

The southern software centers, Bangalore in Karnataka state, Chennai (formerly Madras) in Tamil Nadu, and Hyderabad in Andhra Pradesh, constitute the so-called "Silicon Triangle of India." Other important hubs include

Mumbai (formerly Bombay) and New Delhi. In the 1990's, the central government established the Software Technology Parks of India, a visionary project to provide infrastructure and administrative support, including reliable high speed access, for software development companies.

Hyderabad Software Industry

Software Technology Parks of India, Hyderabad was established in 1991-1992. Registration of firms in the Park rose from "a handful" in 1991 to over 1000 in 2000, and to approximately 1400 in 2002. In the early 1990's the Park's business grew at an annual rate of 100 percent. In 2000- 2001 and 2001-2002, the annual growth rate tapered off to 81 percent and 42 percent, respectively. 170 *Exports:* Export revenues grew from less than $1 million in 1992 to nearly $250 million in 1999- 2000.

In 2002-2003, export revenues attained 3,668 crores (equivalent to approximately $700 million), an increase of 26 percent over the previous year. A recent press note indicates that 820 out of more than 1,400 entities in the Park are contributing to exports. Info-Tech Enabled Services (ITES) exports, such as business process outsourcing and call centers, are increasing and now account for about 40 percent of total revenues. The number of professionals engaged in export firms in the Park rose to about 64,300 in early 2003.

The distribution among types of exports in 2003 is as follows: Approximately 79 percent through datacom facilities, 20 percent through consultancy projects, and the remainder through physical media. According to STPI, the value of software exports through datacom facilities is expected to rise in response to increased bandwidth, access to new markets, and increased outsourcing to India. Although most of the exports in 2002 were directed to the U.S. and Canada, Europe, Japan, Australia, Asia, and the Middle East also are destinations. *Outsourcing:* Hyderabad is emerging as a fast growing hub for outsourcing. In 2002-2003, companies such as Nipuna, Dell, 24/7, Cognizant, Activecard, Click2learn, Swift Reponse, and Redpine Signals, Inc., established a presence in the Technology Park.

3. Outsourcing and IT enabled services

Outsourcing, according to a 2003 article in CIO Magazine, is "one of the best ways for CIOs to cut application development and maintenance costs..." Reportedly, between 50 and 67 percent of all Fortune 500 companies currently outsource to the Indian sub-continent, although many at this stage are only undertaking pilot projects. IT-enabled services (ITES) embrace call centers, medical transcription, data digitization, and web content development and animation, and are expected to grow substantially.

According to a World Bank study, in 2000 India employed between 50,000 and 100,000 workers in IT-enabled services, producing about $500 million in export earnings. The amount of software services work performed in India for U.S. companies was expected to double in 2003.

Summarizing, one study notes that "The Indian IT industry is largely software service and export oriented, and often, the term "Indian IT industry" is used synonymously with the Indian software industry." According to a study by the Stanford Computer Industry Project, India's formidable human resource base historically drives national software strategy. Its world class technical training bodies, such as the Indian Institutes of Technology and the Tata Institute of Fundamental Research, also played a pivotal role.

> The Ministry of Information Technology decided in 2003 to establish a $20 million Internet security center in New Delhi. The center—supported by CERT at CMU—addresses computer security incidents, publishes alerts, and promotes information and training. Software Technology Parks India (STPI)—an autonomous body of the government—has a stake in the proposed center. The Center for Development of Advanced Computing (C-DAC) and the DRDO have been at the forefront of information security technologies. The Networking and Internet Software Group of the C-DAC, for example, is working on the development of "core network security technologies," which include C-DAC's Virtual Private

network, crypto package, and prototype of e-commerce applications. FIRST-India (Forum for Incident Response and Security Teams) is a non-profit organization for facilitating "trusted interaction amongst teams from India conducting incident response and cyber security tasks. Membership is open to private and public sector organizations in India, including the Defense Public Sector Undertakings.

India's efforts to enhance and restructure technical intelligence collection, give greater prominence to information warfare operations, and permit private sector participation in defense and military contracts constitute an expanding web of connections in the evolving national security picture. However, leadership and expanding market share in the global software industry represents a double-edged sword with respect to India's national security. On the one hand, an emerging national software export strategy centered on military hi-tech spin-offs (i.e., patterned after current practice in Israel) promises to extend the benefits of state-of-the art technology while creating economic growth. On the other hand, the more ubiquitous indigenous computer software becomes and the more India's national security depends on it, the greater is the potential vulnerability to malicious intrusion or tampering. India's prominence in the IT field (as both software developer and exporter) together with the government's announced plans to modernize the Indian armed forces have spawned significant military, business, and academic ties with entities in a host of countries, including the United States. India's Prime Minister, in a June 2003 visit to Shanghai, proposed that "Indian and Chinese firms work together" in the IT software sector.

Scientific and technical trade and cooperation links with Russia and Israel are of particular interest with respect to developing or enhancing New Delhi's electronic warfare and information operations. Russia, an acknowledged leader in cyber warfare matters, has enjoyed close cooperation with India in computer research going back to the Soviet era. New Delhi's Department of Science and Technology and Russia's Academy of Sciences have sponsored and facilitated several bilateral research efforts for more than a decade. India's Center for Development of Advanced Computing (C-DAC) and Russia's Institute for Computer Aided Design formed the RICCR (Russia-India Center for Advanced Computing Research) in late 2000. According to information posted on the RICCR website, the Center promotes and facilitates collaborative research in the following areas: software development for high-speed computers with parallel architecture; program codes; ecology, geology, and seismic data processing; weather forecasting and climate modeling; economics; and computer satellite systems, among others. India C-DAC has committed its PARAM super computer to this cooperative research.

More recently, Moscow and New Delhi have taken active measures to strengthen traditional ties in the military defense and armaments field. In approving opportunities for cooperation in information and communications technologies, biotechnology, electronics, banking and financial services, the two sides have decided to address potential complementarities in the emerging global economic system.

CONCLUSION

The main thrust of the data presented is that India's armed forces have initiated a shift in military doctrine to embrace more directly offensive and defensive cyber warfare, leveraging India's strengths in IT research and software development.

India has a robust hacking network. In addition, the government has announced several operational steps, such as founding a National Defense University with a key focus on computer software, and establishing a new intelligence communication and electronic surveillance agency. In parallel with these steps, India's traditional pre-occupation with protecting military secrets has given way to closer government/industry collaboration to keep pace with competitive challenges within the region and at the global level. New Delhi actively seeks military-technical and scientific cooperation and exchange with strategic partners such as Israel and Russia that reputedly possess exceptional cyber capabilities. In addition, there is significant open discussion relating to adoption of the Israeli model of military/industry strategic cooperation, i.e., a national software export strategy centered on product-supplier relationships and military hi-tech spin-offs. As noted earlier in this chapter, much of the computer software industry in India is clustered in "Technology Parks" in a few of the principal cities, such as Bangalore, Chennai, and Hyderabad. Security protection is relatively robust because of the importance of the industry to the overall Indian economy.

Public and private sector interests in India accord priority to cyber security issues and concerns and during the last several years have implemented significant policy measures to address them. With more software used to run infrastructure and commerce in the advanced economies being "outsourced" to India and other developing countries, the risk of unauthorized intrusions or programming compromises rises. A malicious intrusion scenario, for example, might entail rogue employees in India's software development industry tampering with code to insert a back-door or "time bomb."

10

Scenario in Iran

The United States jams our radar systems; this is part of their Satanic behavior with their huge array of technological capabilities. We would not be surprised if they do it again. We have to find ways to get electronic counter-countermeasures (ECCM). We have taken certain measures to produce ECCM equipment.

1989 Interview with "Head of the Electronics Industry" in Iran in Military Industries in the Islamic Republic of Iran: Assessment of the Defense Industries Organization John M. Shields May 1996

Taking into consideration that the government...has been planning for development of information technology and communications in Iran, this issue has attracted the attention of the defense sector in the past and at the moment...Due to the interest of the defense sector in these fields, a university complex will be established to gather the necessary manpower. Along with that, all capabilities in information technology and communications manufacturing in software education and infrastructure and research are concentrated in the defense sector... – Iranian Defense Minister Ali Shamkhani

Malek Ashtar University of Technology Speech February 2003

The Farsi language broadcasts by the VOA as well as Los Angeles-based ParsTV and Appadana TV are uplinked in the United States via Telstar-5...It is then turned around at Washington International Telport in Alexandria, Va., and uplinked again to Telstar12 over the eastern Atlantic Ocean...It is Telstar-12 that is being jammed, say investigators for companies working with the broadcasters, cutting off broadcasts not only in Iran but in Europe and the rest of the Middle East as well...A representative of one of the Iranian-American broadcasters said he suspected the jamming came from Cuba, which has excellent relations with Iran, but offered no proof. — Robert Windrem, NBC News, July 2003

Iran's civilian Information and Communications Technology (ICT) culture is highly complex. The government, cognizant of the importance of the knowledge sector and the efficiencies associated with the Internet, is determined that Iran will not be excluded from the global Information Technology economy. The educated and generally literate populace, aware of external cultural developments and trends through contacts with the Iranian diaspora and through foreign travel, clamors for access to information and entertainment. Internet service entrepreneurs chafe at the antiquated and obsolescent telephone infrastructure. Conservative elements of the clerical regime nevertheless fear that unfettered access to information will lead to unrest and potential resistance.

Telecommunications and Internet services in Iran generally are considered rudimentary compared to leading countries in the Persian Gulf region. One expert attributes Tehran's failure to realize its full potential to "internal religious and political contradictions."

According to the CIA, Iran has over 5,000 Internet hosts in 2004, compared to 15,931 in Saudi Arabia and 56,283 in the United Arab Emirates. As regards personal computers, the International Telecommunications Union (ITU) states that Iran's penetration rate was 7.50 per 100 persons in 2003, compared to 13.67 in Saudi Arabia and 11.99 in U.A.E.183 Despite Iran's mediocre standings in Internet and PC penetration, in recent years, the government has allocated significant resources to "catching-up" in the Information and Communications Technology (ICT) sector. The defense sector, in particular, enjoys priority access to financial and human resources dedicated to research and development in electronic warfare and related fields.

BACKGROUND

An oil-rich, semi-authoritarian, Islamist power, Iran is determined to overcome a long-standing self-perception of military and technological inferiority. To achieve this, the government in recent years has taken steps to both transform its foreign policy and security doctrine and acquire sophisticated weaponry. In addition to reported investment in WMD (weapons of mass destruction) precursors, Tehran is purchasing state-of-the-art advanced conventional systems while actively pursuing digital technologies and military-related information technology (IT) research and development.

Estrangement from Washington traditionally gave the leadership a useful pivot with which to garner popular support for its regional policies and ambitions. It also provided a justification, or excuse, for developing asymmetric warfare capabilities of all types. More recently, the collapse of Saddam Hussein's army has reinforced Tehran's ambition to become a key political player in Central Asia. Rising U.S. presence in the region is a thorn in the regime's side, perhaps strengthening the leadership's ambitions to play a credible "denial role" in the area.

While the Iranian leadership's primary goal is to continue to preserve and protect the Shi'a revolution, strategic and geopolitical considerations, rather than ideology, have in recent years assumed greater prominence in Tehran's formulation of its national security policies. In addition to strategic military investments, economic growth and job creation have become leading concerns. Islamic and nationalist objectives have receded in importance in determining the goals of internal development. In describing this shift, experts note the government's more pragmatic approach: "Iran's policies...are increasingly prudent, with the Islamic Republic trying to calm regional tension and end its isolation...The Islamic regime has supported the status quo with regard to territorial integrity, has avoided major military provocations..."

Moreover, according to analyst John Battilega, Iran's primary national security concerns are "local," relating to maintaining the internal security and territorial integrity in an unstable, threatening region. Battilega says Tehran seeks to avoid technological and economic isolation, which could doom any prospect of achieving the power base necessary to become a major political "player" in Central Asia.

In this framework, the government has sought pragmatic ties with neighbors in Central Asia, such as Russia and India, to protect its economic interests and raise its political profile in the region. The regime, through its intelligence services, continues to provide covert support to anti- Israeli terrorist groups. Available open source evidence suggests that Tehran will continue to play an opportunistic role, particularly as regards the significant covert activities of its intelligence services supporting international terrorism.

U.S. GOVERNMENT REPORTS AND FOREIGN OFFICIAL STATEMENTS

U.S. officials have consistently included Iran on a list of "rogue" states with the capacity and motive to launch a cyber attack against U.S. interests. In public testimony, former CIA Director George Tenet, for example, has pointed to the efforts of potential foes of the U.S. to interfere with U.S. computer networks. Richard Clarke, former chairman of the President's Critical Infrastructure Protection Board, has noted that Iraq, Iran, North Korea, China, and Russia are already training people in cyber warfare.

According to a declassified threat assessment in the U.S. Navy's Strategic Planning Guidance published in 2000, "Russia, China, India, and Cuba have acknowledged policies of preparing for information warfare," while "North Korea, Libya, Iran, Iraq, and Syria have some capability." Persian Gulf military expert Anthony H. Cordesman writes that Iran is improving its capabilities in information warfare, "although it seems unlikely that it is capable of advanced attacks on protected US military and government computer, information, and battle management systems." However, with regard to generalized cyber attacks, "Iran probably has more capability to attack the US private sector and the systems of the Gulf States."

Jay Valentine, former head of Infoglide, a database analysis company and contractor to the U.S. government, noted in 1999 that "There are at least six nations right now who have active groups, paid by their governments, trying to formulate tools and procedures to cause computer terrorism in U.S. corporations...Those countries are Syria, Iran, China, India, Pakistan, and Israel." More recently, the July 2002 Riptech Internet Security Threat Report indicated that, among seven countries designated as "state sponsors of terrorism," Iran was the source of 90 percent of attacks against Riptech clients in the first half of 2002.

In terms of countries with fewer than one million Internet users, Iran and Kuwait were "by far the most prolific" in terms of originating attacks, according to an early 2003 study released by Symantec. For more than a decade, Iran's military leaders have expressed inadequacy in the face of modern "information warfare" (as practiced by the U.S. and other powers). This, and other factors, induced the leadership to restructure defense priorities and domestic R & D efforts in the 1990's.

According to a study sponsored by the National Intelligence Council in 1999, Iraq and Iran are examples of states that "will likely explore the usefulness of information technology in pursuit of asymmetric conflict...To counter U.S. military capabilities—current or those that emerge from the RMA [Revolution in Military Affairs]—these states will explore ways to exploit U.S. vulnerabilities, including through the employment of information warfare and cyberterrorism."

In 2002, Iran had approximately 250 Internet Service Providers. Most of these are government owned or belong to state agencies, such as Universities and think tanks. The few ISPs that operate independently from the government reportedly provide access only cautiously to individuals and charge prices that essentially limit the use of the Internet to users in upper economic brackets. Publicly available computer terminals are said to have spawned a new "sub-culture" in the principal cities, such as Tehran.

One media report indicates that the proliferation of cyber cafés, coupled with rudimentary attempts by the government to filter content and control public access, has spawned a hacker mentality. Disgruntled or bored youth, according to this source, take out their frustrations through clandestine computer hacking. The Iranian government in 2001 reportedly was drafting rules and preparing software-filtering equipment to control Internet service and content. The leadership deems Internet use by researchers and University students a positive and necessary step. The ISPs associated with these state entities use leased lines under government control. On the other hand, some cyber cafés, using ISPs linked to satellites, remain out of the government's reach.

FOREIGN MILITARY RESEARCH

As stated above, Tehran accords high priority to military modernization to shore-up perceived security vulnerabilities. As one analyst put it in 1996 with respect to the defense sector: Tehran is "widening the technological threshold of its industrial complex." In recent years, the government has allocated a significant share of its oil revenues to military R&D required to manufacture or exploit weapons of mass destruction, advanced conventional weapons, and diverse electronic warfare technologies.

In the aftermath of the 1991 Gulf War, Iran grasped the value of information technologies for military ends. Tehran moved to ensure its armed forces are "digitized." With respect to militarytechnical training, for example, a July 1997 report from Tehran stated that 15,000 new recruits were being tested for admission to the regular Army's officer training college; those who pass the entrance exams will be eligible to pursue a broad range of academic subjects, including computer software.

Defense Minister Ali Shamkhani stated in December 2000 that "Iran relies on its indigenous strength and domestic hardware and software potentials for national security." More recently, Defense Minister Shamkhani signaled the importance of IT investments in boosting military defense capabilities. The Ministry of Defense seeks to strengthen the link between Information Warfare infrastructure requirements and academic research in the IT sphere.

In February 2003, Shamkhani visited Malek Ashtar University of Technology in Isfahan province to discuss information technology. According to reliable sources, Shamkhani participated in the first Iranian state conference on "the development of technology in defense." He announced that a "University complex" in these fields will be established to attract the necessary manpower in keeping with defense sector improvement and modernization. "All capabilities in information technology and communications manufacturing in software education and infrastructure and research are concentrated in the defense sector, and this capability cannot be seen in any other sector," the Defense Minister noted.

Malek Ashtar University, in Shahinshahr, Isfahan Province, is also known as the University of Sciences and Technology. Cursory examination of open source documents reveals that the University is engaged in a range of R&D activities, including aerospace, information and communication technology, and genetic biotechnology. Anecdotal evidence indicates links between institutes such as the Advanced Information Communication Technology Center (Sharif University of Technology) and the ICT Department at Malek Ashtar University with respect to teaching in the field of "advanced computer networks... filtering and firewalling..."

INFORMATION TECHNOLOGY INVESTMENT

Despite U.S. export sanctions, Iran has access to computer hardware and software of various types and sophistication. For example, although exports of Silicon Graphics work stations to Iran are banned, a Tehran-based company in 1993 nevertheless imported such a work station which ran SoftImage graphics software developed by a Canadian company. According to an ITU statistical series on computer penetration in individual member countries, Iran had 56 PC's per 1000 people in 1999. This number rose to 63 per 1000 or 4 million computers overall in 2000, and to 75 per 1000 or 4.9 million PC's in 2003. Iran reportedly imports large amounts of computer software. Indigenous firms, such as SENA Soft, are involved in "updating" this software. The Iranian Software Producers Association signed an agreement in 2003 with Dubai Electronic City to permit Iranian software firms to cooperate with foreign companies in Dubai.

Beginning in the 1990s, several U.S. software producers, such as Microsoft and IBM, explored the market in Iran. According to several sources, Iran Electronic Industries (aka SA Iran) is the major producer of electronic systems and products in Iran. In the military field, IEI's activities embrace a wide range, such as optics, electro-optics and laser communications, telecommunications security, electronic warfare, radar tube manufacturing, and missile launchers. IEI's website asserts that the Corporation has "six subsidiaries and 5,000 experienced personnel including 700 qualified and highly trained engineers in different disciplines. IEI has developed a high capability in research and development (R&D) which is the technological backbone of the company." IEI's subsidiaries include: Shiraz Electronics Industries, Sharif University of Technology/Iran Electronics Research Center, Information Systems of Iran (ISIRAN), and Electronic Components Industries (Microelectronics.) In addition, IEI is linked to Isfahan University of Technology (IUT), particularly in the aerospace field.

Another Iranian military production entity, the Communications Industries Group, is a subsidiary organ to the Defense Industries Organization (DIO). The Group, which manufactures equipment for Iranian military, law enforcement, and internal security bodies, was formed in 1989 as part of an overall reorganization of the military industries. It also reportedly has links to Iran's civilian Ministry of Posts, Telegraph, and Telephone (PTT). CIG is believed to oversee the activities of: 1) GAM Electronics and Communications Industries, and 2) Tactical Communications Industries, formerly known as ICI (Iran Communications Industries). According to the GAM website, GAM is a private corporation with offices in Tehran.

Since 1978, it has "designed, developed, and supported computer applications and systems for government and private enterprises." ICI, according to one source, is Iran's "leading manufacturer of military communications equipment and systems. More than 75 products in the field of tactical communication and encryption systems meet a wide range of the army's requirements."

Computer penetration is projected to rise in the future in response to expanding Internet access. A Taiwanese firm, BenQ, estimates that approximately 800,000 PCs will be sold in Iran in 2003. BenQ collaborates with Iran's largest PC producer, Isiran.

Recently, Malaysian and other Southeast Asian producers have targeted Iran as a market for laptops and desktops.

EXTERNAL CONNECTIONS

Iran's military has moved to cultivate relations with foreign suppliers for advanced technologies. As area expert Anoushiravan Ehteshami writes: design and programmable logic controllers. "Iran's Telecom and Internet Sector: A Comprehensive Survey," June 15, 1999, Ch. 5

In recent years, Iranian leaders have spoken of the need to become progressively more self-sufficient in R&D and to produce major weapons systems. This view has been repeatedly reinforced by the (United States) policy of 'dual containment' and Iranian isolation. However, without considerable outside assistance—and in the absence of an efficient infrastructure—this is still proving too difficult to realize materially. Iran's arms-making potential, therefore, will depend as much on its own efforts and available resources as the continuing good will of its closest military partner, Russia.

Reporting from Moscow (thus far unconfirmed anywhere else in the open source literature) indicates Iran decided in mid-2000 to invest in a "25-year military development program." Little is known about the details of this reported program, however. In keeping with the shift in 1997 toward a security strategy based mainly on cold calculation of national interest (to borrow a phrase from Daniel Byman's *Iran's Security Policy in the Post- Revolutionary Era* published in 2001), Tehran actively seeks economic and military contacts with foreign technology producers.

The election of President Vladimir Putin in May 2000, for example, is reported to have triggered "a new era" in bilateral Russo-Iranian trade relations.

Since then Tehran has made significant moves towards the acquisition of Russian defense technologies and production licenses. India, another country embracing information technologies both for civilian and military uses, has agreed to cooperate with Iran on information technology, training, and international terrorism issues. As outlined in another section of this study, both Russia and India have declared cyber attack doctrine and operational capabilities.

In the period immediately after the 1979 revolution ousting the Shah, Iranian government interest in the electronics industry as a main pillar of the defense industrial base rose in response to the perceived evidence of a weak indigenous R & D infrastructure. A key bottleneck, however, was the flight of scientists and technicians to the U.S. and Europe in the 1980s. In response, the Rafsanjani government took steps to: establish educational and research centers, both within Iran's Universities and within the armed forces; identify overseas partners for technology sharing, student exchanges, and collaborative R & D; and provide incentives to lure educated Iranians back to serve the nation.

During the Cold War, Iran was often able to use East-West tensions to further its foreign assistance agenda. Following the break-up of the Soviet Union the Iranian leadership was no longer able to leverage one great power against the other. In 1997, the Khatami government initiated significant contacts with Moscow, Pyongyang, Beijing, New Delhi, selected EU members, and others. Of these overtures, ties with Russia and India deserve further attention. Several sources indicate that senior Russian and Iranian leaders recently have "coordinated" on long-term political strategy and policies with respect to the Middle East and Central Asia (including development of the Caspian Basin). Russia's motives for pursuing closer ties with Iran are complex and subject to interpretation. According to an academic assessment published in Tehran after Defense Minister Sergeyev's December 2000 visit, Russia aims to:

- Use Iran to prevent NATO from expanding into Central Asia
- Frustrate and re-balance ambitions of regional competitors, such as Turkey
- Thwart U.S. objectives to dominate the Persian Gulf.

Iranian President Khatami asserted in Moscow in March 2001 that Russian-Iranian ties are of a deep-rooted nature, "are not a limited tactical move..." An account of Khatami's visit published by Iran's Chamber of Commerce, for example, quotes the President:

"The officials of the two countries decided to broaden and deepen their ties in all fields.

So, they signed a treaty of basic relations, which will set the ground for all the future cooperation. On the Russian side, the Director of Moscow's Center for Iranian Studies, Rajab Safarov, commented in July 2002 that "Russian-Iranian military technical cooperation should not be a subject of bargain and should be interpreted as 'natural trade and economic interaction'..." Beyond the rhetoric, however, informed observers suggest that closer Russo-Iranian ties rest largely on pragmatic necessity. The two countries' interests in the defense sector, for example, are complementary (and mutually profitable): Russian industry depends significantly on foreign consumers since it cannot survive solely on domestic procurement, while Tehran has made a key commitment to upgrade and transform its military and has sufficient oil revenues to pay. As one expert notes:

Arms sales generate only an estimated $3 billion per year, clearly insufficient for maintaining and converting the fast-decaying remains of the once mighty Soviet military industrial complex...Under these conditions, Iran is very attractive –it represents one of the largest Asian arms sales markets and is generally off-limits to Western producers."

The election in Russia of Vladimir Putin in May 2000 triggered a drive in Iran to strengthen bilateral military cooperation. Recent media reporting discusses a significant Iranian military development program. The total value of the arms sales program, of which Russia might expect one-third of the business, is estimated at $25 billion. In late 2000, reports from Moscow noted that Russia's involvement in the program would proceed in phases:

(1) fulfill the previously contracted conventional arms sales to Iran booked in 1989-1991;

(2) negotiate an agreement in 2001 covering sales of advanced conventional defense systems.

Of greater potential interest to Iran in the longer run, however, is the training and access to technological "know-how" prescribed in the framework military cooperation agreements and related documents. (Often such access to training is linked to purchases of military hardware.) Reportedly, Tehran has entered into agreements with the Soviet military in which each year Iranian military officers will receive training in Russian academies.

Finally, as noted above, Iranian universities, such as Malek Ashtar University of Technology, have ties to Russian universities and research institutes that provide funding and technical expertise to Iranian researchers. In addition to long-term bilateral cooperation agreements in the military sector, Moscow and Tehran have shown increasing interest in government-sponsored scientific exchange, building on established arrangements in this field.

In general, each side enjoys significant scientific resources and a well-developed institutional framework of research centers and scientific academies. Iran's Academy of Science, for example, opened its doors in 1990. It was constituted to promote science and technology, study the experience of other countries that might apply to available facilities in Iran, exchange views and research with other countries, and award scholarships and sabbaticals to establish links with scientific academies elsewhere. Provision of scientific training by Moscow reportedly is an important element of overall bilateral cooperation with the Iranian government.

In March 2001, for example, President Khatami visited Russia to discuss mutual strategic interests and to prepare several specific agreements in the energy, trade, military-technical, and scientific-technical cooperation fields. The two sides signed a memorandum of understanding regarding the development, manufacture, and launch of a geostationary telecommunications satellite. In July 2002, Moscow reportedly committed to provide Iran additional assistance in the nuclear development field as part of a 10-year cooperation effort. According to a *New York Times* story from Moscow, "the initiative (not yet approved by either side) also calls for expansion of economic, industrial, and scientific cooperation with Iran."

With respect to scientific developments potentially relevant to electronic warfare, Russia was awarded a $200-300 million contract to build a telecommunications satellite called the Zohreh. The Zohreh—with capacity to broadcast about 12 channels (seven for television and five for telecoms)— is to be the first of six satellites funded by Tehran to be stationed in geostationary orbits to "boost Iran's telecommunications services."

Although some procedural and legal issues reportedly still must be resolved between Moscow and Tehran, the plan was to launch the satellite using Iran's solid fuel rocket, Shahab-4, reported to have been "in the engine design and test phase" in 1999. According to U.S. Navy Vice-Admiral Thomas Wilson's Congressional testimony in March 2002, "During the next ten years, many states will seek to augment their weapons of mass destruction, missiles, satellite reconnaissance, and global positioning systems, designed to counter key U.S. concepts."

During an official visit to India in January 2003, President Khatami signed a formal declaration setting forth the "vision of strategic partnership between India and Iran..." Several reports indicate closer ties will be built on "mutual trade," i.e., Iran will increase sales to New Delhi of crude oil while India will export information technologies (software) and agricultural commodities to Iran. The "New Delhi declaration" embraces several aspects of bilateral cooperation, such as economic, energy, science and technology, information technology, training, and addressing the problem of international terrorism. The two sides also agreed to explore opportunities for cooperation in agreed areas and called upon the business communities of the two countries to promote bilateral trade and investment.

During his visit to India, President Khatami observed the activities and programs of HITECH City in Hyderabad, a primary center for information technology in India that has hosted business visits by a variety of world leaders. According to various accounts, HITECH city specializes in both software production and formal training of computer specialists. Reportedly, the city exported approximately $11 million in computer software in 2002. Khatami also visited the eSeva Center in Andhra Pradesh, accompanied by the Minister of Defense and the President's information and communications technology special envoy, Dr. N. Jahangard. eSeva specialists explained the Andhra Pradesh e-governance initiatives.

In addition, Iranian intelligence could penetrate or exploit the considerable Iranian expatriate communities in the U.S., U.K., and other countries. The Iranian diaspora, consisting mainly of citizens who left the country to reside in North America or Europe in the early 1980s, reportedly plays a significant supporting role in promoting the IT sector. Many of the refugees who fled after the Islamic Revolution are trained engineers, skilled in computer science.

Some have returned to Iran either to assist in improving the telecommunications infrastructure or to invest in Internet cafes. Evidence of information sharing can be seen in e-mail discourses between Iranian expatriates in the U.S. and University research centers in Iran, for example. In view of its ambitious telecommunications plans, the government in mid-2002 officially invited Iranian IT experts living abroad to apply for jobs to supplement the indigenous supply of technical or engineering manpower.

CONCLUSION

Iran is opening up to information technologies in response to both military and economic needs. Disentangling the various contradictory influences and impulses with respect to information technology provides insights into Iranian strategy.

It appears the government's current policy objective is to "transform" the IT sector, albeit with a monopoly over the telecom backbone. Selected activities (such as state enterprises and University research centers) receive official backing, but elsewhere government regulates through the licensing and control of private ISPs, installation of content filtering devices and other monitoring devices.

Access to personal computers (PCs) and the Internet, even in cyber cafés, is mostly limited to Iran's elite through price rationing. Government limits and restrictions foster widespread "black" activity, such as the purchase of private satellite dishes, software piracy, and computer hacking. The mixture of IT investment, computer talent, and underemployed youth has spawned a culture in Tehran that is potentially ripe for exploitation or manipulation by Iran's intelligence services. Iran's sense of military and economic inadequacy, isolation, and vulnerability in the post-Cold War world is driving on-going interest in non-conventional weapons and technologies, including advanced information and communications technologies.

In this framework, there is considerable anecdotal evidence that Iran has begun to emphasize the link between defense modernization and academic research in the computer engineering field. This evidence suggests the government is sponsoring the development of a cyber warfare capability as a potential force multiplier. We assess that Tehran may be actively exploring a cyber warfare capability, based on the following:

- Leadership frustration with Iran's outdated and under-manned conventional military, especially in the aftermath of the 1991 Gulf War.
- Presence of a highly-educated elite committed to acquisition and exploitation of state-ofthe- art communications and Internet technologies.
- Evidence that the regime is funding, training, and harnessing human resources in the ICT field, drawing, for example, on Iranian expatriates trained in computer network engineering, information warfare, and security matters.
- Ministry of Defense funding of dedicated R&D facilities linking the armed services and technical universities (such as Malek Ashtar) concerned with information technologies and national security.
- Evidence suggesting that the clerical regime has taken steps to obtain technical help and training in the computer hardware and software fields from Russia and India—acknowledged leaders in cyber warfare matters.

Government Plans in the ICT Investment Field

In July 2002, the Secretary of Iran's Supreme Information Technology Council, Nasrollah Jahangard, announced that the regime plans to spend the equivalent of $125 million in 2002 to develop information technology and to create jobs. According to the PTT's Acting Deputy Minister for Planning and Development, future infrastructure goals are as follows (through the first phase of the Third Year Plan):

- Providing data network services in 420 points embracing over 180 cities
- Building required infrastructure for "inter-organizational" networks and point to point communication with the capacity of 7000 ports and speed of 64 Kbps up to 2Mbps, covering 1 million end-users
- Providing Internet service and IP national network with a total capacity of 10,000 ports, covering 1000 ISP's and 1 million end-users
- Establishing more than 200 ADSL ports for live video and multimedia services at a speed up to 8 Mbps in 8 large cities259 According to Iran's Acting Deputy Minister, the government aims to acquire the capacity to serve 15 million Internet users by 2005 (including 60,000 high-speed line subscribers.) The core network layer will consist of:
- 12 router switches in 10 Iranian states
- Domestic and international STM-16 and STM-4 lines for linking core network switches
- Allocating 10 gateways to PSTN network to transmit domestic and international voice traffic in VoIP form for 8 states in Iran International connections are planned as follows:
- Fiber optic link with capacity of STM-4 (622Mbps) through Jusk-Fojaireh
- Fiber optic support link with capacity of STM-4 (622 Mbps) through Bandar Abbas- Gheshm-Dubai
- Satellite connections with capacity of 34 Mbps in 8 Iranian states
- STM-1 link with Turkmenistan, Azerbaijian, Armenia, Pakistan, Turkey, and Iraq Overall, the goal of the PTT by 2005 is to connect 300 cities to the national data network. Capacity of each urban connection and international lines would be 80 Gbps and 3.4 Gbps,

11

Scenario in North Korea

Our party's military-first ideology explains the need to push ahead with the revolution and construction through the constant enhancement of the revolutionary army's position and role. By comprehensively embodying the demands of military-first ideology, great Comrade Kim Chong-il is wisely leading the advance of the 21st century in order to achieve the victory of the independent cause.

Excerpt from Democratic Peoples Republic of Korea's Military First Doctrinal Declaration, published in Nodong Sinmun, March 21, 2003

I believe that the North Koreans, whatever their limitations, have a capacity to think deeply and innovatively about military affairs...And what I have observed over the years convinces me that they are devoting considerable attention to cyber war."

John Arquilla, RAND consultant, *Wired News*, June 2, 2003

In a report to South Korea's National Assembly's National Defense Committee, the country's Defense Ministry warns that North Korea has developed an advanced cyber warfare capability that could be used to gather intelligence or launch cyberattacks against South Korea, the United States or Japan. According to the report, North Korea has trained 500 computer hackers in advanced cyber attack techniques, and the recluse state's cyber warfare capabilities "have reached the levelof advanced countries."

Agence France Presse report from Seoul, October 4, 2004

The DPRK does have several dozens of modern telecommunications facilities and academic research institutes with sophisticated telecommunications equipment, allowing them access to and use of modern telecommunications technologies, including wireless radio and telephone, satellite communications, and the Internet...The real puzzle is how the North Korean telecommunications personnel are still able to maintain in good working condition most of the telecommunications facilities and equipment, despite enormous material, technical, and financial difficulties facing them today.

Alexandre Mansourov, "Bytes and Bullets: Impact of IT Revolution on War and Peace in Korea," October 2002

BACKGROUND

Episodes such as Operation "Eligible Receiver," a 1997 Pentagon exercise in which a red team assembled by the U.S. intelligence community posed as North Korea, have fostered popular interest in Pyongyang's putative cyber capabilities. In reality, the Democratic People's Republic of Korea (DPRK) represents a complex, enigmatic puzzle. On the one hand, the regime obsesses about national security and espouses a rigid "military first" doctrine that dictates priority funding to the Korean People's Army (KPA). On the other, North Korea's documented dependency on outside economic and technical aid and illicit foreign trade suggests economic backwardness and impaired military readiness that calls into question offensive capabilities.

It is generally accepted that the Hermit regime led by Party Chairman Kim Jong-il has long been paranoid about national defense and military preparedness. In addition to sparring politically with Seoul, the civilian and military leaders obsess about the possible military threat from South Korea—supported by the United States.

The presumptive threat "justifies" popular sacrifice. Given North Korea's modest GDP (estimated at only $22 billion in 2002, about equivalent to El Salvador or Lithuania but with a population 6 times greater) and meager natural endowments, the government's room for maneuver is severely limited. Aid agencies note the

DPRK's dependence on outside food and fuel assistance and dearth of investment capital.

Visitors with access to cities and regions beyond the capital assess civilian transportation and communications infrastructure as rudimentary at best. A decade ago, Pyongyang adopted a military strategy based on asymmetric advantage to leverage its meager financial resources, i.e., leveraging a relatively modest investment in resources to obtain a disproportionate impact in influence or deterrence.

In this context, the DPRK began to develop or acquire sophisticated military technologies such as long-range missiles and nuclear devices, which would not only deter adversaries in Northeast Asia and earn the regime potential export revenue, but also provide diplomatic bargaining chips in securing concessions from its neighbors. At the same time, the regime stepped-up investment in militaryrelated R&D in the computer hardware and software domain.

The DPRK currently allocates an estimated 25 to 35 percent of its GDP to military expenditures. Despite the budgetary weight given to the military, experts assess the armed forces are only "modestly digitized." For example, Alexandre Mansourov, a former Soviet diplomat stationed in Pyongyang, observes that the Korean People's Army (KPA):

Is still predominantly an 'analog and tube' force equipped with 'appropriate' technology, often going back to the days of the Korean War, not 'cutting edge' technology. The level of IT expertise within the KPA and the North Korean defense industry is low, and we tend to overestimate it.

> Assessing North Korea's military strengths, including its cyber warfare capabilities and intentions, entails distinct challenges. First, the reclusive, Stalinist leadership and a closed society render reliable information difficult to obtain. Second, DPRK leaders are reputedly masters of propaganda and deception. Deliberate "disinformation" campaigns are often used when the government wishes to hide lapses or tout accomplishments that may have never been achieved. Due to the government's

authoritarian control, disinformation activities are often easier to conceal than in societies that are more open. Public relations campaigns notwithstanding, foreign observers generally agree that North Korea's underlying natural resource base, transportation and communications infrastructure, and technically competitive workforce are minimal.

Beneath the veneer of military-technical exploits, the reality is that North Korea is one of the poorest countries in the world. Disinformation is not solely in the domain of the North, however. South Korea's intelligence services reportedly engage in propaganda and deception. Elements in South Korea's defense sector have a vested interest in misrepresenting the potential threat from the North. Placing fabricated or exaggerated reports in the popular media about Pyongyang's military plans is a means to promote continued U.S. military presence in South Korea, generate defense industry contracts, and sustain local investment in military research and development.

A report that some experts attribute to the Defense Security Command in Seoul states, for example, that in 1986 a five-year program under the name Mirim College (later renamed the Automated Warfare Institute, according to South Korea's National Intelligence Service) was created for DPRK military forces.

The mission of the facility at Mirim is reportedly to "educate a corps of professional military technicians for creation and management of military computer system[s], and ... other fields such as electronic warfare...The institute's general curriculum is divided into five majors, including command automation, computers, programming, automated reconnaissance, and electronic warfare."

Reportedly, about ten percent of each class is assigned to work for "the People's Armed Forces Ministry surveillance bureau, where their duties consist of searching the Internet and also of carrying out hacking activities."

Disinformation from both countries complicates efforts to discern the truth about intentions and plans in the Hermit regime.

U.S. GOVERNMENT REPORTS AND FOREIGN OFFICIAL STATEMENTS

During the research for this report, no public DPRK statement of the regime's cyber war plans, capabilities, or intentions was found. Some evidence suggests, however, that KPA officers continue to engage in liaison and training exercises with their counterparts in China—a state that not only is an avowed proponent and practitioner of Information Warfare but also possesses a dedicated training facility, the Communication Command Academy in Wuhan.

Western security experts have included North Korea in their assessments of countries that are developing a cyber attack capability. In 2002 Richard Clarke, a former Special Advisor to the President for Cyberspace Security, testified that North Korea was one of the nations "developing information warfare units, either in their military, or in their intelligence services, or both." Former Australian Defense Force officials believe that North Korea is actively probing Australia's cyber infrastructure.

An unclassified Canadian Intelligence Service publication, in reference to American military and Congressional reports, states "North Korea, Libya, Iran, Iraq, and Syria have some IO [information operations] capabilities." Western open source discussions of North Korea's military doctrine emphasize surprise and a rapid thrust into the South. Reportedly, the KPA's overall objective is to "disturb the coherence of South Korea defenses in depth—including its key command, control, and communications, and intelligence infrastructure." The countries neighboring North Korea have adopted a higher cyber alert status in response to a perceived threat increase.

South Korea's recent cyber defense initiatives, for example, reflect concern over potential vulnerability. The ROK military staged its first mock battle to practice Internet-related warfare in August 2001. Although there is no open source reference to an attack scenario involving North Korea, the cyber battle—during the annual joint U.S.-ROK Ulji Focus Lens exercise—taught the military to defend computer networks from possible hacking and virus attacks. The drill reportedly ran through a cyber warfare defense system called Infocon at South Korea's JCS Headquarters. The ROK's military is operating a Computer Emergency Response Team and has recently automated the security procedures for its officers.

> South Korea's network vulnerabilities are also well known. For example, it is widely recognized that the Slammer worm almost crippled all Internet access in South Korea.
>
> ROK officials reported in early 2000 an increasing number of overseas web intruders exploiting South Korea's weak computer defenses to launch attacks on foreign sites. "Statistics showed that in January alone South Korea chalked up 32 cases up from 18 cases a year earlier, in which foreign hackers intruded into its computer systems and used them as launching pads to assail foreign websites," a KISA spokesman said. "We have a good network environment in this country but we are suffering from a great shortage of people in charge of security," the spokesman continued.
>
> South Korea represents an attractive target for potential cyber attackers in North Korea. Seoul is an acknowledged leader in broadband technology. A May 2002 briefing by the ROK Ministry of Information and Communication noted that South Korea has "the world's best infocommunications infrastructure and a dramatic increase of Internet users." At the end of 2001, South Korea had an estimated 25 million Internet users, and more than 7.8 million broadband subscribers.
>
> Seoul, according to the Ministry of Information and Communication, is experiencing both an increased dependency on IT systems (for business and education) and greater interdependence (and also vulnerability) because of various government, university, and business networks.

South Korea's relatively unprotected networks and systems might provide a platform for clandestine attacks against Seoul or third countries. A theoretical possibility would be a cyberterrorist attack either directly against South Korea or exploiting the ROK as a proxy for a wider attack.

Linguistic, cultural, and other affinities between North and South would certainly facilitate hackers in Pyongyang compromising servers in South Korea. As noted above, academic IT experts and researchers in Seoul and Pyongyang often exchange information about professional matters of common interest.

In this context, university computer servers reportedly are especially vulnerable to hacking because security measures are lax and universities invest in networked broadband technologies. Overall, the meager unclassified evidence suggests that the DPRK has a rudimentary electronic warfare capability (e.g., jamming). It is possible Pyongyang possesses a capacity to compromise IT networks or hack into protected South Korean or United States databases. However, this finding represents little more than conjecture based on doctrinal considerations, such as the military first strategy, and documented testing of adanced missile and other military technology components.

MILITARY AND INTELLIGENCE AGENCY RESEARCH

CIA and other published sources estimate annual military expenditures in North Korea at slightly over $5 billion. This estimate compares with $12.8 billion in South Korea, $9.7 billion in Iran, $8.97 billion in Israel, $4.47 billion in Singapore, and $3.113 billion in Norway. These comparative figures should be considered only as general orders of magnitude, however, because of issues with input data and different assumptions and accounting methods employed. According to South Korea's Ministry of National Defense, sources of funds for the DPRK's military budget include weapons exports and profits "reinvested" in the budget from direct production of weapons and farming activities. Profits from illicit activities such as narcotics trade and remittances from the Chosen Soren (Korean nationals resident in Japan) reportedly also contribute significantly to supporting military investment.

Reliable published information on Pyongyang's programmatic or weapons systems outlays under the overall military budget, however, is non-existent. Regardless, it is clear that the DPRK annually has far less to spend on its military priorities than its neighbors in East Asia. To compensate, the regime resorts to various stratagems to obtain hardware, software, and engineering plans on the cheap from sympathetic foreign governments and private entities. U.S. military and civilian experts assess that the DPRK is adept at collecting proscribed foreign technologies necessary to compete militarily in East Asia.

For example, in addition to exploiting unwitting high-tech investors and visiting academics, North Korea employs various assets, such as embassy defense attaches overseas and intelligence collection services engaged in industrial espionage, to obtain proprietary information and prototype hardware. The Chosen Soren, through front companies and similar techniques, procures state of the art hardware and software on behalf of North Korea.

> Chosen Soren, the association of Korean residents in Japan, was founded in May 1955. Media sources estimate the organization has about 200,000 members. Its structure embraces a headquarters in Tokyo, regional head offices and branches, and 23 business enterprises. The name "Chosen" derives from the period of Japanese occupation of the Korean peninsula. Korean residents in Japan who choose not to adopt South Korean citizenship remain "Chosen nationals" under Japanese law.
>
> Through several illicit activities and enterprises under its control, the Chosen Soren remits hard currencies to North Korea. According to published reports, the Japanese police testified in 1994 that about $600 million annually was remitted to Pyongyang, although the annual amount has since declined.
>
> Gakushu-gumi is Chosen Soren's underground organization. It is connected to the North Korean Workers

Party. Reportedly the Gakushu-gumi engages in intelligence activities of various types, such as information gathering and diversion of advanced technologies for use by North Korea. The State Security Agency (SSA), under the direction of Kim Jong-nam, the eldest son of the DPRK leader, covers a range of counter intelligence and security duties normally associated with the secret police. According to an informed source, the SSA "has counter intelligence responsibilities at home and abroad, and runs overseas intelligence collection operations...The agency also guards national borders and monitors international entry points."

Media reports state that the Chairman's son, Kim Jong-nam, head of the National Defense Commission, consolidated the SSA's overseas intelligence gathering unit, which engages in hacking and monitoring foreign communications, into the Korean Computer Center (KCC) in Pyongyang. Recent reports indicate that the KCC is the hub of the Hermit regime's information technology planning. The facility reportedly is technically equipped and houses some 800 employees. Despite industrial country agreements restricting access to dual-use technologies such as advanced computers, the KCC and other North Korean facilities nevertheless obtained these illegally from Europe, Japan and other suppliers. A South Korean firm, BIT Computer, reportedly has a contract to train the KCC's work force. According to a journalistic account:

The KCC, which used to be understood merely as a research institute developing software, is confirmed to have carried out, under Kim Jong Nam's initiatives from the outset, functions of a 'clandestine overseas information command center' under the jurisdiction of the SSA. Having been involved since the late 1980s in the SSA's overseas information gathering through communications monitoring and computer hacking, Kim reportedly found it necessary to reinforce the information gathering functions and develop the computer industry at the same time.

One of the current functions of the KCC, according to a recent article on IT developments in North Korea, is to monitor the web sites of major government agencies and business establishments: "Its activities include communications monitoring and hacking, putting even innocent seeming work like language and voice software in a different light." The DPRK reportedly is interested in blueprints or technical specifications (or any vulnerabilities and loopholes) in foreign systems and technologies. South Korea's technology firms, as well as academic and quasi-government defense research agencies, represent potential targets.

Assuming published reports about the SSA's involvement in the work of the Korea Computer Center are accurate, these reports would support the case that Pyongyang is pursuing a cyber attack capability involving computer hacking against foreign targets. An academic center with a number of legitimate activities would provide a reasonable cover for computer software development and other techniques applicable to cyber warfare.

INFORMATION TECHNOLOGY INVESTMENT

The senior leadership in Pyongyang is paying growing attention to the IT sector. A reputed "media junkie," Chairman Kim Jong-il has experimented with the Internet and the World Wide Web. According to numerous journalistic accounts, the DPRK leader has personally promoted inward direct investment in computer software and communications technologies. He also supported the creation of a domestic intranet to facilitate communication among military, political, and academic elites.

In the last decade, the DPRK is reported to have studied Internet firewall applications to shield sensitive domestic communications and databases from outside intrusion. In addition, the Chairman's son Kim Jong-nam, controls the programming activities at the North Korean Academy of Sciences, the Pyongyang Information Center, Yakchon Research Institute, Kim Il Sung University, and Kim Chaek Institute of Technology. In the mid-1990s, the gradual reduction in tensions between Seoul and

Pyongyang and the loosening of international trade restrictions helped accelerate the rate of political and economic change on the peninsula and in the region as a whole.

Various reports indicate Kim Jong-il and his associates—based on outreach to China, Japan, and other neighbors—embraced the IT sector as a potential source of future economic competitiveness and growth. For example, the demise of the Soviet Union and transformation of China to a quasi "market" economy forced Pyongyang to fend for itself to a greater degree and develop alternative sources of foreign exchange.

The leadership calculated that participation in the global digital economy as a software exporter might generate foreign exchange over the longer term and offer North Korea an escape from its endemic economic woes. At the same time, however, the regime recognized that distributed communications connectivity at the grass roots level was potentially dangerous if it implied loss of central political control. The DPRK in recent years has successfully attracted IT infrastructure and related scientific investment from South Korea, China, and Japan, even though the DPRK has a long standing reputation as an opportunist and "deadbeat" in international commercial and investment circles.

As mentioned earlier, the information technology sector in North Korea is designed primarily for military, governmental, and industrial use; expansion and development of telecommunications networks and facilities are not consumer-driven. Gunter Unterbeck is vice president of KCC Europe, a firm that delivers Internet service to the state-run Korea Computer Center. According to a report in *Newsweek*, Jan Holtermann, a fellow German who co-founded the company, "in January [2004] announced a contract to provide Internet service in partnership with the state-run Korea Computer Center. The Germans have since invested an estimated $1 million in computer equipment and a satellite link to Internet servers in Berlin. The link works, but so far Pyongyang has not yet opened it to the public."

North Korea's civilian telecommunications technology lags far behind that of South Korea. According to figures in the CIA *World Factbook*, the North has 1.1 million main telephone lines in use compared to 24 million in the South. A recent South Korean report noted that the phone systems in Pyongyang and major cities are automatic but systems in rural areas remain hand operated.

Pyongyang may have as few as 2700 public telephones in a city with a population of about two million. More fundamentally, as Peter Hayes of the Nautilus Institute has pointed out, the DPRK's lack of basic necessities—such as a reliable electrical grid—poses an obstacle to infrastructure development. The primitive state of the domestic telecommunications infrastructure contrasts sharply with North Korea's emerging effort to provide to favored official elites international fixed line, wireless, and satellite communications options. Basic service reportedly is available to senior party, government, and military officials and to foreign guests. Recent developments in fiber optics, mobile telephones, and rudimentary Internet and email connectivity are of particular interest.

During the last decade, a growing number of South Korean and Japanese business investors and academic computer experts visited Pyongyang. In the course of such visits to DPRK institutes and universities, several recorded their observations. One expert, for example, reported observing PC's and work stations in the following range: 386, 486, Pentium, NEC 9801 series, SUN, Sony, DEC (Alpha Chip). Civilian computer access is extremely limited. According to a report, North Korea is said to have "only about 100,000 plus computers for private use, most of them in the 386 class."

Reportedly, North Korea produces 32-bit microprocessors and is actively researching 64-bit computers. Pyongyang announced in May 2001 that it had produced 1300 "up-to-date" computers in February and distributed them to local educational institutions. A June 2001 report from a DPRK news organ in Tokyo indicated that North Korea "has opened its first PC manufacturing plant and has already produced hundreds of Pentium and Celeron-class machines." The computers reportedly are being installed in educational institutes intended to provide computertraining courses to talented youth.

In September 2002, Panda Electronic Group of China and the DPRK's Ministry of Electronics Industry established a joint venture to develop, manufacture, and market computers and peripherals. A 2003 report outlines a yearly production figure of 135,000 computers. TASS, the Russian state-controlled news agency, reported in July 2003 that computers assembled in North Korea were displayed for sale at an international industrial exhibition held in Vladivostok.

> There is credible evidence that the leadership in Pyongyang gives priority to applied scientific research. The quality and breadth of technical and professional journals in the electronics, information technology and related fields demonstrates the regime's commitment to advanced sciences.
>
> Second, Pyongyang continues to exploit the post-Cold War relaxation of tensions in East Asia to attract foreign direct investment in communications infrastructure improvements. Several North Korean academic institutions offer scientific research and training programs that in some cases are directly applicable to integrated information technologies and computer systems, software development, programming, and information warfare. Computers and software reportedly are accessible to leading academic research bodies. Both theoretical and practical work has been advanced through the use of this advanced technology.
>
> As with the investment liberalization measures currently under way in the Info-Tech sector, the leadership seems to have adopted China's approach by employing academic research institutions to facilitate research in military information warfare programs. In recent years, for example, key technical academic institutions, such as the Academy of Sciences and Kim Il Sung and Kim Chaek Universities, have opened computer colleges and expanded computer teaching and research faculties. Sources deemed to be reliable also assert that similar North Korean institutions, such as the Korea Computer Center and the Pyongyang Informatics Center, are directly

engaged in national security work, especially information gathering and potential cyber warfare activities such as malicious hacking. Reportedly, these institutions enjoy significant budgetary resources. The following passages outline examples of the programs and research in these institutions.

The Academy of Science's computer division reportedly is engaged in theoretical and practical research in computer science. According to an informed observer, its long-term plan embraces development of computer programs for domestic use and export; manpower training; and distribution of software technology and products. Among the Academy's current research interests are: Korean character recognition, machine translation, data compression, relational data base systems, bank management systems, and voice recognition. Reportedly, the Academy has been responsible for many application and edutainment programs, some of which are marketed by the Paeksong Trading Corporation.

According to a North Korean media report, a new school of "information technology" was established at the Academy in early 2002. Training embraces subjects such as programming digital controls, semi-conductor design, and precision machinery, with a teaching staff that includes prominent scientists and technicians drawn from various institutes within the Academy.

Kim Il-sung University is engaged in research and development in cooperation with computer science faculties elsewhere. The university's computer center was established in 1985. An informed observer states that the university in 1994 had more than 200 PC's for student use. The university has been responsible for development of the following software: Intelligent Locker (Hard Disc protection program); Worluf Anti-virus (broadband anti-virus program); SIMNA (simulation and system analysis program); a war game program; Hepatitis Diagnosis and Prescription System; and FC 2.0 (A highly portable C++ program development tool).328 Kim Chaek University of

Technology, founded in 1948, underwent a significant reorganization in the late 1990s. According to a 2002 article, the university has established three colleges addressing computer science, information science and technology, and machine science.

Over 2000 students graduate from the University annually. In an interview published by The People's Korea, a Tokyo based unofficial web site of the DPRK, Chong Gwang Chon the Chief of Academic Studies at Kim Chaek University said "our University has been doing academic exchanges with neighboring countries such as China…It is planned to increase opportunities to hold exchange meeting [sic] with foreign Universities such as Universities in Europe. Among the software programs listed at the university are Computer Fax (communications software) and Materials Security Software (SGVision.) SGVision is an image-reprocessing program with a steganographic function.

Pyongyang Informatics Center (PIC) was established in 1986. The PIC reportedly hosts more than 120 research scientists and is equipped with an average of 1.5 computers per person. This institution is reportedly a leader in Korean language processing and word processor development. The latter program accepts Japanese, Chinese, and Russian characters, in addition to Korean and English. The PIC is responsible for developing the Chang-duk system for MSDOS and Windows. The Center reportedly has an internal LAN using Novell Netware 3.11. According to a 2002 article, the PIC programming institute is "teaching the development and technology of computer network and multimedia programs, database (Software Information Center) construction programs and others…with a goal of around 2000 people each year."

The DPRK continues to exploit the post-Cold War decline in tensions to seek direct investment in the IT sector and technical assistance from abroad. Pyongyang places high priority on importing advanced technologies and parts for eventual integration into equipment for export. To achieve this, the government recently reorganized and consolidated its foreign trade promotion bureaucracy to facilitate joint ventures and imports from China and South Korea. The Kwangmyongsong Guidance Bureau, for example, through the Kwangmyongsong General Corporation, plays a role in channeling parts from abroad to computer manufacturers in North Korea.

North Korea, for a variety of motives, including a desire to compete in the global Info-Tech economy, is striving to advance in digital technologies and related R & D. Although the Korean Workers Party must remain vigilant in the face of the information revolution to avoid losing political control over the populace, the regime is clearly allocating significant resources to improvements in telecommunications infrastructure, hardware and software acquisition and development, programming research, and related technical training and education. The contribution of foreign assistance to this endeavor is crucial.

CONCLUSION

The totalitarian, paranoid make-up of the regime in North Korea renders leadership intent in the cyber field, military plans, and degree of technical sophistication among the elites difficult to pin down.

A gradual loosening in travel restrictions and international trade in recent years has spawned discussion in the media regarding Pyongyang's interest in digital Internet technologies; acquisition and exploitation of advanced (Western) computer blueprints; experimentation with email and Intranets connecting local universities and scientific institutes; computer science training; and formation of government/academic/enterprise R & D networks patterned after institutions in China.

There are numerous reports beginning in the 1990's describing the DPRK leadership's ambitions to achieve a "digital economy." The unclassified evidence to date, however, suggests that this goal is nothing more than a distant dream on the part of Kim Jong-il and his immediate advisors. As one authority recently observed:

Grossly underdeveloped electronics and computer industrial infrastructure, morally and physically obsolete and dysfunctional national telecommunications infrastructure, perennial national macro-economic crisis and virtual collapse of the nation-wide power grid, a closed and highly politicized society, and inter-agency rivalry present considerable obstacles in continued development of IT-based C4ISR and EIW capabilities.

Nevertheless, the "military first" doctrine, coupled with a proven capability to focus resources, train personnel, and illicitly procure foreign technical assistance, suggests it is possible that the regime has a rudimentary, exploratory or "pilot" capability to hack or compromise unprotected IT networks or data bases in South Korea or other neighboring countries. This finding represents little more than conjecture, based on extrapolating from North Korea's proven engineering achievements in its missile and related high-technology military programs.

ANNEX 1: INFRASTRUCTURE INVESTMENT

After initial technical and other assistance from the ITU and UNDP in the early 1990s, the DPRK erected a factory for local production of fiber optic cable for use in domestic and international communications. The factory has a research institute to develop replacements for imported materials. By 1998, the DPRK was reported to have connected 36 cities and counties with coaxial fiber optic cables. A 2001 media report noted that North Korea had connected Hamhung, Chongin, Najin, and China's Hunchon with fiber optic lines. In addition, in August 2001 Loxley Pacific (headquartered in Thailand) won a 30 year telecommunications network concession for the "Rason International Telecommunications Center." The latter is used to provide access to international networks from the DPRK. According to sources in South Korea, it is now possible to get international direct dial service to 170 foreign cities from Pyongyang. AT&T has been servicing calls between North Korea and the United States since 1995.

Mobile telecommunications service is mostly limited to military purposes. Early in 2002, the DPRK tested a pilot mobile telecommunications service for 300 users run by Loxley Pacific. The test system is reported to have been based on the European

GSM mobile system. This is potentially controversial, however, because South Korea relies on the U.S.-based CDMA system.

The DPRK's limited access to the Internet comes from satellite links provided by a company in South Korea and by landlines from China. According to an informed academic, although North Korea has been assigned the Internet domain name "kp" and Pyongyang may have successfully tested an Internet connection with Australia, the link was not implemented for "political reasons."

There are a few North Korean websites hosted in China and Japan, for example <http://www.korea-dpr.com/> and <http://www.dprkorea.com/>. Kim Chol Hwan, CEO of South Korea's Gigalink Ltd., stated in 2001 that the DPRK has completed the construction of a firewall to protect its intranet (inter-linking domestic science institutes and universities) from eventual connection to the Internet.

According to media reports, the North has conducted a study on firewalls with Japanese scholars. This is seen as part of preparations for accessing the Internet. In late 2001, China's Shenyang Public Information Industry Co. Ltd announced the availability of e-mail services to North Korea. Charges for sending and receiving e-mail through this service, called Silibank, are based on the amount of data sent. This service is aimed at corporations rather than individuals. Users must provide contact information including nationality, identify business partners in North Korea, and pay a registration fee of $100.

The Silibank e-mail service is available only to registered users and relies on two servers, one in Shenyang and the other in Pyongyang. Outside the DPRK, users connect to the server using an e-mail client such as Microsoft Outlook to send and receive e-mail over the Internet. Representatives of a Seoul software company, Hoonnet, reported in 2002 that North Korea's Chosun International Communications Center recently opened an Internet network employing landlines. The fiber optic cable allegedly connects Pyongyang and Sinuiju with the Chinese cities of Dandong, Beijing, and Shanghai under a contract with China Telecom. According to this source, the North Korean computer server is in Pyongyang where the so-called "Chosun Internet Joint Venture Company" is located.

The advances made in the telecommunication field have also been seen in computer technologies. The relaxation of tensions on the Korean peninsula beginning in the mid-1990's facilitated South Korean technology exports to the North. Trade between the countries increased from $18.8 million in 1989 to $333.4 million in 1999. According to a recent report from Seoul, through 1999 South Korean civic groups sent a total of 450 sets of computers to North Korea, including 100 sets delivered in September 1998 to Kim Chaek University of Technology by South Korea's Kyungnam University. Such exports are limited by law to 386 class computers.

The following paragraphs highlight a few of the joint business ventures in the IT sector, academic research partnerships, and technical assistance programs involving Japan, China, ROK, and other partners.

Japan

As stated above, the Chosen Soren is a principal conduit of technical assistance to North Korea. It is said to act as North Korea's unofficial embassy in Tokyo. Reportedly, it also assists the DPRK in foreign intelligence operations. The Chosen Soren develops businesses and "front companies" abroad that benefit the Pyongyang regime by generating hard currency. One such business venture is Unikotech, established in July 2000 with an initial capitalization of 100 million yen.

The firm plans to sell software developed by the Korea Computer Center. According to several sources, Unikotech is a joint venture between IMRI (a South Korean producer of computer monitors) and CGS Company, a computer software producer in Tokyo.

A press release notes that CGS and KCC in Pyongyang "have been exchanging technological cooperation over the past decade." CGS President RyangYong Bu reportedly played a key role in restoring advanced computer hardware to the KCC following the fire at its headquarters in 1997.

China

Beginning in 1994, experts and specialists from North and South Korea began a bottom-up approach to address information technology issues. An International conference on Korean computer language was held in Yanbian, China in 1994 and each year thereafter. Agreement was reached in four areas: IT vocabulary, keyboard arrangement, character ordering, and coding system.

As discussed previously, "top down" initiatives—involving government ministers and/or CEO's of private companies—have accelerated in the last few years, reflecting both a loosening in international political tensions and the high priority accorded to IT expansion.

DPRK leaders have pursued especially close IT cooperation with China. Kim Jong-il has visited China at least twice to study information technology reforms. In May 2000 Kim visited Legend Computers, Ltd. in Shanghai. Three months later, Pyongyang established an English-language website (providing information on North Korea) on the Internet in Beijing. In 2001 Kim visited China for a week. He toured Shanghai's Pudong Sci-tech district accompanied by 20 high-ranking officials, including the Head of the General Political Department of the KPA.

Reportedly, Kim Jong-il's outreach to China has been facilitated by the close relations between his son, National Defense Commission Chairman Kim Jong-nam, and PRC former Chairman Jiang Zemin's eldest son, Stanford-educated Jiang Mianheng. The latter is considered a leading architect of the PRC's IT industry, including the introduction of Linux in China. Jiang Mianheng, Vice President of the Chinese Academy of Sciences, visited IT firms in South Korea in September 2002.

He held discussions at a Samsung Electronics factory, met with the Chairman of the Samsung group, and visited Hanaro Telecom. In April 2002, Pyongyang exhibited its software products at the first session of North Korea Computer Software Expo in Beijing. The products exhibited included a computer operating system developed by Pyongyang, as well as letter/character identification, translation, and fingerprint recognition software.

The Expo was co-sponsored by the North Korean Academy of Sciences, Panpacific North Korea National Economic Development Promotion Association, and Reese International Group. Panpacific represents the association of Koreans resident in Japan.

Republic of Korea

In the IT domain, many businesses have been interested in inter-Korean opportunities. According to media accounts from 2001, "representatives of IT firms in the South have visited the North in droves this year, as if floodgates have opened." Observers comment that the South Korean business rush north is competitive and uncoordinated. An illustrative list of proposed projects includes:

- NTrack, a South Korean e-commerce company, has joined with the North's Kwangmyongsung group to build the first ever IT center in Pyongyang. The center is purportedly planned as a $3 million complex where IT components will be produced and North Korean IT experts trained. A 15-story business center is planned for 2002. The DPRK provides the site, water, and electricity, while Ntrack is responsible for all materials, technical manpower, and finance.
- BIT Computer Corporation (Seoul) signed an agreement in June 2001 with the Korea Computer Center to establish satellite Internet links. Under the terms of the contract, BIT would become the sole supplier of satellite Internet equipment to North Korea for five years. BIT President Chol Hyun Jung said the entire venture had the approval of Kim Jong-il. The President of BIT computers, a medical data start-up, lectured at the KCC in February 2001 to 500 local IT experts. KCC reportedly asked for teaching materials.
- Giga Link, Cubic TRC, and Herbmedi.com plan to create a trial broadband network at the Pyongyang Informatics Center. Under terms of the arrangement, they will also sell software developed in the North to customers in Seoul.
- Samsung Group, on November 9, 2000, announced plans to invest $1 billion to build an electronics complex in the

DPRK by the year 2008. The complex will likely be in the Western North Korean port city of Sinuiju. After the first phase of construction which will be completed in 2002, Samsung said it would be able to produce $500 million worth of appliances which will mostly be re-imported into the South. Once completed, Samsung will be able to produce $3 billion worth of electronics products annually at the industrial complex.

Government entities both north and south of the 38th parallel are coordinating some activities.

For example, an ROK Ministry of Unification has been established in Seoul. The ministry's purpose is to coordinate, facilitate, and regulate steps leading to potential North-South unification. In this context, government-sponsored bodies, such as the Information Technology Forum for Unification (ITFU), have been created. According to a Website, it is a "forum for professionals in the IT domain." The stated purpose of the ITFU is:

- Research and analysis of North-South Korean IT interchange trends
- Formulation of an alternative policy on North-South Korea IT cooperation
- Move to international standards on a uniform basis
- Transfer technology/skills/intelligence between the North and South
- Further support between North and South through IT.

DPRK government officials have visited the ROK on a number of occasions to study its economy. For example, Mr. Park Nam-ki, Chairman of North Korea's State Planning Commission, visited South Korean information technology companies in October 2002. Mr. Pak is reported as saying "I hope Samsung will bridge cooperation between North and South Korea... IT brings North and South Korea close". Samsung is the world's largest manufacturer of computer memory chips. Reportedly, the visiting delegation included Chang Sung Taek, the North Korean leader's brother in law. Numerous steps have been taken by academics in the South (acting in their personal or official capacities) to forge cooperative relations and programs with counterparts in the North.

Pohang University in South Korea, which also performs national-security related research for Seoul's Agency for Defense Development, is one such institution. Professor Chan-mo Park of Pohang, a specialist in virtual reality, has lectured in Pyongyang at the Pyongyang Informatics Center. He recently initialed an agreement with PIC officials to conduct joint research in IT software, including virtual reality programs. He has also described (in writing) contacts and conversations with leading North Korean physicists and other prominent scientists in the IT field. Media reports of South Korean academics teaching computer courses in the North have surfaced in the last year.

Kyungnam University, in South Korea, hosts the Institute for Far Eastern Studies (IFES) in Seoul. According to the IFES website, the institute is staffed by more than 100 scholars and researchers and, as such, is the largest institute of its kind in the country, distributing research materials to about 1000 members. The website indicates the institute will fulfill its function as an "open library" for those who are interested in North Korean issues by providing information on the Internet.

IFES reportedly offers a 10-week program aimed at fostering economic opportunities on the Korean peninsula. A segment of the course, taught by a Hanzbiz executive, addresses IT industry cooperation between the two Koreas. IFES also offers a 16-week course (on-line) which covers the Internet and North Korea. In March 2001, a Christian charity in Seoul agreed with the North Korea Education Ministry to operate jointly an Information Technology University in Pyongyang. According to press reports, North Korea has promised to provide land, while the planning, building, and running of the institute—due to open in 2003—would be arranged by the two sides. Kim Jin-kyong, President of the Yanbian, China University of Science and Technology (which has a large ethnic Korean population) has been appointed director of the Institute.388 Russia Russia, after a hiatus of almost a decade due to a bilateral political rift, resumed high-level contacts with the DPRK beginning with a visit to Pyongyang in 2000 by President Putin. In 2001, Defense Minister Kim Il-Chol paid an official visit to his counterpart in Moscow. According to journalistic accounts, the North Korean delegation discussed military cooperation and also consulted with the Vice-Premier in charge of Russia's "military-industrial complex," Ilya Klebanov.

United States

Kim Chaek University of Technology is now in its second year of cooperative research with the Maxwell School at Syracuse University in New York State. According to the Maxwell School's *Information & Computing technology Newsletter*, the "two universities have agreed to conduct joint research in the area of integrated information technology." The Maxwell School expects to "host visiting researchers" from the DPRK.

The Chronicle of Higher Education reported in May 2003 that the North Korean scholars are working on "computer and network security," planning to publish papers, and construct "facilities identically configured." Overall, the DPRK continues to spare no effort to acquire state-of the art technologies and technical assistance in the form of "know how" from a variety of external sources. Whether the government leadership's ambitions in the information technologies field can be converted into a practical national economic strategy remains an open question. As one informed observer notes, "I think they [The DPRK leaders] see technology pay-offs for their military and for the party. And over the longer term, they hope to be able to find a niche of sorts in the global markets, where they might, for example, be writing software.

12

Scenario in Pakistan

BACKGROUND

Well-documented hacker activity in Pakistan and likely ties between the hacker community and Pakistani intelligence services suggest that Pakistan possesses a cyber attack capability. However, the evidence is lacking in the open source domain to determine the exact nature of the capability, and it is quite possible that the government of Pakistan has made only a minimal investment in its cyber warfare program. The evidence collected for this report indicates that the main target of this offensive capability is India—Islamabad's rival in the Kashmir dispute.

Pakistan's developed IT industry, well-educated computer programmers, and somewhat supportive government that is concerned with security in Kashmir and parity with India could provide an environment that may support a cyber warfare program. Since 1947, the year Pakistan gained independence from India, tensions between the two countries have alternately risen and abated, recently peaking with the 2001 Kashmiri conflict and the security stalemate stemming from the development of nuclear weapons. The resulting conventional arms conflicts and nuclear weapons build-up have greatly destabilized the region by creating an insoluble security dilemma.

The primary focus of conflict has been over Kashmir, the disputed area to the east of Pakistan and to the north of India. Both countries claim the territory. Armed conflict has resulted, with minimal progress towards a resolution of the territorial dispute. Achieving military objectives and nuclear parity with India are the prime national security concerns of a nominally democratically elected government in Islamabad that is highly influenced by the military.

In the Kashmir conflict in South Asia, cyberspace is becoming increasingly contested. Pakistan and India each control Internet sites that spread propaganda in line with their stance in the conflict. There has been an increase in the popularity of sites that feature propaganda for both sides, including chat rooms, polls, interactive message boards, photos, and other types of propagandist literature.

Messages such as "Indians, you people are losers... this is a piece of advice to Indians to free their hands from Kashmir and stop dreaming about it", posted after an attack on www.zeetv.com (a site owned by Indian media magnate Subhash Chandra), are typical of the political intent of the cyber war going on between Pakistan and India. Although Pakistan denies that it is funding these efforts, Islamabad does provide open diplomatic support for Kashmiri freedom fighters and there is rumored contact between the Pakistani intelligence services and Pakistani hacker groups.

The problem of a potent Pakistani cyber warfare program is two-fold. First, it could pose destabilizing effects in the South Asian region, with attacks on the civilian IT infrastructure and businesses, as well as cyber intrusions into highly-restricted nuclear and and other national security-related operations. The extent of damage caused to Indian websites, for example, has been considerable. In 2002, over 90% of Indian businesses with an online presence detected a security breach within the previous year and of those, 80% of businesses reported financial losses due to those computer security breaches.

Simple defacements and other trivial annoyances from cyber war could spill into the realm of truly detrimental losses. A second potential problem is that of a wider-scale cyber "arms-race" on the subcontinent. The Canadian Security Intelligence Service identifies the hacker war between Indian and Pakistani citizens over Kashmir as an example of a cyber war that has already left the theoretical realm. Pakistan's cyber warfare ability, left uncontained, could develop into a program that rivals in offensive capability the more developed cyber warfare pioneers such as China and Russia.

U.S. GOVERNMENT REPORTS AND FOREIGN OFFICIAL STATEMENTS

As of this writing, no official U.S. government reports have discussed Pakistani cyber attack capability. In 1998, an article published in the Pakistani *Defence Journal* by Syer M. Amir Husain proclaimed a genuine need for a Pakistani cyber warfare capability. The article followed the milw0rm raid on India's nuclear secrets stored at the Bhabha Atomic Research Centre (BARC) and a 1996 attack launched from the U.S. by three expatriate students, which penetrated a Pakistani military computer system. Husain cited these two incidents as revealing the necessity of an indigenous cyber warfare program.

The article detailed potential uses of such a program: industrial espionage, prevention of telecommunications disruptions, the potential launching of denial of service attacks, propaganda and defamation, intelligence/data mining, and support for Pakistan's armed forces. The article recommends creation of a team similar to the Computer Emergency Response Teams (CERT— ex. CERT from Carnegie Mellon) that operate in the U.S. and also details how to construct a cyber warfare program.

The Pakistani government is certainly concerned with national IT security and has legislation in place to arrest, process, and prosecute cyber criminals. In 2003, when Interior Minister Faisal Saleh Hayat was asked if the country's top secret documents stored in computers were safe from hackers, he responded "We have already made foolproof arrangements at our institutions that are of sensitive and strategic interest."

Indeed in 2002, a special unit of the Punjabi police force was designated as the "Electronic Crimes Unit" (ECU) with broad powers to fight cyber crime directed against Pakistani targets. Its goals include prevention, detection, recovery, and deterrence of cyber crimes and the authority to prosecute anyone who commits hacking "intentionally, without authorization to access any computer of any institution, department or agency of the government which is exclusively for the use of that outfit, and such conduct which may adversely affect the use/operation of such computer."

Cyber attacks on Pakistani government websites have resulted in efforts to improve network security. In October 2003 the Pakistani government formed a "Cyber Crime Wing" comprised of the representatives from the Ministries of the Interior and Telecommunications. This new center, along with the National Response Centre which formed a few months earlier, is responsible for securing the computer networks of government officials. The new ministry was formed as a response to the efforts of Indian hackers earlier in the year, when they delivered viruses (dubbed "Indian Snacks") in emails to Pakistani officials. The ability of the Pakistani government to effectively secure its own computer systems is a primary concern of the Ministry of Information. The Pakistani government has also formed a National Response Centre for Cyber Crime (NR3C). The stated mission of the NR3C is that it should serve as:

"the national focal point for gathering information on threats to critical infrastructures. It is the principal means of facilitating and coordinating the federal government's response to an incident, mitigating attacks, investigating threats, and monitoring reconstitution efforts. The NR3C includes investigators and analysts experienced in computer crimes and infrastructure protection. It is under process of being linked electronically to the rest of the federal and local governments. The NR3C provides law enforcement and intelligence information and reports to relevant federal, state, and local agencies. Before disseminating such information, the NR3C coordinates with the intelligence community to protect national security interests."

FOREIGN MILITARY AND INTELLIGENCE AGENCY RESEARCH

The Pakistani military has not released any official publications in English on cyber warfare as of this writing. There has been theoretical discussion on the possible advantages of pursuing a cyber warfare capability: Major Ozair Ahmed, in a 1998 *Defence Journal* article titled "Concept of Knowledge Warriors and Software

Soldiers," writes that military information operations are more than just:

> "battlefield intelligence or tactical attacks on the other side's radar or telephone network, but [it is] a powerful lever capable of altering high-level decision [sic] by the opponent. In knowledge warfare, each side will try to shape enemy actions by manipulating the flow of intelligence and information."

Major Ahmed argues that Pakistan "requires a different breed of computer specialists who will program, process and operate the military hardware and software behind the scene, these would be the nation's other asset Software Soldiers." Much of the article references a policy memo that the U.S. Joint Chiefs of Staff presented on May 6, 1993, enumerating various uses of electronic command and control capabilities (C2). However, this memo did not address cyber warfare in detail. Therefore, it is difficult to ascertain the weight of the article. Nonetheless, Ahmed does make a point about Pakistani recruitment of hackers that is consistent with the real life instances of recruitment of Pakistani hackers by its intelligence services.

> "There is definitely a requirement to have a select group of trained people to be used as software soldiers. These are usually software developers, programmers and mostly machine operators on pre-defined machinery. Such talent is picked up normally from the student community."

Although it may seem that the Pakistani military or intelligence services have considerable powers to wage cyber warfare, their skills may not be as powerful as perceived. In 1996, a group of three Pakistani teenagers operating out of the U.S. hacked into a former Pakistani Air Force chief's personal account and downloaded all of his files. The aforementioned milw0rm hacking incident brings into question just how capable and technologically adept Pakistan's Inter- Services Intelligence Directorate (ISID) is at protecting its own networks and, in turn, its offensive cyber warfare capabilities.

In 2002, the official Pakistani government website was taken down by a rudimentary denial of service attack from Indian hackers employing the Yaha Worm—exploiting an easily fixed software vulnerability.

In an incident of some embarrassment, officials in the Pakistani science and technology ministry said the information ministry lacked sufficient technical expertise to prevent attacks from determined hackers. A suggestion for better cyber security, ostensibly made because Pakistani website hosting services exhibited inadequate security measures, recommended finding a host for the website "through a third country where the rates are cheaper and the hosts have the responsibility for protecting the website."

In response to the threat posed by Pakistani cyber warfare units and freelance Pakistani hackers, India has implemented data security training and IT support for its army officers. The threat that "India could be severely battered if a concerted cyber-offensive is launched by an enemy country" (the enemy country being Pakistan) was sufficient to prompt the Indian Army to outline its IT security goals in the "IT Roadmap-2008."

An Indian army institute in Hyderabad was established in 2001 to teach officers the fundamentals of information warfare. India's response has grown more focused over the years, an indication of what the government likely perceives as Pakistan's growing cyber warfare capabilities. The Indian Defense Information Warfare Agency (DIWA) was formed in 2003 and will reportedly handle all "information warfare, including psychological operations, cyber war, electro-magnetic spectrum and soundwaves" activities for the Indian army. New Delhi's response suggests that Pakistan does indeed pose a threat against computer networks.

Pakistan's Interior Minister Faisal Saleh Hayat stated that the U.S. Federal Bureau of Investigation is training Pakistani Federal Investigation Agency (FIA) officials in various methods to combat cyber crime. According to the report, Minister Hayat said a "cyber threat was a serious issue since it originated from unknown places and its impact could not be assessed in the initial stage" and that "in the recent past nearly all the government sites had been under DOS [sic] attack."

PAKISTANI HACKERS

Although many of Pakistan's hackers operate independently and within self-contained units, there may nevertheless be ties between elements of this hacker community and Pakistani intelligence services. Within the population of Pakistan, there is a small and dedicated group of technically adept individuals that could be recruited into the intelligence services. Without a doubt, the hackers have political intentions behind their attacks. Some observers believe that several Pakistani hackers have been contacted by Pakistani intelligence services and some of these hackers now operate in service under the ISID's direction. India has repeatedly accused Pakistan of recruiting hackers for use by intelligence services.

"There is a new breed emerging, in the age-group of 14-35 years, which feels it can create equal havoc with a mouse and an AK-47," says [Indian] Deputy Commissioner of Police Himanshu Roy, head of Mumbai Police's cyber crimes unit.

It should be noted that our research did not locate any sources that definitively confirm Indian claims that Pakistani intelligence-supported hackers have carried out cyber attacks against India. Hacker activity in Pakistan has been well documented. A number of website defacements that these hackers performed have gained international notoriety. Computer hackers in Pakistan regularly attack computer systems and networks in India and have continually defaced Indian government websites. Pakistani groups such as Death to India, Kill India, and G-Force Pakistan look to spread information on how to hack into Indian websites and networks. Other named Pakistani hacker groups include "Nightman" and a group run by "Doctor Nuker."

G-Force Pakistan has been fingered in attacking the Indian Science Congress site, the National Research Centre, and the Indian National Information Technology Promotion, while Doctor Nuker has targeted the Indian Parliament and Nightman has attacked the Lal Bahadur Shastri National Academy of Administration. Indian intelligence officials say that these groups are run by adolescent Pakistanis and are not part of a military-backed cyber warfare scheme. However, they claim that these adolescents have begun to be recruited by Pakistani intelligence officials to wage cyber war against Indian targets.

India has continually asserted that the ISID has been in the past, and is currently in the business of recruiting skilled hackers to wage cyber warfare. According to Indian intelligence officials, one Pakistani hacker, the so-called Doctor Nuker, was identified by Pakistani intelligence as having superior hacking skills and directed to attack critical Indian government servers.

Ravi Prasad maintains that Indian intelligence should not dismiss the possibility of being attacked by cyber foes, especially Islamic militant groups operating out of Pakistan. India's security establishment has also ignored cyber warfare capabilities possessed by Islamic militant organizations. The Rand Corporation recently warned: "Osama bin Laden's Egyptian followers can immediately cripple the information infrastructures of Russia and India."

Clark Staten, Executive Director, Emergency Response and Research Institute, Chicago, warned that Pakistani terrorist organizations had developed offensive capabilities in cyber warfare. Pakistani officials may not be well versed in IT protection, but Pakistanit hacking exploits have certainly had effects on U.S. webpages. Especially evident has been the Islamic fundamentalist rhetoric voiced since 9/11 which has frequently appeared in the content of website defacements.

The notorious GForce Pakistan hackers attacked several Defense Test and Evaluation Processional Institute website homepages, defacing them with pictures and text messages with terrorist and Islamic themes. The vandalized sites included <http://www.dtepi.mil>, <http://enduringfreedom.dtepi.mil>, <http://nasa.dtepi.mil>, and others; all sites that were supposedly being served by KCnet, a U.S. ISP based in Kansas City. The GForce message also included threats to deface 1,500 more U.S., British, and Indian websites.

In 2000, more than 40 Indian sites had been attacked by Pakistani hackers. That number has increased in the past few years, due to increased availability of open source hacking knowledge, more exploits for software, and presumably because more attention has been paid to the development of cyber warfare capability. According to Attrition.org, a top computer security organization, 72 top-level domain names (TLDs) in India were hacked in 2000, accounting for a 1700% escalation of cyber warfare activities between Pakistan and India compared to a year before. In January 2003, an 18-year-old Indian "ethical hacker" and noted cyber security expert Ankit Fadia stated that 40-50 Indian websites, including sensitive government and corporate sites, are hacked by Pakistani cyber criminals every month.

Fadia has served as a cyber security consultant for numerous intelligence agencies, defense departments, and government and private organizations. He has also aided Indian law enforcement in tracking Pakistani "hacktivists," often anti-Indian. Fadia underscored the need for cyber security awareness and training in India, mainly as a response to the Pakistani development of cyber warfare techniques and strategies.

According to the Internet security firm mi2g, individual hacker groups are joining together to launch cyber attacks against the U.S., Israel, and India. The ongoing conflict in the Kashmir region in the Indian subcontinent has been reflected in the tension online. The Unix Security Guards and the World's Fantabulous Hackers were responsible for 111 cyber attacks on sites located in India. D.K. Matai, mi2g's chairman and CEO said: "The most important lesson learnt from these events is the coming together of pro-Islamic groups to simultaneously participate in joint digital attacks on U.S./UK, Israeli and Indian targets.

Historically, the U.S. has been allied with Pakistan. It seems that recent political and cyberspace events are both pointing towards a closer alignment of interests in the near future between the U.S., India and Israel."

INFORMATION TECHNOLOGY INVESTMENT

The IT industry of Pakistan has enjoyed the support of the government since the late 1990s. Pakistani IT investment seeks to develop current state-of-the-art infrastructure. The "legacy systems" of older communication networks are currently being upgraded. Information technology training is broadly available in colleges and universities. Islamabad estimates that there are twenty-one million computer literate Pakistanis. E-government initiatives are being developed in addition to changes in the legal and regulatory regimes. These four factors create an environment that may support a cyber attack capability.

The Pakistani government has initiated significant efforts to improve its economic conditions by investing in information technologies. Pakistan launched its first communications satellite, PAKSAT-1, in 2003. According to an August 2002 report card on IT investment progress by the IT division of the Pakistani Ministry of Science and Technology, significant progress has been registered. This included the expansion of the availability of Internet bandwidth to a larger portion of the population and the development of a "world class infrastructure" within 24 months of initial deployment of IT policy. The IT division plans to launch a public key infrastructure program to support electronic commerce. In addition, a payment gateway and electronic clearinghouse initiatives are being developed.

A lower-level threat that should not be minimized is the possibility that Pakistani software companies have embedded code to make the software vulnerable to attack. As countries such as the United States, Britain, and India outsource their programming of software to countries such as Pakistan, Philippines and Russia, the risk of rogue programmers using their access to commit acts of cyber terrorism rises. The possibility of abuse by hackers, organized crime agents, and cyber terrorists in countries not necessarily allied with the United States is great, and grows as more and more programming is outsourced to these countries for economic reasons.

CONCLUSION

Pakistan's efforts appear to be focused on countering India's cyber warfare capability (the viceversa is also true). However, the U.S. is still at risk of cyber attack from hackers that reside there. Pakistan has served as our ally against al-Qaeda in the current war on terrorism, and has at least served nominally as our ally in the past. However, the unstable situation on the sub-continent and the anti-U.S. sentiments harbored by some Pakistani citizens, combined with the mixed loyalties of elements within the ISID, increase the possibility that a cyber attack against the U.S. will come from Pakistan. Following 9/11, the hacker group GForce Pakistan attacked several U.S. .mil websites and defaced them.

Pakistan poses a threat to cyberspace with its growing army of young talented hackers. Regardless of state backing, these hackers have shown a penchant to involve themselves in realworld situations such as the Kashmir conflict and countering anti-Islamic sentiments in the West following 9/11. With the possible backing of the state, taking into account the reported ISID contact with Pakistani hackers, it would seem Pakistan may be investigating the possibility of building a more potent cyber warfare program capable of disrupting Indian computer networks. The immediate threat is to India's burgeoning IT industry and to the supervisory control or data acquisition computer programs that control sensitive, national security-related industries, such as nuclear installations.

13

Scenario in Russia

Information warfare is a way of resolving a conflict between opposing sides. The goal is for one side to gain and hold an information advantage over the other. This is achieved by exerting a specific information/psychological and *information/technical influence on a nation's decision-making system, on the nation's populous* [sic] *and on its* information resource structures, as well as by defeating the enemy's control system and his information resource structures with the help of additional means, such as nuclear assets, weapons and electronic assets.

Russian military officer in conversation with Lieutenant Colonel (ret.) Timothy L. Thomas

"Russian Views on Information-based Warfare," *Airpower Journal*, 1996

The circumstance that, as specialists believe, over half of the world population will be living in cities in the first third of the 21st century and can especially suffer in case of wars began to play a role of no small importance here. Therefore it is believed that to win victory with minimum victims among the civilian population and minimum property damage, it will be necessary to employ very precise lethal and nonlethal kinds of weapons in order to exert sufficient pressure on the opposing country's leadership directly or through the population masses of cities. Electronic weapons in particular can prove to be specifically such a means.

Major M. Boytsov

"Russia Information War," *In Foreign Navies*, February 6, 1996, FBIS-UMA-96-026-S

BACKGROUND

Russia's military services, working with experts in the IT sector and academic community, have developed a robust cyber warfare doctrine.435 "Information weaponry," weapons based on programming code, receives paramount attention in official cyber warfare doctrine. The authors of Russia's cyber warfare doctrine have published discussions and debates concerning their official policy. It is likely that Moscow will continue to scout U.S. military and private sector networks and websites to obtain information about configuration of communications nodes.

However, analysis of open source materials is inadequate to predict whether a Russian cyber warfare program would target U.S. networks, especially taking into account closer political and economic ties between the two nations in recent years.

The collapse of the Soviet Union in 1991 led to economic turmoil and a significant "brain drain" affecting various Russian industries and academic circles. Despite the wide-scale turmoil, the Federal Security Service (FSB), the Federal Agency for Government Communications and Information (FAPSI), and the high technology sector in Russia should not be taken lightly as regards potential to underwrite and develop a cyber warfare program. Russian intelligence services have a history of employing hackers against the United States. In 1985 the KGB hired Markus Hess, an East German hacker, to attack U.S. defense agencies in the infamous case of the "Cuckoo's Egg." Both FAPSI and the FSB, KGB successor organs, are believed to have potent information-gathering programs, which has led to increased suspicions over possible attempts at espionage.

The U.S. Department of Defense (DoD) remains wary of the threat posed by Russian hackers. These hackers reportedly took two million DoD computers offline in what the Pentagon suspected to have been a Russian electronic espionage campaign (then dubbed 'Operation Moonlight Maze'). However, there have also been cases of analysts over-estimating Russian cyber-capabilities. In February of 1998, break-ins into U.S. Department of Defense networks and the subsequent investigation (dubbed Solar Sunrise) were mistakenly attributed to Russian secret services. In actuality, the attacks were perpetrated by two Northern California teenagers under the direction of a handler in Israel.

The fact that FBI agents and then deputy Secretary of Defense John Hamre suspected that Russian secret services were behind the attacks, however mistaken, was understandable based on Moscow's past behavior and other evidence. Currently, the three most significant struggles faced by the new Russian government are development of a cohesive democratic government, restructuring of a collapsed economy into a viable free-market alternative, and quelling of an open rebellion by Chechen rebels. Renewed government attention to rebuilding aging infrastructure has led to an increase in economic confidence and a subsequent upswing in the Russian economy. In terms of this cyber warfare country assessment, the Chechen conflict is the most important because it has forced the Russian intelligence services to wage cyber war on the technologically adept Chechens.

Oleg Gordievsky, the former London KGB section head, claimed at the 1998 Global Cybercrime Conference that "there are organized groups of hackers tied to the FSB and pro-Chechen sites have been hacked into by such groups... one man I know, who was caught committing a cybercrime, was given the choice of either prison or cooperation with the FSB and he went along." At the conference in 1998, Gordievsky said that not only did his agents perform information operations; they also participated in industrial espionage. Gordievsky claimed that 12 of his 29 agents were involved in conducting intelligence on the attitudes of banks towards possible investment in Russian-owned industries. Sergei Pokrovsky, the editor of the Russian hacker magazine Khaker confirmed that the FSB employs hackers for both foreign and domestic espionage.

There are several indicators suggesting an active Russian cyber warfare capability at present. For example, active Russian foreign intelligence services possessing a high-level of technical expertise and the actions of government-sponsored hackers against the Chechens are suggestive; this evidence, in addition to the development of relevant doctrinal concepts, directly confirms research on cyber warfare.

Here, as was the case in the China country study, one must be careful to discern what constitutes disinformation and what parts of cyber warfare doctrine have actually been implemented. Extrapolating from the meager open source data is intriguing but risky. The Russian press is quick to point out that American fears of an offensive cyber attack from Russia are largely unfounded. Such fears should not be so easily allayed. As evidenced by the Chechen conflict, Russian secret services under sponsorship of the government will not hesitate to use cyber warfare to further their agenda and to protect what they deem to be matters of national security.

U.S. GOVERNMENT REPORTS AND FOREIGN OFFICIAL STATEMENTS

Operating under government control, the Academy of Sciences in Moscow has been linked to unsanctioned intrusions into U.S. private sector IT networks. Although the military and intelligence services have faced severe budget cutbacks in the past few years and Russia itself is in the midst of an arduous economic restructuring, its information operations and cyber warfare research capabilities are still significant and potentially pose a considerable threat to worldwide computer security.

Existing open source literature and published statements by intelligence experts point to Russia as a nation-state whose abilities in cyber warfare are, next to the United States, the most developed among technically capable countries. According to official U.S. analyses, Russia is an example of a country heavily involved with developing its own cyber warfare capability. Of the 15 criteria enumerated in a Defense Science Board report on technical prowess, Russia was listed as having a significant capability in seven categories and a good capability in four. This performance continues, even in the face of widespread economic difficulties.

In a summary of cyber warfare capabilities by *Jane's Intelligence Review*, Russia was reported to have a majority of the listed strengths in the areas of electronic attack and electronic protection. Testimony from both Lawrence Gershwin, top intelligence and science officer at the National Intelligence Council and George Tenet, then Director of Central Intelligence (DCI), coupled with official CIA analysis on cyber warfare, have raised the prospect of an extensive Russian cyber warfare program. Richard Clarke, former White House senior advisor on cyber security, has also testified to the existence of Russian cyber warfare capabilities. The NSA has also fingered Moscow as having an "aggressive" cyber warfare program. U.S. intelligence officials believe that Moscow has been sponsoring cyber warfare research.

U.S. government analysts also believe that the Russian military is the spearhead of cyber warfare program development and that Russian intelligence services are involved with cyber warfare research and usage. In 2000, CIA analyst John Serabian cited unnamed Russian sources as revealing a burgeoning cyber warfare research program operating within the Russian Federation. Following the release of this CIA report, several newspapers in Russia printed vehement denouncements of American claims that these cyber warfare programs would be used for offensive purposes. Following attacks on U.S. e-commerce sites, the CIA and Pentagon both reported to the press that they were aware of the ongoing development of cyber warfare programs in Russia, insinuating that Russian hackers had something to do with the attacks in question. In response, Russian journalists, citing military sources, were quick to point out that there was absolutely no evidence to link Russian cyber warfare with these attacks and that U.S. intelligence services, by having an "external computer threat" to direct actions at, would be able to make their investigative positions extremely "advantageous."

In Moscow, information security and defensive cyber warfare development matters have been discussed as early as 1996 in the Duma Subcommittee for Information Security, when there was some suspicion that recently purchased telecommunications devices from the United States were implanted with devices that could cause irreparable damage to Russian telecommunications systems when triggered by remote device. In response, information security in Russia became an urgent matter, with efforts to secure cyber space a top priority.

In 1999, an administration in charge of computer and information security was set up in the FSB. Additional new faculty with expertise in the areas of computer and information security were hired for the FSB academy.

Russia's official cyber warfare doctrine appears to be a product of fear of U.S. superiority in the cyber field. Former Russian Federation Secretary of the Security Council (Minister of Defense), Sergey Ivanov said that the Russian government was in support of the development of "international law regimes for preventing the use of information technologies for purposes incompatible with missions of ensuring international stability and security." The possession of an advanced IT capability by the U.S. military and intelligence services apparently raises Moscow's fear of losing an all-out cyber war between the two nations. Ivanov said that "in our view, there is a danger of the outbreak of 'cyberwars' using worldwide computer networks and other lines of communication, which demands that preventive steps be taken."

He further stated that these technological breakthroughs could lead to an "arms race," one that Russia could compete in but could not possibly win. In 2001, General Vladislav Sherstyuk, the RF Security Council deputy secretary, said that the appearance of a new information area of confrontation is capable of provoking the beginning of the next spiral of arms race. The development of strikecapable military computer viruses, in contrast to strategic nuclear missiles, requires no special expertise beyond what is available in the general civilian realm.

As early as the mid-70's (some experts place these events around the mid-80's), the Russian military had begun researching the next revolution in military affairs (RMA). According to Mary Fitzgerald of the Hudson Institute, Marshal Ogarkov, then Chief of the Russian General Staff, first used the phrase "revolution in military affairs" in publication, referring to the usage of electronic command and control in military units. Since then, Russian military theorists have evaluated the "impact of computer viruses, [and] other types of information weapons, logic bombs, special microbes, and micro-chipping."

The Russian technology sector and academic community, in conjunction with the Russian military, have developed cyber warfare doctrine beyond what any other country, save the U.S., possesses. The Russians recognize that information warfare requires the simultaneous conduct of offensive and defensive measures in order for cyber warfare to be successful. According to a prominent Russian expert, the fact that cyber warfare provides a new means to affect the military and civilian population of a target changes its principles, tactics and permissible conditions from that of conventional warfare.

Software weapons receive great attention in the Russian cyber warfare doctrine. Development and use of such weapons requires long-term planning, technical expertise, and intelligence on targets, all of which Russian secret services such as FAPSI and the FSB possess. The list of weapons includes the viruses (the best of which break down security and self-propagate), reprogramming memory chips (causing loss of long-term stored data), Trojan horses, rewriting software programs through remote-access tampering, and destruction of critical infrastructure from remote areas.

FOREIGN MILITARY AND INTELLIGENCE AGENCY RESEARCH

During the investigatory phase of Operation Moonlight Maze, Michael Vatis, then head of the FBI's National Infrastructure Protection Center (NIPC), attributed hacking and data theft in Pentagon networks to Russia. Vatis said that the hackers had stolen "unclassified but stillsensitive information about essentially defense/technical research matters," and that the intrusions had occurred in "Defense Department, other federal government agencies, and privatesector computer networks."

During Moonlight Maze, U.S. Senator Robert Bennett argued that the threat from this area was very real and even supposed that the three-year long attack on government networks also stretched into hacking of networks in the private sector. Senator Bennett believes that the unsanctioned intrusion was perpetrated by people physically located at the Russian Academy of Sciences.463 The FBI attempted to determine whether the Academy of Sciences was responsible for the attacks; trace-backs and initial collection of forensic evidence revealed compelling details that could be inferred as actions attributable to an active Russian information operations program. The 1998 intrusions were traced back to seven dial-up connections in Russia. With respect to two attacks in July 1998, intrusions were detected from Lab 1313, a then unknown group that was using an Internet connection from the Russian Academy of Sciences.

These two attacks attempted to steal information from Meganet Corp., a private company which develops cryptographic software. This was a significant detail because most cryptographic software is not available for export. During the investigation of Moonlight Maze, analysts found that there were many instances in which technical defense research data was downloaded and transferred back to Russia.

In a possibly related incident that occurred in February of 1999, a Hewlett Packard printer at the Navy's Space and Naval Warfare Systems Command Center (Spawar) in San Diego was programmed to send copies of printed documents to a remote location in Russia. Spawar provides electronic security for the Marine Corps and other government federal agencies. In conjunction with its responsibilities for the cyber security of various government agencies, Spawar also provides the Navy with intelligence codes. Oleg Kalugin, a former head of Soviet counterintelligence now resident in Maryland, has reported that such facilities were prime targets for Russian intelligence.465 Kalugin notes that FAPSI, which specializes in electronic methods of espionage, would use the Internet to spy on assets in the United States. The technical data that is reported to have been stolen is in line with what FAPSI would be looking for. "That's what they're good at," Kalugin said. "Russia is quite good at producing technology but can't afford to finance the research."

Moscow's information security defenses to counteract cyber warfare have also been a focus of the vast military-industrial complex that exists in Russia. According to official but unconfirmed information, the government of the Russian Federation sent out a directive in March of 2000, ordering Russian enterprises to provide new information security measures as well as preparatory operational security measures, usage of American operating systems (UNIX and Microsoft Windows) by the Russian military.

However, there are Russian technology experts who decry this government intervention into IT security saying that it will stifle the ability of the technology sector to develop adequate tools to counteract cyber attacks. Maksim Otstanov, head of the Laboratory of Civilian and Financial Cryptology of the Institute of Commercial Engineering, said that "government intervention in present-day Russia, unfortunately, most often leads to the fact that operators of telecommunications services are 'weighted down' with an unthinkable number of licensing conditions, which leads to their consolidation and erosion of the smaller segments of the market."

Secret service officials in Moscow are also growing increasingly concerned about the low level of funding that FAPSI's 'Electronic Russia' (Russia's national IT security program) is receiving and going to receive in the future. An article released in late 2002 included FAPSI opinions on the current state and the future of Russian national IT security:

The program Electronic Russia allocated about 2.5 percent of the total funding of the program for measures related to developing information and data protection systems in 2002; and about 0.66 percent in 2003. In the opinion of FAPSI [Federal Agency for Government Communications and Information] representatives, this money is not enough either to analyze the degree of protection of the program, or to develop means of information protection. The Agency believes that the funding of this work should be 20 percent, as in similar programs in foreign countries.

Russian Involvement in the Chechen Cyber War

An analysis of the information war between the Chechens and the Russian military during the mid-1990s to the year 2000 shows that the Russian military and intelligence services possess cyber warfare capabilities. In the first conflict (1994-1996), the Chechens originally had the upper hand in the public relations war because the Russian government denied the press access to many of its own military actions, allowing the Chechens to spin events through their own media outlets. The Chechens, on the other hand, welcomed the presence of the press as a way of getting out their message and favorably shading their coverage.

By the start of the second conflict (1997-2001) however, the Russian government saw the need to control the information coming out of Chechnya.

Moscow decided to control both the amount and type of information being released. Both groups in the conflict used news websites to portray their accounts of events. Along with Chechen-controlled websites such as kavkaz.org, there were also sites that were run by allies outside of Russia, such as qoqaz.net.my based in Malaysia.

This network of sites allowed allied third parties to access information such as pictures and statistics and disseminate the information on the web. What did each side do with an electronic broadcast capability?

Moscow used officially sanctioned state-controlled radio and television broadcasts to show its side of events. The Russians also used websites to spread their message, including infocentre.ru that prescribed how reporters should be reporting news about the conflict. The Russians also published a book version of events and their history of the conflict.

On the other side, the Chechens had a different response to cyber warfare. On their site, www.qoqaz.net, it was possible to download videos of attacks on Russians, view photos of Chechens in action and of Russian prisoners of war, find news items, read profiles of Chechen commanders, and read interviews with various Chechen leaders and fighters.

In case this site was down, alternate sites were listed: www.qoqaz.net.my, www.qoqaz.com, and www.qoqaz.de. The evidence from these two conflicts shows that as cyber warfare and the IT communications revolution develop, it becomes increasingly difficult to control the kinds of information that becomes publicly available, which, counter intuitively, warrants the development of more cyber warfare capability.

In 2002, Chechen rebels claimed that two of their websites, kavkaz.org and chechenpress.com, crashed under hack attacks by the Russian FSB security service. The website crashes were reportedly timed to occur concurrently or shortly after Russian

Special Forces troops stormed the Moscow Theater in which the rebels had taken hostages. "On October 26 ... our Web Site kavkaz.org was attacked by a group of hackers," said a spokesman for the Chechen rebel site run by Movladi Udugov. Following the attack on the site, which is based in the United States, Udugov said that he was "amazed Russia's special services can operate so freely on U.S. territory."

The attacks on one site, chechenpress.com, fell under the category of brute-force denial of service (DoS) attacks, while on the other site, kavkaz.org, the attacks appeared much more sophisticated. According to Chechen sources, the website was hijacked by hackers from the FSB.

The FSB hackers reportedly accomplished this by changing the domain registration of the site and then eliminating the data for the site from the hosting server. Upon learning of these attacks, the rebels moved the information on the sites to kavkazcenter.com. However, that site was attacked just a week later, also apparently the work of FSB hackers.

Russian Cyber Warfare Doctrine Compared

Moscow's cyber warfare does have similarities with its Chinese counterpart and other cyber warfare programs. A common aspect for almost all cyber warfare programs is that the ultimate goal of an offensive doctrine is the planning of and subsequent execution of an effective cyber "first-strike" against the enemy. This "digital pearl harbor" (discussed theoretically) is an ideal cyber attack strike when it is able to defeat the enemy without the attacker actually having to resort to physical battle. According to Professor Major General Vladimir Belous, "it can be predicted that the battlefield of the future will begin to shift more and more into the area of intellectual effect. An aggressor country is capable of developing, and under certain conditions executing, a scenario of information war against another state in an attempt to demolish it from within. In that way it is possible to force the enemy to surrender without using traditional kinds of weapons."

Russian cyber warfare doctrine also addresses the optimum time to strike. Prior to an "information strike", all targets should be identified (including enemy information systems), enemy access to external information should be denied, credit and monetary circulation should be disrupted, and the populace should be subjected to a massive psychological operation— including disinformation and propaganda.

This would be accomplished by careful pre-strike planning and long-term investments in reconnaissance and covert penetration into enemy systems.

> "Computer networks and databases are penetrated in advance before the beginning of combat operations by agent and other methods, and microorganism cultures are introduced that eat away electronic components. The employment of information weapons in the concluding phase of a major regional conflict is similar to their use in peacekeeping operations. Estimates have shown that the use of information weapons must be constantly accompanied by the limited use or threat of use of conventional weapons, especially high-precision weapons."

Officially, the Russian government has a globally non-interventionist stance regarding the application of cyber warfare. Former Minister of Defense Ivanov spoke on the new military doctrine of the Russian Federation in 2001. One of the questions asked of him was whether there had been any measures undertaken to create a capability to wage cyber wars using computer networks and other types of communication.

The response was somewhat circular and evasive with the first part of it stating that the "fundamental stance of Russia is to observe the principles of non-application of force, non-intervention in internal affairs, respect for the human rights and freedoms, and not permitting achievements in the sphere of information sciences and telecommunications to be used for purposes that are in contravention of the UN Charter."

A thinly veiled barb at the "overwhelmingly" advanced state of U.S. cyber warfare capabilities, Ivanov's statements were made in response to the "existence of the Anglo-American Echelon global spying system."

When asked about the Echelon program, the National Security Agency's (NSA) SIGINT gathering system, Ivanov said that "FAPSI, the Ministry of Defense, the FSB of Russia, the State Technical Commission of Russia, and other federal executive authorities are taking suitable steps aimed at raising the level of protection for information being transmitted."

This statement provides evidence that Russia has at least some measure of a defensive cyber warfare capability. However, Russian intelligence and security services and the Russian government deny accusations of official involvement as regards an offensive capability.

Boris Labusov, spokesman for Russia's SVR (Foreign Intelligence Service), asked, "Do you think Russian special services are so stupid as to engage in such activities directly from Moscow? For decades, everybody has written about how clever the KGB and Soviet intelligence are. Why should one think we suddenly became less clever enough not to allow themselves to be traced?" According to Russian media analysis, fears of Russian hackers may have been the factor that spurred funding for NIPC in 1999, as the Clinton administration sought to develop programs for the defense of computer networks.

CONCLUSION

Much of the initial Russian research and development in cyber warfare has been conducted in response to what the Russian government considers an aggressive development of a U.S. information warfare program. Although relations between Washington and Moscow have improved since the end of the Cold War, beneath the new peaceful rhetoric some tensions remain. Russian actions against the Chechens have drawn increasing ire from the international community and recent refusals to back the U.S. military action in Iraq signal that the relationship between the two countries remains fundamentally wary.

If the recent revelation of Robert Hanssen as the most damaging mole in U.S. history is any indication, Russia's active secret services still have considerable resources and energy to spend on espionage in the United States. This, coupled with an advanced cyber warfare doctrine, documented technical expertise, and dedicated intelligence services (as discussed above), makes Russia a considerable cyber-threat to U.S. computer systems. As described in this study, Moscow has demonstrated a willingness to use cyber warfare against perceived threats, as evidenced by the actions of the FSB against Chechen rebel websites in the ongoing conflict.

Although it is unlikely Russia would launch a pre-emptive cyber strike on the U.S. absent a state of war, it is highly likely that Russian intelligence services will continue to scout U.S. military and private sector sites in order to gain information. Add to this the fact that intelligence gathering from a remote location is very hard to trace and also fairly inexpensive, cyber warfare represents a viable solution to the Russian government's cost-cutting in the areas of military and intelligence services.

- Means of effect on components of electronic equipment and its power supply.
- Temporary or irreversible disabling of individual components of electronic systems.
- Means of power electronic suppression: ultrapowerful microwave generators (gyrotrons, reflex triodes, relativistic magnetrons, turbutrons); Explosive magnetic generators; Explosive magnetohydrodynamic generators. Means of power effect through an electrical network.
- Software for disabling equipment (hard drive head resonance, monitor burnout and so on).
- Software for erasing rewritable memory.
- Software for affecting continuous power sources and so on.
- Means of disabling electrical networks.
- Means of effect on programming resource of electronic control modules
- Disabling or changing the algorithm of functioning of control system software by using special software.
- Means of penetrating information security systems. Means of penetrating enemy information networks. Means of concealing information collection sources. Means of

disabling all or specific software of an information system, possibly at a strictly given point in time or with the onset of a certain event in the system.

- Means of covertly partially changing the algorithm of functioning of the software. Means of collecting data circulating in the enemy information system. Means of delivery and introduction of specific algorithms to a specific place of an information system. Means of effect on facility security systems.
- Means of effect on programming resource of electronic control modules.
- Stopping or disorganizing the functioning of data exchange subsystems by an effect on the signal propagation medium and on the algorithms of functioning.
- EW assets, especially ground-based and airborne (helicopter and UAV) communications jammers (possibly with elements of artificial intelligence.) Droppable expendable jammers.
- Means of effect on data transfer protocols of communications and data transfer systems. Means of effect on addressing and routing algorithms. Means of intercepting and disrupting the passage of information in its technical transfer channels. Means of provoking a system overload by false requests for establishing contact.

The Russian military seeks to use the Federal Agency for Government Communications and Information (FAPSI much like the National Security Agency or NSA) to combat unsanctioned access to government and military materials.

The Russian military and FAPSI have also been looking into using viruses as a method of warfare, especially as a force multiplier unleashed at the start of the conflict. A primary goal of the Russian intelligence agencies is to gain superiority in "information accumulation, processing and adaptation..., and especially in reconnaissance and electronic warfare systems."

The Russians also seek to achieve significant capabilities in disrupting the enemy's information support system.

All of these things are used in attempting to control the actions of the enemy; they amount to the general Russian view of information warfare. Priority problems for the Russian military that they are attempting to tackle include: "creating a telecommunications environment and its lash-up with nationwide communications and data-transmission systems; developing and incorporating base problem-oriented systems; equipping the armed forces staffs and organizations quickly with the basics of information technology and personal computers, advanced communications and telecommunications gear, and improved organizational techniques to adopt a "paperless" information technology; improving tools and methods for developing software and the use of computer assisted technologies; assuring technical, information, linguistic, and program compatibility; improving the system of training, retraining, and skill enhancement of military specialists; and creating standardized, advanced means of information technology.

14

Local Networks

BACKGROUND

The past half-decade has witnessed several malicious Distributed Denial of Service (DDoS) virus attacks which—despite the widespread use of defensive firewalls—have either prevented authorized access to a system resource or delayed system operations. The Melissa Macro Virus demonstrated that attackers can affect one's computer from the Internet even if a fire wall is in place. First observed in March 1999, Melissa was a malicious Trojan that infected over 100,000 hosts in four days. It started with executable software.

The Love Bug virus reportedly crippled millions of computers world wide in 2000 by clogging the e-mail systems of many businesses with unwanted messages. Originating in the Philippines, it first emerged in Asia and "spread to Europe and the United States overnight." According to press reports, the virus not only destroyed data on infected machines but attempted to activate another program from a Philippine website that stole passwords from victims' computers.

In June 2001, a computer security company identified a vulnerability in a web server program that could lead to a buffer overflow exploit. In July 2001 the Code Red Worm was released, targeting the White House. It has been estimated that over 200,000 computers participated in the attack. Code Red worms search for systems running Microsoft Internet Information Server (IIS) that have not patched the unchecked buffer vulnerability in idq.dll or removed the ISAPI script mappings. The worm exploited the vulnerability to inject itself.

Although these exploits proved to be annoyances, albeit costly ones, they did not cause irreparable systemic damage or adversely affect U.S. national security. Attacking unencrypted U.S. defense networks (DoD logistics, for example), on the other hand, could compromise significant military logistics operations or force costly reconfigurations or "work arounds" with potential security implications.

The foregoing examples demonstrate that firewalls are insufficient protection and are often thwarted by the actions of internal users (who unwittingly allow malicious code to enter a system or network) In addition, attackers often use scanners to search for open shares and services on a system; such scanners often use packet crafting and source address spoofing to circumvent firewalls.

Worms Coupled with a Denial of Service Payload

The SQL Slammer worm, which first appeared in January 2003, exploited a vulnerability in the Resolution Service of SQL Server 2000 and Microsoft Desktop Engine 2000. The vulnerability allows for the execution of arbitrary code on the SQL Server computer due to a stack buffer overflow.

The worm is a self-propagating code, i.e., if a packet is sent to a vulnerable machine the victim machine will become infected and also begin to scan for new hosts. A recent research paper by a South African computer security firm described in detail a hypothetical attack combining malicious computer code joined with a destructive payload. The essence of the scenario is that a publicly available search engine, a few selected e-mail addresses, and an off the shelf computer code could cripple an entire internal network. This scenario was adumbrated in a 2001 analysis that pointed out that a worm similar to Code Red "could do much more serious damage with only minor design modifications [to include a destructive payload]...If maximum destruction is a hostile adversary's goal, worms are a cost effective way to significantly disrupt the Unites States' national information infrastructure."

Creating a worm to target a specific country

SensePost, a South African computer security firm, has identified several vulnerabilities to a potential worm that permitted a full host compromise. Among the vulnerabilities are:

Microsoft IIS (5) Unicode/ 2x decode

Microsoft IIS (4) MSADC

Microsoft IIS (5) printer extensions

Microsoft IIS (5) WebDAV

Microsoft SQL with blank SA configured

Blank local administrator passwords on Microsoft Windows hosts.

According to SensePost, a worm based on the above-mentioned vulnerabilities, combined with a Denial of Service payload, could completely disable a large internal network. In delivering the payload, the key is to find e-mail addresses to target. The author wrote scripts that use Google to search for public references to e-mail addresses on the WWW. The scripts allow the author to search for e-mails from a given country and, in particular, seek individuals employed by telecommunications and financial firms, energy utilities, government departments, armed services, or hospitals in that country. According to the SensePost document, running the scripts demonstrates that there are many email addresses available, especially on bulletin boards. If a malicious user could infect one government node with a worm (even the desktop computer of a low ranking official), he could infect the government system as well.

PHYSICAL INFRASTRUCTURE ATTACKS: THE VULNERABILITIES OF SUPERVISORY CONTROL AND DATA ACQUISITION SYSTEMS (SCADA)

"Process control" information systems associated with critical infrastructures (such as banking, electricity, water, oil and gas) are considered likely targets for cyber attackers. Supervisory Control and Data Acquisition systems rely on embedded "process control" programs. Individual SCADA systems may be unique, but the knowledge associated with Distributed Control Systems (DCS) and Programmable Logic Controllers (PLC) are accessible to most computer programmers. Over the past decade, an evolution in data communications and process control has introduced potential systemic vulnerabilities.

The data connections from DCS and PLC systems to the plant network are vital to production, yet can be an invitation to compromise if "problems on the business network can be passed on to the process network" through a utility's Ethernet and TCP/IP networking.

According to some experts, hackers are learning about PLC's and DCS's. Recently, an individual hacked into a PLC in a semiconductor manufacturing plant, shutting down a reverse osmosis system. Reportedly, several brands of controllers can be compromised by tools in the "average teenage script kiddy tool kit."

SCADA Systems

Supervisory control and data acquisition (SCADA) programs are used in control of administrative systems from nuclear power plants to traffic control systems to gas pipelines. What is most troubling about SCADA is its user-friendliness and its potency in total control of most applications. While most SCADA operators are probably not trained IT professionals, the ease of use and the GUI interfaces that SCADA employs make it extremely easy to access and to use.

The main exploits of SCADA systems will come from worms and viruses that make their way into the system and Trojan horses which offer remote access to SCADA servers. Another exploit comes from a terrorist-hacker being physically at the terminal, versed in the operation of the SCADA system from using online user manuals. The plethora of information about SCADA packages includes free .pdf documentation of user interfaces, user logon creations, alarm systems, etc as well as online tutorials, paid training sessions at the company sites, and other methods of learning the ins-and-outs of SCADA software and hardware packages.

APPENDIX B: TERMINOLOGY ISSUES

"Cyber" refers to the virtual world in which attacks take place, although the wall between the virtual world and the so-called real world is rapidly crumbling. Actions in the virtual world (sending e-mail, electronic commerce in the retail or in business-to-business, and electronic controls and software that control physical devices such as train switches, air-traffic control devices, and waterway regulation) have physical impacts on the real world. The "warfare" part of the term is derived from the various characteristics of cyber warfare that resemble conventional warfare. War is usually defined as the organized use of violent force by groups to forward a political goal. This academically sanitized definition is sometimes qualified by the requirements that combat and actual deaths need be involved to define some phenomenon as warfare, but here the term warfare is used as an illustrative analogy. Cyber warfare involves units organized along nation-state boundaries, in offensive and defensive operations.

Differences in Terminology

National security experts, military analysts, academia, and terrorism researchers have each come up with terms describing the cyber attack phenomena. Depending upon the stated mission or the scope of each group, the terms serve to clarify the exact nature of the phenomena they are attempting to describe. Although in the short term these terms clarify, the plethora of terminology used to identify essentially the same phenomenon serves only to confuse the reader. The primary differences lie in the kinds of actions and kinds of actors that are at the heart of each specific definition.

The term *information operations* is preferred by national security and military experts to describe the strategies employed in the military arena in order to defeat the enemy using electronic and other high-tech means. It is also meant to be the term used during times of peace. Not all of the actions within information operations would be considered cyber warfare. According to the operational definition of information operations that is used by the Joint Chiefs of Staff, information operations encompasses all of the "actions taken to affect adversary information and information systems while defending one's own information and information systems. Also called IO."

Here the primary nuance, information operations, as well as information warfare, is focused on the control of information (interpretation of observed phenomena) and the ability to disrupt its acquisition and dissemination. Information operations also encompasses the capturing of signals intelligence and deployment of planes carrying leaflets in an attempt to influence an adversary using propaganda, known as psychological operations. The term *information warfare* is preferred in the military as well as in the academic study of the implications of the innovations in the Information Age upon warfare. Information warfare is "actions taken to achieve information superiority in support of national military strategy by affecting adversary information and information systems while leveraging and defending our information and systems."

Information warfare seeks to deny the enemy the acquisition of information and improve upon one's own information resources. As can be expected, the usage of this term by military experts is during wartime. Military experts also use the term information warfare specifically with respect to the military's attempt to lift the fog of war by integrating units with a wireless network in order to maintain better battlefield control and sight.

Information warfare largely stays in the cyber realm, where data is electronic and can be accessed remotely, but information warfare can expand beyond bits and bytes. The Department of Defense's definition of information warfare is "actions taken to achieve information superiority by affecting adversary information, information-based processes, information systems, and computer-based networks while defending one's own information, information-based processes, information systems, and computer-based networks."

Cyber terrorism, the subject of Dan Verton's recent book, *Black Ice*, is nearly identical a phenomena to cyber warfare. According to Professor Dorothy Denning, "cyberterrorism refers to the convergence of cyberspace and terrorism. It covers politically motivated hacking operations intended to cause grave harm such as loss of life or severe economic damage. An example would be penetrating an air traffic control system and causing two planes to collide." The primary difference between cyber terrorism and cyber warfare lies in the condition of the actor, whether or not the actor is state, non-state, or sub-state. There are two roots to the confusion involving the usage of the term information warfare and other similarly vague terms.

During the early-1990's, military analysts and general staffs around the world recognized that warfare was changing due primarily to the integration of computing capability into conventional warfare. This is warfare in the Information Age, or high-tech warfare. These innovations in and of themselves do not constitute cyber warfare, however the disruption of such capabilities would be considered cyber warfare. The second root of confusion regards the idea of knowledge as a biased and manipulable resource; a post-modernist view of the epistemological consequences of data integrity in the Information Age. Control of information in times of warfare, masterfully thought-out and espoused by the Chinese philosopher Sun Tzu shapes the missions of the modern intelligence community. Information control and control of media access, the main mission of psychological operations, are also integrated in the information warfare term.

15

Information Warfare: The Unethical Use of Cyberspace

Over 35 years ago, computer scientists of the United States Department of Defense, and four western-state universities were constructing the precursor to the Internet. Named ARPANET, for Advanced Research Projects Agency Network, one of the projects goals was to study how communications could be maintained in the event of an all-out nuclear attack, as this was the middle of the Cold War.

After realizing that ARPANET would not be immune to a nuclear assault, the computer scientists using it recognized that assisting human communication was the most fundamental advance that the ARPANET made possible. Today, the Internet provides incredible opportunities for the hundreds of millions of users around the world. Globalization is due, in part, to the connections nations and corporations have been able to establish on behalf of the Internet. Previously, most computerized information was stored on disks or hard drives, but the Internet has allowed for easier access of data by storing information on networks so that it may be accessed from, and sent to any connected location.

Expanding at a phenomenal rate, 200 million Americans used the Internet in 2000, and the number of websites doubles every 37 days, according to the Federal Bureau of Investigation. The convenience and ease of transmitting information around the globe in seconds makes the Internet priceless for business, government agencies and anyone else who can go on-line. The Internet is now one of several regions that create the ever-growing entity known as Cyberspace. Governments, corporations, and educational institutions the world over became conscious of the potential of cyberspace, in which they could communicate, conduct business, and share information in ways previously unavailable. The benefits of this new medium were appealing not only to those using computers for productive means, but for those who sought to unlawfully use information in order to cause damage in a variety of ways. And thus, the unethical use of computers helped create Information Warfare.

According to the Institute for The Advanced Study of Information Warfare, "Information warfare is the offensive and defensive use of information and information systems to deny, exploit, corrupt, or destroy, an adversary's information, information-based processes, information systems, and computer-based networks while protecting one's own. Such actions are designed to achieve advantages over military or business adversaries."

Although a global menace, a focus on the causes and effects of Information Warfare threatening Canada, and mainly the United States will demonstrate the extent to which this phenomenon may reach. Granted, militaries and governments rely on computers for day-to-day operations, this essay will focus more on the aspect of computers that are used and depended on by the general public.

Although virtually every nation in the world could be the victim or purveyor of an Information attack, the most likely target is the United States. The US military is arguably the most powerful in the world and most enemies cannot match their arsenal and power. Rather than try to build an equivalent military, a more efficient alternative of attack would be through computers, with Information Warfare, i.e. cyber terrorism and cyber warfare.

The most severely threatening and destructive forma of Information Warfare are indeed the most difficult to defend against, says the Canadian Security Intelligence Service (CSIS). Terrorist groups and criminal hackers are often far more educated in the area of computers than law enforcement agents, and they have the knowledge and equipment to stay ahead of advances in protective security. Targets could include governments of all levels, military and police forces, political groups and prominent individuals; basically anyone with a computer hooked up to a modem. Using the Internet for terrorist activity reduces the chances of detection or capture. Terrorists can cause disruptions and economic damage to their target by attacking computer systems, rather than using weapons that inflict physical damage. Industrialized nations that are heavily reliant on computer systems are vulnerable to Information Warfare attacks.

A 1999 report by the Center for Strategic and International Studies, "Cybercrime…Cyberterrorism…Cyberwarfare" warned of the severe risk to the critical infrastructures in the United States. Current defenses are inadequate to protect against an attack as the Pentagon estimates that a coordinated attack by fewer than 20 strategically placed computer experts, with a budget of $10 million, could cripple the United States. Within a matter of seconds, a cyber attack could cripple a nation's government and economy, not to mention its society. It is interesting to note that the Internet was created by the US military and now they must protect themselves and their country from others who want to attack the US by means of computers and the Internet.

All industrialized nations, especially those of the Group of Eight Industrialized Nations, G8, are becoming increasingly dependent on their critical infrastructures, which virtually keep nations running. Critical infrastructures, of the government and private sector, are essential to the routine operations of the economy and government, and are both physical and cyber based. Technological advances have linked many infrastructures, such as telecommunications, energy, banking and finance, transportation, water, sewage and emergency systems, and these systems are becoming progressively automated. The reliance and importance of infrastructures have created potential targets for physical and cyber attacks.

The vulnerability of critical infrastructures, and the unique risks associated with networked computing have been recognized by the U.S. for some time, but not until 1998 was this issue applied the urgent status it deserves. The Presidential Decision Directive 63 was approved by Bill Clinton, and a national infrastructure protection policy was developed. The National Infrastructure Protection Center (NIPC), run by the FBI, and the Critical Infrastructure Assurance Office (CIAO), run by the Department of Commerce were created in order to protect and examine infrastructure vulnerabilities. Both the NIPC and CIAO are an administrative types of protection, whereas major cyber-terrorist attacks or network sabotages are handled by the Federal Computer Emergency Response Team (Fed Cert), which is likened to a SWAT team. By creating these agencies, and addressing the threats they face, the US government has made cyberspace security and Information Warfare a top priority. None of these agencies mention the moral and ethical implications of Information Warfare, as this aspect is not evident to be a military or law enforcement concern.

The Canadian Security Intelligence Service is concerned with foreign governments, terrorist groups and politically motivated extremists who may now use Information Warfare instead of traditional method of attack. Terrorism and industrial espionage, among many other malicious acts, are unethical regardless if committed with the aid of computers or not. However, using a computer, the Internet or other forms of IT to facilitate Information Warfare can be considered even more unethical than traditional methods of terrorism and related offences. Compared to the U.S., Canada is less economically and politically influential on the rest of the world, and is fortunately not an enemy to as many foreign states. However, this does not give Canada immunity from transnational Information Warfare. Director of the FBI, Louis J. Freeh, characterized Canada as a "hacker haven" as a result of our "sophisticated information technology system and our open society."

John Deutch, Director of Central Intelligence, testified before an American congressional committee and warned that, "an electronic Pearl Harbour was now a real threat" because, "criminal hackers were offering their services to so-called rogue states with various schemes to undo vital US interests through computer intrusions."Previously, terrorist groups used to take credit for their actions so their objectives would be well known, but a new trend is to avoid responsibility, which is quite easy with cyber attacks, so tracking such organizations is becoming increasingly difficult.

Information Warfare has international implications and virtually any one with access to a particular district of cyberspace is at risk. Several of the many features that make the Internet so unique, such as the speed at which information can be transferred, the ability to remain anonymous, and the ease of accessibility, attract many people, including the criminally minded. The broad range of crimes committed on the Internet, or with the aid of computers, poses new challenges for governments and law enforcement agencies around the world.

Transnational computer crimes, such as cyber terrorism and cyber warfare, are pertinent global matters that must be prevented if cyberspace is to prosper in the future. The future of cyberspace depends on the prevention of the most destructive types of crimes. Therefore, governments, aided by law enforcement agencies and private corporations must address and prevent the most severe threats to cyberspace. Again, ethical implications are not considered.

Not only must industry continue to develop security policies and safeguards for their networks and systems, but it should also continue its efforts to identify security flaws that threaten the Internet. These massive companies, such as Microsoft, Cisco, and Oracle have the knowledge, resources and personnel to create effective solutions. The technology to monitor vast areas of cyberspace, in real time, are available, as well as methods to detect network intrusions. These companies have the ability to inform governments of potential attacks, if and where there is a gap in an infrastructures security system, and they can block against many types of attacks and intrusions.

These abilities could be extremely beneficial for cyberspace as a whole by protecting governments, infrastructures and economies. As well these types of technologies could be incorporated into combating smaller scale crimes. The reason these measures are not commonplace is the initial costs incurred. As well, many companies do not want their vulnerabilities to be known for fear of further violations and loss of consumer confidence. Countless businesses, e-business and real space as well, rely on IT corporations for their products and innovations. Perhaps even more importantly, these corporations provide the global market with the hardware and software needed to access and effectively use cyberspace, and subsequently make the economy even more computer dependent.

These companies made and continue to manufacture the products now in use by terrorists and others who engage in Information Warfare. Although their products intended use is not for such malevolent activities, American and Canadian made products can be used by terrorists to carry out their attacks on the American economy and government networks. These major corporations have a moral obligation to research and fund protective measures that can prevent and shield infrastructures, themselves, governments, not to mention cyberspace as a whole.

The private sector cannot depend on law enforcement agencies for protection. Raymond Kendall, Secretary General of Interpol, (International Criminal Police Organization, consisting of 178 nations) told senior executives of large and growing companies, "The private sector must shoulder the responsibility for its own defense because government agencies do not have the technology necessary to do the job."

Military and law enforcement agencies are the protectors of society, but this may not be the case for cyberspace. They do not have the expertise, time, or resources to effectively deal with the concepts of Information Warfare, as the major firms of the IT industry do. Both government and private sector must put more effort and consideration into the threat of an Information attack, as they both could be the targets. As well, existing computer ethics should be stricter and enforced if the unethical and immoral use of computers is to be significantly reduced. Perhaps the makers of ARPANET should have included ethical guidelines into their creation, as the future of Cyberspace is in jeopardy as the threat of Information Warfare looms.

16

Conclusion

"Whatever the direction the cyber threat takes, the United States will be confronting an increasingly interconnected world in the years ahead…A major drawback of the global diffusion of information technology is our heightened vulnerability. Our "wired" society puts all of us—US business, in particular, because they must maintain an open exchange with customers—at higher risk from enemies. In general, IT's spread and the growth of worldwide digital networks mean that we are challenged to think more broadly about national security."

The evidence laid out in the previous six country studies shows that governments and foreign militaries have varying means and motivations in pursuing cyber warfare capabilities. Different countries have different motives in penetrating or "intruding" on our systems. Among these are intelligence gathering, software theft, compromise of data integrity, and perception management.

This chapter brings together several features of the cyber warfare landscape that assist in placing the country assessments in this report in better perspective. Conceptually, a hack (into an electronic network) could begin with an approach as simple as hiring a skilled individual to exploit a vulnerability in software on a desktop computer.

As cyber warfare programs progress and evolve, the conceptual becomes increasingly complex. Nevertheless, as an overall principle, we distinguish between attacking networks (the "target") and using the Internet (as a carrier) to attack critical infrastructure.

Although the countries examined in the report may demonstratre varying degrees of potential, a logical deduction is that these countries will use their capabilities in an offensive fashion, a deduction that becomes more and more of a concern as network technology becomes a ubiquitous part of the invisible infrastructure that makes daily life possible in advanced industrial countries.

In this chapter, we discuss how serious the vulnerabilities to critical infrastructure are. The current state of affairs suggests that the U.S. public and government and corporate leaders must be vigilant to an apparent rise in the number and sophistication of politically motivated software attacks. Based upon this analysis, we outline policy recommendations and courses of action to help create a more secure cyber infrastructure.

BACKGROUND: THE NATION-STATE ADVANTAGE

According to the U.S. intelligence community, "only government sponsored programs" are developing the cyber tradecraft with the future prospect of targeting U.S. critical infrastructures.484 While intrusions and attacks are not the exclusive province of large, hierarchical organizations, larger organizations do have advantages in resources and longer timehorizon probes, i.e., probes designed to foil U.S. government and military systems encryption. The time-horizon for nation-states operating in this fashion is much longer because many of the reconnoitering activities are considered innocuous. Terrorists, on the other hand, generally have limited resources and thus will place their resources where the impact is largest (e.g., physical attacks).

A hostile nation-state conducting a cyber attack on the United States is likely to conceal its identity to minimize the likelihood of retaliation. In these circumstances, a hostile government might adopt the tactic of sponsoring terrorists or mercenary hacker cells who can attack without leaving clear national signatures.

In addition to hiring or sponsoring cyber warfare "agents," a nation-state can spoof or conceal the origin of the digital "hops" through cyberspace in conducting an attack. Current technology permits a variety of methods to conceal points of origin. Such "laundering" techniques (described in the figure below), by masking the origin of the attack, tend to weaken conventional deterrence predicated on the threat of swift and accurate retaliatory response.

- *Spoofing*: This represents an attempt by an unauthorized entity to gain access to a system by posing as an authorized user. There are several spoofing techniques involving faking the IP address of a legitimate neighbor using knowledge of the number of hops involved. More recently, a program called NCovert uses spoofing techniques (forging the source of the IP address to appear like the intended recipient of the information) to conceal the source of data that passes over a network.
- *Wireless*: Proliferation of wireless access points permits access to the Internet by anyone within range of an unsecured 802.11b site. A recent article discussed "Wardriving" in which individuals try to identify poorly-secured networks by driving with a laptop.
- *Universities*: These usually have extensive Internet connectivity. PCs are often readily accessible to unauthorized persons and the large number of users requires significant bandwidth with minimal monitoring.
- *Internet Cafés*: These provide services in locations where users are often transiting a country or where individuals may not be able to afford a computer and Internet connectivity. Little attempt is made to register or identify patrons.
- *Direct Access Satellite*: Direct satellite access requires authentication which can be traced back to a registered user having paid for that access. If the actual user, however, is different than the registered user then the authentication process is meaningless.

HOW VULNERABLE ARE WE?

This section introduces the general concept of targets and vulnerabilities and assesses some of the parameters. In the previous section we examined individual segments of the critical infrastructure in greater depth. How and what would nation-states attack using a cyber capability and how important a factor is internet architecture i.e., topology? The popular media discuss a Digital Pearl Harbor in which an adversary would attack the Internet, dismembering the cyberspace "backbone," plunging the economy into chaos and putting U.S. national security at risk. Conventional wisdom has it that the Internet backbone is quite resilient because of built-in redundancies. While a slow-down in service might occur, traffic would continue to flow through alternative nodes.

However, recent research and findings has shown that the Internet and networks in general may not possess the redundancies once thought, a result primarily due to the major Internet hubs that have grown as a result of the increase in Internet usage. In a major geographic study of network topology, Grubesic, O'Kelly and Murray concluded that because of the competitive nature of the Internet service, the "Internet backbone provider industry has created a situation where many backbones are prone to disconnection if there is a major failure in a hub city for a given network," which could have a potentially "economically catastrophic [effect] for businesses, cities, and regions."

An additional factor that is often overlooked is that potential attackers have an interest in maintaining the integrity of the Internet because it provides a vehicle for launching cyber attacks against critical nodes or systems in the United States and elsewhere. Moreover, the Internet allows one to mount an attack at a remote distance in a "relatively anonymous fashion, and in potentially undetectable ways." It is therefore necessary to distinguish between the "carrier" of an attack (i.e., the Internet) and the target of an attack (i.e., a computer network or other embedded computer control and supervison systems.) In the most extreme of cases, the Internet itself could become the target of a concerted attack, however, as many attacks are executed across the connections fostered by the Internet, it is unlikely that such a concerted attack could be sustained.

Second, with respect to topology, compromise of national-level networks (including government, corporate/financial, and military/national security) carries more extreme economic and related consequences. Successful attacks have targeted a broad gamut of local and national sites ranging from air and ground transportation and the banking system, to physical infrastructure (such as dams and power grids), to government services and military systems. The degree of disruption in these examples varied. In some cases, the attacks amounted to mere nuisances while in others the effects were economically costly.

It is therefore important to distinguish between targets that can be localized geographically and those, such as the systems of federal and state government agencies or the telecommunications infrastructure of the public switched network, which are regional and even national in scope. Reportedly, most telephonic and other communications and data networks in the United States tend to be restricted geographically (i.e., localized) and reparable relatively quickly. An attack that undermines confidence at a broader, national level, however, is likely to have more extreme economic or psychological consequences (impairment of "trust").

This category might include town governments, small businesses, and local hospitals.

1. Scanning (little or no disruptive consequence but could lead to wider implications)
2. Reconnaissance of vulnerabilities
3. Website defacements (hacktivism such as defacing the website with web graffiti)
4. Data, identity, and sensitive information theft (e.g., an individual's social security number)
5. Undetected alteration of data (your birthday on a website)
6. Denial of service attacks (attacks on a single website that do not permanently disrupt availability)

National Level Impact

[Government Services]

Illustratively, this category would embrace agencies such as U.S. Social Security Administration; National Institutes of Health; Center for Disease Control; Department of Energy; Federal Reserve System, and more.

1. Web defacements (malicious intent, such as changing the site listing of indications of the SARS virus on the CDC website)
2. Semantic hacking (interference with search engines and news websites, such as CNN)
3. Denial of service attacks (sustained interference with a web service or site)

[Economic]

This category includes multinational corporations; global financial institutions; and critical components of the U.S. economic infrastructure (transportation, electricity, water, telecommunications, etc.)

1. Undermining the integrity of the banking system and inter-bank trust
2. Corrupting corporate data tables and degrading delivery schedules
3. Industrial espionage (stealing all of Ford motors car schematics for 2004)
4. Hacking SCADA systems

[National Security]

Examples of organizations in this category include the Pentagon, Armed Forces, intelligence organizations, FBI, and the National Labs (Sandia, Lawrence Livermore, among others).

1. Denial of Service attacks degrading military procurement, transport, and logistics
2. Theft of classified data (e.g., plans about troop deployment in Iraq for March 2003)
3. Psychological and disinformation campaigns

Vulnerabilities in Existing Critical Infrastructure

Skeptics claim that computer networks are not vulnerable to cyber attack. Criticism comes in a variety of flavors, ranging from complete denial of the existence of vulnerabilities to the argument that although vulnerabilities exist, the built-in redundancy of networks make them inherently able to withstand concerted attacks from multiple locations. Another observation some experts have made is that cyber attacks are easily defended against, that the attack itself becomes regionalized or isolated as quickly as it appeared. Skeptics feel that any talk of cyber warfare having a "devastating" effect on computer networks has the appearance of being alarmist and Cassandra-like.

This claim is strong and bolstered by the available open source evidence, suggesting that some of the effects of cyber attacks are local and do not warrant the efforts of a concerted program to solve vulnerabilities in the critical infrastructure and networks of states.

What these critics lack is vision and imagination; it is a logical prediction that as network connectivity and dependency on the Internet increases, the number and the overall disruptive effect of vulnerabilities and exploits will also increase. Before attempting to assess the degree of disruptiveness of attacks, we must set the boundaries of the universe of possible attacks.

First, according to the National Research Council, cyber offense is aimed at four IT categories:

(1) Internet;

(2) Telecommunications infrastructure (e.g., telephone, fax, satellite communications; wireless cell phones, etc.);

(3) Embedded real time computing (e.g., avionics; supervisory control and data acquisition systems [SCADA] systems controlling physical plants such as hydroelectric dams, power grids, pipelines, etc.); and

(4) Dedicated computing devices (e.g., desktop computers).

INTERNET

Cyber attacks against computer networks can occur along any point of the network, encompassing a wide range of possible entrance points including central routers (forming the crux of the Internet's connectivity), Domain Name Servers, central servers operated by Internet Service Providers, all the way to vulnerabilities at the end-user level. The Internet, similar to the cosmological concept of an open universe, has no beginning and no end when discussing the "direction of a cyber attack."

Telecommunications Infrastructure

The vulnerabilities in a single part of cyber space may be the same in other parts of cyber space, as the ubiquity of software applications and operating systems makes it likely that a zero-day exploit could cause significant damage because of the inability of programmers to fix all vulnerabilities within networks and software. A zero-day exploit is particularly damaging because it targets a previously unknown vulnerability, precluding any attempt by programmers to patch the targeted vulnerability. Viruses and worms spread in a nondiscriminatory fashion, affecting servers and end-users alike and diffusion occurs in the network from both central locations and peripheral locations. There are also vulnerabilities involved with software and electronic mail, server software and other applications.

Embedded Real Time Computing: The increased reliance on SCADA systems in water treatment facilities, hydroelectric dams, electric grids, oil pipelines and other utilities increases the possibility of it becoming a target of cyber attack. Because these systems are often linked to commercial IT systems, a vulnerability on a company's network can be translated into a vulnerability that could link to SCADA systems. Dedicated Computing devices: Computing devices such as desktop computers and network servers, in particular those that are connected by "always-on" connections, are vulnerable to intrusions.

> In the open source realm, documented accounts of cyber attacks have been plentiful in light of the security danger such reports pose. There have been many serious instances of cyber attacks causing SCADA systems and other computer networks to malfunction as a result of accidental or targeted and malicious intent. The summary below, presented by category, details incidents of recent attacks against and disruptions of critical infrastructure and sensitive computer networks.

Air and Ground Transportation

In January of 2003, Continental Airlines based in Newark, NJ was forced to ground flights due to system inoperability caused by the SQL "Slammer" virus.

Banking Systems

In January of 2003, Bank of America had 13,000 ATM machines rendered inoperable due to the SQL "Slammer" virus.

Dams and Waterways

A well-documented and oft-quoted incident refers to a known case in 1998 when a 12-year old hacker broke into the computer system controlling Arizona's Roosevelt Dam's floodgates. According to sources, the hacker had complete control of the command SCADA system for the dam and could have flooded the city of Phoenix.

Another well documented incident refers to the April 23, 2000 arrest of Vitek Boden, a man who successfully intruded into a Queensland, Australia wastewater management system 46 times. For two months, the attacks were a mystery to investigators as Boden dumped hundreds of thousands of gallons of waste into parks, rivers, and commercial properties.

A December 2002 report from Mechanical Engineering cites examples of "wardriving" into SCADA-controlled utilities. According to Paul Blomgren, manager of sales engineering at cybersecurity firm Rainbow Mykotronx based in Torrance, California: "Our people drove to a remote substation," he said. "Without leaving their vehicle, they noticed a wireless network antenna. They plugged in their wireless LAN cards, fired up their notebook computers, and connected to the system within five minutes because it wasn't using passwords." "Within 10 minutes, they had mapped every piece of equipment in the facility," Blomgren said. "Within 15 minutes, they mapped every piece of equipment in the operational control network. Within 20 minutes, they were talking to the business network and had pulled off several business reports. They never even left the vehicle."

Telephones

On February 7, 2002 President Bush was notified of a serious vulnerability with the Abstract Syntax Notification 1 (ASN.1) data transmission standard that the FBI assesses could have been exploited to disable telephone networks and "halt all control information exchanged between ground and aircraft flight control systems."

Power Grids and other Energy Related Infrastructure

In April of 2000 the "ILOVEYOU" virus rendered a petroleum refinery in Texas inoperable.506 In January of 2003, the SQL "Slammer" worm disabled the monitoring computers at Ohio's Davis-Besse nuclear power plant in Toledo, Ohio.

Government Services and Military Systems

In 1994, a 16-year old English hacker took down hundreds of Department of Defense systems.

Thankfully these systems were not classified. In September of 2003 the "Welchia" virus disabled the State Department's Consular Lookout and Support System (CLASS) which contained more than 15 million records from the FBI, State Department and U.S. immigration and provided consular offices assistance in processing visas to foreigners.

Along with documented successful cyber attacks, there have also been several mass cyber exercises simulating an organized nation-state adversary carrying out cyber warfare against American assets and critical infrastructure.

Figure 4: Simulations

Exercise Eligible Receiver

In 1997, a NSA exercise employing 35 computer specialists used hacking tools from 1,900 documented hacker websites to disable large parts of the U.S. power grid. They were also able to disrupt the C2 system of Pacific Command based in Honolulu. The exercise, conducted over 2 weeks in June of 1997 by the Joint Chiefs of Staff and the Department of Defense, attacked unclassified Defense Department computer systems and pieces of critical infrastructure in the United States. The Department of Defense owned approximately 2.1 million computers (1999) and hundreds of local area networks in the unclassified realm that were the targets of attack. The report that was released by Defense Department individuals in light of the results of the exercise pointed to a lack of knowledge about what hackers could do with computers and information readily available on the internet.

Digital Pearl Harbor

This seminar-style (no actual computer intrusion was performed) wargaming exercise was made possible through the joint efforts of IT professionals, Gartner Inc., and the U.S. Naval War College. The conference was conducted in July of 2002 over a period of three days to determine whether cyber terrorists could attack the United States in a "Pearl Harbor" type attack in terms of timing, magnitude, and planning.

The exercise presupposed that a cyber terrorist organization would have access to $200 million and 5 years of planning along with Internet access to do their research in order to launch an attack of this magnitude.

The results of the attacks on financial institutions, telecommunications networks, the Internet, and the electric power grid showed that different areas would be affected differently due to security measures already in place. While it was fairly easy to shut down large portions of the Internet, create havoc on the financial markets, and shutdown the electrical power grid to a large region of the United States, it was very difficult to take out the telecommunications networks because of existing security.

OPLAN 3600

The name of the Pentagon's plan to defend against acts of cyber warfare. It also details how to enact cyberwarfare against another country.

Energy Department Simulation

According to a Washington Post report, the Department of Energy conducted its own investigation into potential vulnerabilities within the power grid. "What they do know is that "Red Teams" of mock intruders from the Energy Department's four national laboratories have devised what one government document listed as "eight scenarios for SCADA attack on an electrical power grid" — and all of them work. Eighteen such exercises have been conducted to date against large regional utilities, and Richard A. Clarke, Bush's cyber-security adviser, said the intruders 'have always, always succeeded.'"

Livewire National Cyber Exercise

In October 2003, the Institute for Security Technology Studies at Dartmouth College designed and managed "Operation Livewire", a simulation sponsored by the Department of Homeland Security. The purpose of the exercise was to examine the challenges of responding to a largescale cyber attack directed against the U.S. telecommunications, energy, banking, and finance sectors. The simulation involved an East Coast city, a West Coast city, and various private corporations in 14 locations throughout the country. An After Action Report assessed the response of law enforcement at federal, state, and local levels to the simulated attack. Beyond these simulations, several incidents of intrusions and information theft in government computer systems in the late 1990's are now cited as prime examples of the dangers of cyber warfare.

Figure 5: Cyber attacks of importance to national security

Rome Labs Incident

In 1994, the Air Force's Rome Labs computers were broken into by two UK hacker youths, causing an estimated $500,000 worth of damage. At that time Rome Labs was the Air Force's center for command and control research.

Moonlight Maze

In March of 1998, U.S. officials discovered a "pattern of probing of computer systems at the Pentagon, NASA, Energy Department, private universities and research labs, which had begun in March 1998 and had been going on for nearly two years." The attacks were traced to the Soviet Union, to an Internet provider hub that was in close proximity to the Russian Academy of Sciences. Soviet officials denied having anything to do with them.

Solar Sunrise

Originally suspected to be the work of Russian hackers, these attacks were eventually traced to two hackers in California and an Israeli youth working in concert. The attacks occurred in 1998, and the hackers were able to attain troop movement information for the U.S. military in the Gulf region. The nature of the attacks and penetrations were so well coordinated that it led Deputy Secretary of Defense John Hamre to say that it was one of the "most organized and systematic attack" on U.S. systems to date.518

In addition to the effects of cyber attacks on critical infrastructure, cyber warfare could also cause significant damage to a nation's economy. Although some believe that the estimates of the costs of virus outbreaks and disruptive worms are exaggerated, the result of a cyber attack on a company's "just-in-time" delivery system, for example, or a denial-of-service attack on an online retailer is not a monetary amount that can be easily dismissed.

Professor Eric Johnson points out that in today's globalized, digitized world, workers often perform in extended enterprises involving disparate firms widely dispersed and communicating through the Internet. Through a web browser, business decisions and design changes can be communicated across borders and continents instantaneously. "Every one of those interactions could potentially be observed or disrupted by youthful hackers seeking a thrill, or other more malicious individuals pursuing competitive gain."

SUMMARY AND RECOMMENDATIONS TO POLICYMAKERS

In approaching recommendations to policymakers and the IT industry, we suggest the following boundary conditions:

1) Our adversaries or potential adversaries have resources, expertise, training, and know-how that is world class. This factor should not be underestimated. It places a premium on "creativity" in fashioning response measures.
2) Defining a "catastrophic" attack is fraught with difficulty. Absent such a scenario, however, we believe that our adversaries are capable of inflicting significant material, financial, and psychological damage through denial of service and related attacks that inflict a disproportionate

toll on our economic welfare and our standard of living, in some cases. We agree, however, that considerable additional work will have to be performed to calculate more accurately the economic costs that are passed from businesses to the consumer. The cost of "lost trust", on the other hand, is perhaps immeasurable.

3) As the IT revolution deepens and matures, civilian information technologies will increasingly be incorporated in the military and the defense sector. Hostile nation-states could, for example, employ cyber assaults to disrupt or impede the mobilization, deployment, or resupply of U.S. military forces.

We have identified *three general areas of vulnerabilities*, which, if left unmitigated, would be cause for future concern:

A. Critical Infrastructure

Although the civilian critical infrastructure currently has known vulnerabilities, these vulnerabilities have only led to temporary outages, short-term economic losses and inconveniences. However, future outages of longer duration and intensity could cause significant disruptions.

B. Economic and Financial Sector

Again, the commercial sector has suffered only slowdowns and degradation due to unauthorized intrusions, but the rising costs of these actions and the fact that these costs are passed onto the consumer are not trivial consequences. The fact that trust is reduced as the availability of these services becomes more and more unpredictable could lead to longer-term economic losses. Moreover, cyber attacks might also disrupt by corrupting or deleting data.

This has significant implications extending beyond simple congestion or Denial of Service experienced, for example, in recent computer worms.

C. Military and National Security Sector

As militaries and intelligence services rely more and more on IT in order to modernize efficiently, this reliance opens up more holes in critical military infrastructure, while fostering a spiral of deterrence as each side attempts to one-up the other in exploiting a cyber attack capability. Much of the Pentagon logistics chain flows over public-switched networks. Some of the intelligence gathering of U.S. intelligence agencies also flows over public networks. Secure IT is critical in making sure that the data received on both ends of an intelligence transmission is not compromised.

Fundamental considerations remain. Due to convergence, the way that information technology and telecommunications are morphing into a single entity, it will be difficult to discern all of the possible vulnerabilities in a network. Viewed from a global perspective, for example, the development of information technology has been seen as an efficient way to modernize and increase economic well-being. This global implication raises two concerns:

1. Increasing connectivity and networking increases the amount of critical infrastructure that must be protected while simultaneously adding to the number of vulnerabilities in critical infrastructures, and
2. It dramatically expands the number of people that have knowledge and access to this critical infrastructure.

Information Technology is a reciprocal power: it can be used to benefit mankind, and it can be used to harm it.

RECOMMENDATIONS

What should the U.S. be doing about it?

1. *Technology is important—but no panacea.*

In recent years, software and hardware producers have begun to make their products more secure. Stronger operating system kernels, faster anti-virus software and virus detection, tougher firewalls and Internet browsers—these are just some of the steps taken to help cut down on the vulnerabilities present in today's network architecture. However, whatever patches or software re-design are devised and created by software manufacturers, vulnerabilities will always persist because users neglect to use the patches or creative hackers figure out a way to defeat the new security software code. As President George W. Bush once said: "There is no such thing as perfect security."

Technology improvement points:

- Stronger security options in operating systems, more robust and user-friendly anti-virus software, firewalls that are tougher to penetrate, and stronger security configurations for Internet browsers and e-mail utilities.
- Reduction in the number of open virtual ports on a typical computer set-up.
- Faster patches and more innovative patch delivery systems.
- Resolve currently known software and hardware vulnerabilities in operating systems, server software, SCADA systems, and DCS systems.
- Educate and motivate code writers to provide secure code.

2. *Vigilance is critical.*

In the face of more sophisticated and numerous malicious or hostile probes, security awareness must receive greater attention. The Internet and related businesses (routers, servers, computers, et al.) is 80 percent owned by private companies and individuals. These "owners" so far have successfully resisted government regulation.

We recommend: A joint government and private sector assessment of cyber security progress mandated by Congress and overseen by the Department of Homeland Security, every two years, with some authority for oversight of systems related to national security.

3. *Raise consciousness*

As with the effort to bring the "rule of law" to the 19th Century American frontier, gaining acceptance of security procedures at every level of the economy and society will take time. In the last five years, enormous strides have been taken, first to gain an understanding of the interconnections in our digital economy and second to engineer firewalls, patches, enhanced encryption, and other appropriate defenses. It does little good if a software company produces a patch for a security vulnerability if no one downloads it. Publicize "best practices" for computer security; these best practices include:

- Operating systems and software should be updated regularly
- Strong password policies should be enforced
- All unnecessary services should be disabled
- Anti-virus software should be installed and kept up to date
- High fidelity intrusion detection systems and firewalls should be employed
- Passwords should be changed when employees leave a company or government agency
- Access to networks should be given out cautiously and with forethought as to the security implications of such access if the network is part of the critical infrastructure system Further action should be taken after closer examination is undertaken in the following areas:

4. *Indications and Warnings*

More research should be done into the cyber warfare developments of other countries and also terrorist groups. Mounting an effective civil defense traditionally relies on indications and warnings (I & W) which we normally associate with weapons acquisition, movement of people and money, and all the other logistics required for typical combat operations. Traditionally, the more complex the operations, the more prominent the preparations and the greater the opportunity of defenders to detect the signs of impending attacks.

What the country studies in this volume have shown is that traditional I &W may not capture the entire picture with respect to cyber attacks. Further investigation into intent of use and other factors is required to gain a more accurate understanding of observable signatures. In this regard, the U.S. scientific community, and particularly private-sector R&D, has historically risen to face challenges to our national security such as lack of functional I & W signatures. We are confident that in the years to come the U.S. scientific community will fulfill that role again.

According to the National Research Council, cyber attacks that are sustained over time proceed gradually and incrementally require fewer resources; if such attacks are undetected, the cumulative effects could attain dangerous proportions. This suggests that direct, bold assaults may be less effective than more calibrated, subtle methods of attack. In the long run, a slow, gradual process of reconnaissance and infection will be more insidious because it fails to disturb any of the stakeholders involved.528 Increased awareness in this possibility and formulation of detection methods would reduce the possibilities of such an attack occurring.

5. A Partnership Between Government and the Private Sector

As outlined in the conclusion to the *National Strategy to Secure Cyberspace*, a partnership between government and the private sector regarding cyber security is critical for several reasons. According to the *National Strategy* "this unique partnership and process was and will continue to be necessary because the majority of the country's cyber resources are controlled by entities outside of government."

Anthony Cordesman thoughtfully points out that "there is no practical way that the federal government will ever develop the technical skills, and overcome its lack of specialized competence in ways that enable it to defend the vast majority of physical nodes in America's critical infrastructure or critical e-commerce, computer, and information systems. In fact at least 90% of the burden of day-to-day defense must fall on the private user or corporation."

The private sector's profit incentive and the government's lack of technical expertise stands in the way of either one of these organizations "going-it-alone" on the issue of cyber security. A long-lasting and functional partnership between government and the information technology industry, facilitated by the Department of Homeland Security, will help make cyber space more secure.

APPENDIX A: MORE CRITICAL VULNERABILITIES

This section examines the main types of cyber warfare targets more carefully. Much of the discussion presented below derives from previous work published by Dartmouth College's Institute for Security Technology Studies.

CORE INTERNET INFRASTRUCTURE

1. Routers

Internet traffic is passes through several routers that are grouped into management domains called "Autonomous Systems," each with its own number. The Autonomous Systems pass routing information to each other using the Border Gateway Protocol (BGP). Routers interconnect logical networks by forwarding information to other networks based upon IP addresses. They ensure that packets get from source to destination. A study published in 2001 noted that a lack of diversity in router operating systems leaves open the possibility of attacks. A particular weakness involves the Border Gateway Protocol. This protocol, which governs decisions on where to send traffic on the Internet, is vulnerable to information poisoning that could affect routing tables. In a worst case, large volumes of information headed for global destinations would be lost.

2. Domain Name Service (DNS) Servers

Root DNS servers act as a type of telephone directory, matching names of a site into a numerical address. In October 2002, all 13 of the Internet's root DNS servers—three of which lie outside the U.S.—were victims of a distributed denial of service (DDoS) attack. According to media accounts, the attack was an attempt to clog root DNS servers with useless traffic. Many experts contend that the failure of the October 2002 attack to cause permanent damage is a tribute to the resiliency of the Internet. Most of the information contained in the root servers is cached in redundant and hierarchical fashion across the multiple secondary DNS servers.

Bibliography

Alexander, Yonah, and Paul A. Leventhal, Preventing Nuclear Terrorism: The Report and Papers of the International Task Force on Prevention of Nuclear Terrorism, Lanham, MD: Rowman & Littlefield, 1987.

Arend, A.: International Law and the Use of Force, London, Routledge, 1993.

Allison, Graham, Nuclear Terrorism: The Ultimate Preventable Catastrophe, New York: Times Books, 2004.

Basrur, Rajesh M., and Hasan-Askari Rizvi, Nuclear Terrorism and South Asia, Albuquerque, NM: Sandia National Laboratories, February 2003.

Bellamy, C.: Knights in White Armour: The New Art of War and Peace, London, Random House, 1997.

Bukharin, Oleg, The Threat of Nuclear Terrorism and the Physical Security of Nuclear Installations and Materials in the former Soviet Union, Monterey, CA: Center for Russian and Eurasian Studies, Monterey Institute of International Studies, 1992.

Damrosch, L.F.: Law and Force in the New International Order, Boulder, Westview Press, 1991.

Friedman, G.: The Future of War: Power, Technology and American World Dominance in the 21st Century, N.Y., Random House, 1996.

Holsti, K.: The State, War, and the State of War, Cambridge, Cambridge Univ. Press, 1996.

Huntington, S.P.: The Soldier and the State, N.Y., Vintage Books, 1964.

Hoffman, Bruce, Inside Terrorism, New York: Columbia University Press, 1998.

Janowitz, M.: The Professional Soldier: A Social and Political Portrait, N.Y., The Free Press, 1960.

Keane J.: Democracy and Civil Liberty, London, Verso, 1988.

Kaplan, David, The Cult At the End of the World, New York: Crown Publishers, 1996.

Laquer, Walter, The New Terrorism: Fanaticism and the Arms of Mass Destruction, Oxford: Oxford University Press, 1999.

Norton, Augustus R., and Martin H. Greenberg, Studies in Nuclear Terrorism, Boston: G.K. Hall & Co., 1979.

Nair, A. M.: An Indian Freedom Fighter in Japan, Bombay, Orient Longman, 1983.

Noorani, A.G. : Indian Political Trials : 1775-1947, New Delhi, Oxford University Press, 2005.

Potter, William C., Nikolai Sokov, Harold Müller, and Annette Schaper, Tactical Nuclear Weapons: Options for Control, Geneva: United Nations Institute for Disarmament Research, 2002.

Posen, B.R.: The Sources of Military Doctrine, Ithaca, 1984, Cornell Univ. Press.

Rosen, P.: Societies and Military Power: India and its Armies, Ithaca, Cornell University Press, 1996.

Rhodes, Richard, The Making of the Atomic Bomb, New York: Simon and Schuster, 1988.

Schroeer, Dietrich, Science, Technology, and the Nuclear Arms Race, Ontario: John Wiley & Sons, 1984.

Spector, Leonard S., Going Nuclear, Cambridge, MA: Ballinger Publishing Company, 1987.

Index

♦♦♦